ARCHITECTURE AND SCULPTURE
IN EARLY BRITAIN

ARCHITECTURE AND SCULPTURE IN EARLY BRITAIN

Celtic Saxon Norman

ROBERT STOLL

with photographs by Jean Roubier

A STUDIO BOOK

THE VIKING PRESS · NEW YORK

Translated from the German by

J. MAXWELL BROWNJOHN

BRITANNIA ROMANICA
© 1966 BY ANTON SCHROLL & CO., VIENNA
ARCHITECTURE AND SCULPTURE IN EARLY BRITAIN
THIS EDITION © 1967 BY THAMES AND HUDSON, LONDON
PUBLISHED IN 1967 BY THE VIKING PRESS, INC.
625 MADISON AVENUE, NEW YORK, N.Y. 10022
ILLUSTRATIONS PRINTED BY BRAUN ET CIE, MULHOUSE, FRANCE
TEXT PRINTED IN GERMANY BY BOSS-DRUCK UND VERLAG, KLEVE
BOUND IN HOLLAND BY VAN RIJMENAM, N.V.

CONTENTS

ARCHITECTURE AND SCULPTURE IN
EARLY BRITAIN

Few extant buildings give such perfect expression to the full essence of Romanesque, which attained its prime in about 1100, as the castle and cathedral of Durham. Strictly speaking, very few other buildings belong to the first rank of Romanesque architecture. Among those that do are Speyer Cathedral, the Benedictine abbeys of St-Benoît-sur-Loire and St-Savin-sur-Gartempe (Cluny, Cîteaux, Clairvaux and Hirsau no longer being what they were), the pilgrim churches of Ste-Foy at Conques, St-Sernin at Toulouse and Ste-Madeleine at Vézelay, that other great place of pilgrimage, Santiago de Compostela, Pisa Cathedral, and the Basilica of San Nicola at Bari. These buildings were erected, or substantially augmented, in the period c. 1100.

These churches are much more important than others of the same period, and are major constituents of the 'candida ecclesiarum vestis' which can be defined as the visible expression of a spiritual movement and potent impulse that, after the centuries-long process of disintegration occasioned by the collapse of the Roman West, the abdication of the Roman East and the irruption of new races from outside the old Imperium Romanum, welded Europe together—even more thoroughly than under Charlemagne's rule—with the strength of a reinforced and reorganized Christianity.

But they are more than simply that. As architectural structures they bear a special relationship to the world in its role as the sphere of human trial and human behaviour; as monuments to the divine presence they conduct a crucial dialogue with man. They are boundary-stones in the physical and spiritual topography of their age. They stand at the intersections of the various components of spiritual and temporal power which, in their entirety, as an outlook on life, mental attitude and material expression, help to constitute Romanesque.

Durham embodies all the impulses which conduced to the development of Romanesque, and, in particular, of those which are the legacy of ancient Rome. It was a Benedictine monastery which had its roots in the monastic settlement founded on the island of Lindisfarne by Irish monks. It was the objective of countless pilgrims bent on visiting the relics of St Cuthbert, the Anglo-Saxon monk who was reared and educated by the Irish and who, as Bishop of Lindisfarne, took his lead from Rome. It was an influential see and, thus, a token of the strengthened central authority of Rome under Popes Gregory VII and Urban II, one a monk and the other a former

7

prior of Cluny. But Durham was also a Norman fortress situated not far south of the Roman wall which had formed the northernmost frontier of the Roman Empire, a fortress commanded by a bishop whose duty it was, as Earl of Northumbria and Palatine of the English king, to guard the border against an ever-hostile Scotland. Furthermore, Durham constituted a warning to the north of England, which was riddled with rebellious Anglo-Saxon noblemen and continued to be so even after 1080. The north only submitted to the Conqueror and his most energetic champion, Bishop Odo of Bayeux, after it had been ravaged and crippled for generations to come by the bloodiest and most remorseless punitive expedition of the century. Durham was born of prayer and austerity, just as Romanesque in general displays an intimate connection between heaven and earth. Where angels are, there, too, are demons. Vices hover about the figure of the Almighty on the tympanum.

Terrestrial bulk dedicated to the supreme God—such is Durham. It was here, for the first time in the evolution of Romanesque, that the cathedral architect successfully ventured to transmit the thrust of the walls back to earth by spanning nave and aisles with ribbed vaults. Durham was a cathedral, a fortress, monastery and place of pilgrimage. In human terms, bishop, ruler, monk and pilgrims—ingredients of all that is Romanesque—are also, in varying degrees, ingredients of what has been called 'Britannia romanica'.

SCOPE AND DEFINITION

Britannia romanica is here seen as part of a comprehensive whole. Since the area under examination lies somewhat outside the immediate domain of the Holy Roman Empire, the Papacy, the Cluniac reforms and the main routes of pilgrimage, many connoisseurs of Romanesque regard it as a marginal field. Consequently, it has seemed appropriate to pose a few special questions, principally in the Notes at the end of this book. The forces operative in the development of English Romanesque include some which, though absent elsewhere or present only as undercurrents, are nonetheless symbols of England as one of the heirs of Rome.

Art-forms are moulded by attitudes to life. Form has always been engendered by the human spirit, not by force. A work of art is inevitably affected by the nature of the age, by current conditions, by society and its ideas, by the individual and his experience, but it only becomes an expression of the age and its attitude to life, of man and his view of God and the world, when it is moulded by a creative mind. Transcending all limitations, the work then gains validity. Only this justifies repeated inquiries into the meaning implicit in a work. Only then, whether in a cathedral, portal, mural painting or sculpture, do we encounter testimony to the human mind of which the work is a tangible expression.

Admittedly, the term 'Britannia romanica' does not at first sight appear to possess the legitimacy of 'Italia romanica', 'Gallia romanica', or 'Hispania romanica'. Latin provides a common basis in the last three cases, and the impulse towards the formation of the term 'Romanesque' originated within the Romance cultural domain. The French archaeologist, de Greville, was the first (c. 1820) to define medieval buildings with piers, round-headed arches composed of voussoirs, barrel-vaulting and tiers of arcading as a slightly inept and degenerate development of Roman architectural ideas: 'opus Romanum . . . dégradé par nos rudes ancêtres.' His views on the subject of our 'rude ancestors' were quite erroneous—though understandably so, since contemporary knowledge of the true circumstances was still very scanty. Again, 'opus Romanum dénaturé', or however one chose to term it, could only be described as such within the context of an essentially historical and hidebound approach which took classical Roman architecture as its ideal and point of departure while ignoring the fine but differently conceived art of the medieval cathedral builder. Nevertheless, though labouring under certain disadvantages from the outset, the term 'Romanesque' has been invested with new meaning by the intensive stylistic, artistic and cultural research which has been carried out in recent decades.

Latin and Rome manifest themselves under the sign of the Christian Church and the basis of stylistic conception appears transposed, hence the justification for talking of 'Germania romanica'. Moreover, since Charlemagne still recognized the Emperor of Byzantium as a direct successor of the Roman Emperors, the wielders of German Imperial authority expressly regarded themselves— at least from 962 onwards—as directly in line of succession from the Roman Empire. The term 'Romanum Imperium' was first used in the year 1034. It referred, in a very real way, to a spiritual force which had been reconstituted on earth in accordance with genuine tradition but in a new, Christian form—and in this sense the term 'Germania romanica' is legitimate.

No such association with the realm of the medieval Roman Emperors can be claimed for 'Britannia romanica', neither for England, nor Scotland, nor Ireland. The British Isles remained exempt even under Charlemagne, whose policy of imperial unification embraced so much of Europe. True, Britain exerted no political influence on Europe, neither c. 800 nor c. 1000. The centres of power were situated on the Continent, on which the islanders focussed their gaze while remaining aware of their own spiritual and evolutionary vigour. Nevertheless, they gave more than they received during the Carolingian period, when power in England was vested in King Offa of Mercia, the only Western monarch whom Charlemagne regarded as his peer.

On the other hand, the majority of what is now England had been incorporated in the Roman Empire. Built under Emperor Hadrian in AD 122 and abandoned at the end of the 4th century, the Roman wall which ran seventy miles across the island from Tynemouth to the Solway Firth, forming the northern border of the Empire, is still clearly visible today. England is also rich in the ruins of numerous Roman castra, towns and villas. During the Middle Ages, countless Roman stones and bricks were utilized in secular buildings and, more especially, churches. The island's builders had plenty of examples of Roman architectural technique before their eyes, and direct influence is unmistakably apparent in individual cases (Pl, 215, 231), though these are relatively few in number. However, the 'opus romanicum' was a product of other forces as well, not simply a successor—somewhat degenerate, in de Greville's view—of the 'opus romanum'.

How does Ireland fit into this picture? Not subject to any of the foregoing criteria, whether geographical, linguistic or political, it was the only area in the whole of Southern, Central and Western Europe never to form part of the Roman Empire. Roman legionaries and administrators never set foot on Irish soil, even though the depredations inflicted by Irish sea-raiders provided them with ample provocation. The only links between the island and the Roman Empire were commercial. This independence from Rome enabled Ireland to become the only Early Christian cultural zone in Europe, and one which long developed independently of Rome in the ecclesiastical field as well. Yet it was Ireland's independent ideas of Christianity and its dissemination of them among others which helped it to exert such a decisive influence on the evolution of Romanesque in Britain.

THE IRISH

Though never subject to the authority of Rome, Ireland was affected by the spirit of antiquity to a marked degree. Combining it with Celtic and Scandinavian ideas, the Irish moulded it, in their own untrammelled fashion, into something unique which, in turn, left its mark on the whole of medieval Europe. After the influx of alien Germanic tribes into Europe and the British Isles had slowly abated, this evolved from the spirit of late antiquity, which had never entirely disappeared. Again and again, victorious invaders linked their own ways with the stronger culture of vanquished Rome, e.g. the Visigoths in Spain, the Franks in Gaul, and the Ostrogoths and Lombards in Italy, but this set off processes of fermentation and transmutation which extended to the legacy of Christianity as well. From the time of the first missionaries until the advent of the Middle Ages, only Ireland developed in a comparatively calm and contemplative way. This endowed the Irish with the strength and determination to propagate the faith in Europe, first their large island neighbour and then the Continent, where they pushed ever further to the east, north and south, simultaneously renewing their links with the ancient world via Christianity. This process attained particular importance in the 7th century, when Islam obstructed and partially cut existing lines of communication with the patristic schools active in Syria and the Coptic Christians of the desert and Nile Valley, who maintained the Alexandrian tradition. Herein lies a profoundly important aspect of Irish Christianity, and one which was to exert a major influence on the Romanesque style.

There is no firm indication of how Christianity came to Ireland. It may be that Britain introduced the Irish to what it received back again, mainly at their hands, since Christian communities had existed in Roman Britain. The 3rd-century story of Alban of Verulamium bears witness to the presence of Christians there at the time of the persecutions under Diocletian, but it remains uncertain whether Britain, civilized by Rome, ever undertook genuine missionary work in Ireland, with its clan structure and druidical beliefs. The first Christians may have reached Ireland as a result of commercial contacts with south-west France, Spain and the Mediterranean. The sea-routes were in constant use. Tacitus reported that, although little information was available about the interior of the island, traders were familiar with its harbours and coastal approaches. There must have been Christians in these trading posts, immigrants at first and later natives. Prosper of Aquitaine noted in his chronicle (c. 455) that Pope Celestine I had sent Palladius to the Christians of Ireland as bishop in the year 431, but there are no surviving traces of his presence there.

Patrick, the successful evangelizer of Ireland, probably arrived a year later. The son of a Romano-British decurion resident on the west coast of England, he was abducted into slavery by Irish raiders and did not escape for some years. Irish Vitae of the 7th century record a statement by Patrick to the effect that he had been conducted by the fear of God, via Gaul and Italy, to the 'islands of the Tyrrhenian Sea'. Here he may have encountered monasticism in its pre-Benedictine form: the archaically ascetic, hermit-like communities which modelled themselves on the desert monks of Egypt, shunning the world, almost jealously independent, wholly dedicated to the service of God, and consisting at most of a small band of disciples loosely grouped about an older 'holy man'. Patrick transplanted this pre-Chalcedonian monasticism to Ireland, where it quickly sank deep roots in the Irish clan system, with its code of absolute devotion to a specific leader.

Thus began the development of this island of monks and saints, a process whose end was heralded by submission to the episcopal usages of Rome, although, as the crosses of Dysert O'Dea and Kilfenora *(Pl. 135)* show, its aftermath was felt in Romanesque times.

The Irish never came to terms with the Mediterranean spirit—yet another consequence of the fact that Rome had never managed to assert its authority in Ireland. Even Patrick, who regarded himself as a citizen of the Roman Empire during his lifetime, felt his voluntary exile in Ireland, first as a missionary and later as Bishop of Armagh, the place where he died *c.* 461, to be a form of spiritual captivity. Coupled with the spirit of independence, there was the Iro-Celtic urge to roam which finds such vigorous expression in ornamentation and the proclivity for migration and pilgrimage. Only Ireland could have produced St Brendan the Voyager, a simultaneously legendary and authentic figure who set sail for a terrestrial paradise across the seas.

It was this uncompromising attitude which enabled Irish ascetics to persevere in prayer and mortification on remote rocky islets in the Atlantic or in caves such as those beside the upper lake at Glendalough, just as it was lack of compromise which drove them to penetrate the Continent by unknown routes and preach the Christian faith there, moving from place to place in constant pilgrimage.

This sort of outlook could not initially beget any architecture, for architecture is, inherently, a defining and enclosure of space, a subduing of the infinite universe which inspires man with creatural awe and in which he senses the mystery of a divine presence. As a minimal protection against the elements, and from a wish for seclusion, the Irish monks built round stone cells modelled on the palaeolithic stone huts of the Fahan group, some of which still stand today. They also constructed somewhat larger prayer-cells of rectangular ground-plan, mostly of unmortared stone slabs laid in converging courses—oratories which seldom exceeded upturned fishing-boats in size. The early Irish chapel is cell-like in character, but later churches also preserve the structural appearance of the early cell *(Pl. 123)*.

The round tower appeared in about 900. A free-standing structure of emphatically vertical form, it was designed so that the monks outside could be summoned by means of a hand-bell rung from the windows at each of the four quarters, but its sturdy construction and raised entrance also made it a refuge from Viking raids and a repository for mirabilia, relics, and books. However, the Irish reserved their greatest love for crosses. Of the many wooden crosses which they undoubtedly erected, none has survived, but many of the extant stone crosses are entrancingly beautiful *(Pl. 126, 128, 145)*. They are cosmic monuments rooted in the menhir tradition and related to the sun-orientation of the ancient Egyptian obelisks. Here, however, the sun is Christ, the light of the world's salvation. This light streams back to earth from the cross by way of the sermons preached at its foot and the Biblical scenes carved on its shaft. Thus the upright cross becomes the centre of the world, the spot where the earth's axes intersect and meet the divine, vertical axis which governed the disposition of all monastic buildings and, in consequence, the evangelically-minded Irish Church.

The Irish Church was entirely monastic in structure. Bishops were subordinate to an abbot and performed their duties in various places, each according to his competence. Understandably, no genuine cathedrals could come into being under this scheme of things. Buildings referred to as such were merely halls of somewhat more than average size, and ascetically simple compared with contemporary examples on the Continent. Genuine monastery churches and monastery buildings

11

were equally lacking in earlier times, thanks to the basic structure of Irish monasteries, which, with a few exceptions, remained mere clusters of cells until the 12th century. This state of affairs did not change until the arrival of the Cistercians. It was only natural that the wealth of the Irish monasteries should manifest itself less in terms of architecture and sculptural decoration than in paintings and appurtenances made of cloth and precious metal. However, the Irish monasteries' real claim to fame lay in their scholars (so much so that for a while the designations 'Scoti' and 'wise men' became interchangeable); in their schools, which purveyed everything in the way of current knowledge that had been derived from the Fathers of the Church, the Ancient World and the Near East; and, above all, in their scriptoria, which not only evolved an individual and extremely prolific script during the 7th and 8th centuries but illuminated codices with a wealth of imagery nourished on Celtic and Scandinavian sources and tempered by Mediterranean influences.

At the close of the 8th century, having acquired considerable influence over the Carolingian Empire in association with Northumbria, Ireland itself became threatened. Indeed, it may have been this threat which prompted so many Irish monks to abandon their own schools and make for England and the Continent. Lured by hopes of plunder, Norsemen had been appearing off the Irish coast in their long-ships since 795, followed by Danes. They began to settle there in about 840, in Dublin, Waterford and Limerick. They looted, burned, and terrorized the country-side. In the margin of St Gall's 9th-century manuscript of Priscian, the scribe wrote the following verses:

> Wild and furiously rages the storm this night.
> How it has made the billows foam!
> Ah, such nights make me rejoice exceedingly,
> for the robbers from the North come
> only when the sea is calm.

These lines epitomize the fear inspired by the Vikings, though it is also true that their graves have yielded important examples of Irish art, together with jewellery, principally of 9th-century origin, fashioned out of Irish reliquaries and liturgical vessels.

The Irish victories over the Vikings were succeeded by half a century of relative calm—the period which produced the carved crosses of *c.* 900. Raids multiplied again during the second quarter of the 10th century, until the Northerners' sway was finally broken by the destruction of the Viking stronghold at Limerick in about 968. Brian Boru, 'Imperator Scotorum' and the foremost high king in Irish history, was killed in the great and decisive battle of Clontarf in 1014, which spelt the end of the Scandinavians in Ireland.

Thanks to its strong contacts with England and, more especially, the Continent, Ireland had gradually—though at the expense of much individuality—forged links with the Romanesque style which embraced the whole of Western Europe. There was a steady increase in the numbers of Irish who made pilgrimages to Rome and the Holy Land, and 'Scoti peregrini' were always to be found among the bands of pilgrims to Santiago. Sometimes, too, Irish monks felt impelled to stay and settle. Marianus founded a monastic community composed of separate cells on the Irish pattern outside Regensburg in about 1070, though it was not until 1111, with the establishment of the monastery of St Jakob at Regensburg, that the monks adopted the Benedictine rules. Other 'Scottish' monasteries came into being at Würzburg (1135), Vienna (1155), and even Kiev. Needless to say, these contacts exerted a growing and reciprocal effect on Ireland.

The Cistercian abbey at Mellifont *(Pl. 143)*, founded in the year 1142, was Ireland's first monastic building proper. In 1171 the island was conquered by Henry II of England, thereby losing its independence and becoming submerged in the great European process of ecclesiastical and political transformation—only a very minor pawn in the game from then onwards.

What, then, was the contribution of Ireland? The round tower was originally conceived in Ireland, not adopted from Scotland or England. The Life of St Willibald, which dates from the latter half of the 8th century, mentions that many places in England had no chapel, simply a 'high cross, to serve as a centre for daily orisons'. The Picts and Anglo-Saxons adopted this tradition under Irish influence. Many fragmentary stone crosses *(Pl. 120, 121)* are still to be found, mainly in Scotland and the north and west of England, but they are different in character. Their carving displays Continental and even Mediterranean motifs. Their cosmic relationship has diminished; they are closer to man and have become mere monuments. The Irish cross, probably Ireland's most intensely individual creation, exerted no formative influence, either in England or on the Continent.

On the other hand, Ireland did bequeathe England and the Continent its words, attitude and example, its inward independence and individuality. More than any clearly definable factor, it was this spiritual impulse and insistence which survived as an undertone in the achievements of British and, more than that, in the whole of Central European, Romanesque. Nebulous yet unmistakable, it manifests itself at Corbie and Auxerre, at Lucca and Taranto, in Ghent and Lièges, in Mainz, Cologne and Fulda, in Trier and Amiens, at Bobbio, in St Gall, and at Reichenau. From Iona, their island base off the coast of western Scotland, and from the Northumbrian island of Lindisfarne, the Irish helped to mould Christian England.

THE ANGLO-SAXONS

One consequence of the decline of the Roman Empire was that in England, the northernmost outpost of Roman sovereignty, Romano-British civilization and its diversified economic structure—together with villas, towns, military bases and an extensive network of arterial roads—slowly began to disintegrate during the 4th century. Owing to the pressure of alien races on the heart of the Roman Empire and Rome itself, Roman legions were gradually withdrawn from England from about AD 400 onwards until none remained. The Picts pushed southwards from the Scottish highlands, and the Scoti, or Irish—we are now in the period when Patrick was pursuing his missionary activities—boldly assailed the western coasts of England by sea.

Although the Romans had erected defences against Saxon sea-raiders between the Wash and the Isle of Wight, on the so-called Saxon coast, invasion by Germanic tribes could no longer be averted. The first Germans came by invitation, as allies of the Britons in their struggle against the Picts. These were followed by small bands of invaders and, in the middle of the 5th century, by mounting waves of settlers complete with families and cattle. They settled in the cultivable areas of England, which was still largely clothed in forest. For all the great victories attributed to King Arthur by legend, it was the Britons' lot to be exterminated in battle, driven into modern Cornwall and Wales, or degraded to serf status. The extent of their subjugation, which was complete by about 600, can be gauged from the fact that, discounting a few river- and place-names, the language of the Celtic Britons became totally extinct in German-occupied areas. Some intermarriage must have occurred, however, because the emergent Anglo-Saxon character acquired a Celtic substratum whose presence later manifested itself in the Anglo-Saxon penchant for adapting Iro-Celtic and Roman trends in religion and art.

The Germanic tribes—Jutes, Frisians, Angles and Saxons—had already been in close mutual contact in their native areas: to use modern designations, northern Holland, northern Germany bounded by the Ems, Weser and Elbe, Schleswig-Holstein, and Jutland (though the Jutes may actually have hailed from the Rhineland). It is probable that they had also come into contact with products of the Roman world, both plundered and bartered, yet they showed an initial reluctance to live in Romano-British towns such as Verulamium, Colchester, Silchester, London, Lincoln and York. Being agricultural clansfolk, they settled in villages of their own. Wood was their building material, not stone. Their amazement at stone buildings is conveyed by a marginal note in one of the manuscripts of the Anglo-Saxon Chronicle: 'Towns are visible from afar, the skilful work of giants; the most amazing fortress of stone in the world . . .' They dwelt in small rectangular wattle huts, though the existence of long rectangular timber-framed buildings can also be inferred. The latter, roofed with straw or grass and walled with clay-plastered wattling, were 'public' buildings which served as chieftains' halls or meeting-places for councils of elders. Their elongated rectangular ground-plan, steep gabled roofs and stave-work paved the way for certain features of Anglo-Saxon church architecture which emerged after the island had been converted to Christianity.

In the course of a long and sanguinary process, separate tribal groups established petty kingdoms: the Jutes Kent, the Saxons Essex, Sussex and Wessex, the Angles East Anglia and another two which embraced the area north of the Humber and soon combined to form Northumbria. They had a mixed population, like Mercia, the kingdom which grew up in the Midlands and abutted on Celtic Wales in the west. Suzerainty, which was associated with the title 'Bretwalda', or 'Lord of Britain', circulated among the various kingdoms.

During the 7th century, Northumbria not only enjoyed political supremacy under King Oswald and King Oswio but developed into a religious centre unequalled anywhere in contemporary Europe. Based on the monasteries of Lindisfarne, Wearmouth and Jarrow, this cultural prime lasted into the first quarter of the 8th century. Then Mercia gained ascendancy under King Ethelbald, primarily in the political domain. Its most powerful king, Offa (757–96), erected a visible frontier between Mercia and the hostile Celts of Wales in the shape of a massive rampart stretching from the Dee to the Severn. He also concluded a treaty with Charlemagne. This guaranteed safe-conduct to Anglo-Saxon merchants on the Continent and to the pilgrims who were now visiting Rome in increasing numbers.

The sacking of Lindisfarne in 793 marked the beginning of the Viking raids. More and more Danes and Norwegians appeared in Britain and Gaul, as well as Ireland, particularly from the third decade of the 9th century onwards. The year 836, in which Vikings settled at Dubh-Linn in Ireland, saw the death of King Egbert of Wessex, whose victory over the Danes had only delayed invasion by a few years. In 850 the Vikings wintered in England for the first time, making their base on the Isle of Thanet in the Thames Estuary, the spot where Augustine, dispatched by Rome, had first set foot on English soil 250 years earlier. Now followed the great Viking conquests. The newcomers subjugated East Anglia and large tracts of Mercia, and in 878 they established a kingdom centred on York in Northumbria. This meant that the greater part of England was now under their control. The only surviving Anglo-Saxon kingdom was Wessex, which developed during the 10th century into the Kingdom of England. King Alfred, who came to the throne in 871, averted the total collapse of Christian England by defeating the Vikings at Edington in 878, and managed to introduce a temporary lull by concluding the Peace of Wedmore.

It was a stroke of luck, if luck be the right word, that England should have been sent such a ruler at the very moment when she was most immediately threatened by the tough and powerful Danes, with their pagan culture. Alfred the Great richly deserved his surname. This was the first occasion—the second came in the 11th century—when England ran a grave risk of becoming part of a Scandinavian empire, culturally as well as politically. Scandinavian culture continued to exert an effect until well into the Romanesque period, but it was offset once again by Alfred, who took over the work of Northumbria. Alfred was a teacher as well as a political leader, and his ties with Rome and the cultural ideas of the entire Mediterranean area were very strong. He visited Rome twice as a boy. He commissioned a translation of Gregory's *Dialogues* and personally translated Augustine's *Soliloquies*, but his main achievement was an Anglo-Saxon translation of Boethius' *De consolatione philosophiae*, undertaken from a wish to provide his contemporaries with spiritual aid in an age which seemed to him, as the Ostrogothic period did to Boethius, to be a time of ultimate trial. He also showed himself a harbinger of the Romanesque period by embarking on his allotted task wholeheartedly, compassed about by 'many and various cares', as he mentions in his preface, but heedless of his own fate and wholly dedicated to the service of One greater than himself.

Fierce fighting broke out again even before Alfred's death in 899, but his successors—his son Edward and his grandsons Athelstan, Edmund and Eadred—managed to regain control over the areas which had been lost to the Danelaw. Anglo-Saxon England counted for something on the Continent. Otto I (the Great) was married to Editha, Athelstan's sister. A Gospel-book presented by Otto to Athelstan, who was a friend of his, bears the title 'Anglorum basyleos et curagulus totius Bryttanie'. This dates from the period in the 10th century when, led by Archbishop Dunstan of Canterbury and influenced by the reformist movement based on Cluny, England, too, embarked on a process of ecclesiastical revival.

CHRISTIANIZATION AND EARLY PRIME

Although three bishops from Britain attended the Synod of Arles in 314, it is uncertain how much of the Romano-British Christian tradition still survived in England when Augustine, the Benedictine missionary, landed on the Isle of Thanet in 597. Pope Gregory I (the Great) had sent him and his companions to convert the Anglo-Saxons to Christianity. The Romans' withdrawal had undoubtedly undermined the existing Christian communities, and their instability is apparent from the fact that Bishop Germanus of Auxerre had to make two trips to England not long afterwards in order to check the heresy of the British monk Pelagius (d. 418 in Rome).

England had only just managed to withstand the menace of invasion by pagan Germans. Christian communities still survived in the Celtic backwoods but had become largely isolated, as witness the failure of the conference to which Augustine summoned their representatives in 603. Significantly enough, the latter were assisted by Irish clerics from Bangor (Bede, *Historiae ecclesiasticae gentis Anglorum* II/2).

Germanism gained the upper hand in England at precisely the period when Patrick rekindled the Christian faith in Ireland. Columba, the Irish founder of the monastery at Durrow, later settled with twelve disciples on the island of Iona off the west coast of Scotland, whence Christianity was reintroduced into the north of England, notably via Lindisfarne. Columba died on Iona in 597, the year in which Augustine arrived in the south of England from Rome.

The success of Augustine's missionary activities was spectacular. We still possess the text of Pope Gregory's letter to Bishop Eulogius of Alexandria, which mentions that over ten thousand Anglo-Saxons were baptized on Christmas Day 597. They had followed the example of their king, Ethelbert of Kent, but more out of loyalty than conviction. The same thing occurred in Essex, East Anglia and Northumbria, and the undue speed of these conversions inevitably bred a sharp reaction, especially when a baptized king died and his successor happened to be an obdurate heathen. The process was a long one.

Close contact with Rome was maintained, and Pope Gregory dispatched more missionaries. Augustine betook himself to Arles, where he was consecrated archbishop by Bishop Etherius. In addition to the archiepiscopal see at Canterbury, further sees were soon established, one at Rochester (and later London) for Essex, and another at York for Northumbria. East Anglia followed with Dunwich. The demand for church premises increased. A letter from Pope Gregory to Bishop Mellitus of London informs us that heathen temples were to be consecrated as Christian churches after their idols had been smashed. The Roman church of St Martin was still in use at Canterbury when Augustine arrived, since Queen Bertha, a Frankish princess by birth, was a Christian and had brought clerics with her to the Kentish court. A second, dilapidated, church dating from Roman times was restored at Augustine's insistence, and he simultaneously embarked on the construction of SS. Peter and Paul. New churches were erected in the countryside, simple halls, usually of wood but sometimes of stone, like St Andrew's at Rochester or the 'fine church of Paulinus' of which Bede (*H.E.* II/16) reported as early as the beginning of the 8th century that it had 'lost its roof, whether by neglect or hostile destruction, and only the walls still stood'.

King Edwin of Northumbria did not live to see the completion of the stone church erected at his behest. He was killed at the battle of Hatfield in 632, fighting against the heathen king Penda of Mercia. While the pallium intended to symbolize the appointment of a second Anglo-Saxon archbishop was still on its way to York, Paulinus and the queen, a Kentish princess by birth, were forced to flee to the south.

Thus began a chapter in the history of Northumbria which was to exert a decisive influence on the entire development of early Britain. After defeating Caedwalla of Wales, King Oswald (633–42) took up the reins of government with such drive and determination that he quickly became the acknowledged suzerain of all England. Converted to Christianity by the Irish during his foregoing exile on Iona, he had been baptized, so he was the first Anglo-Saxon king to profess to Christian faith from the outset. In place of Roman missionaries, however, Oswald gave a free hand to Irish monks, who pursued their highly fruitful activities in England for the next thirty years. Under Northumbrian leadership, Essex and Central England adopted the Christian faith, and only Sussex remained pagan. There were rifts in the youthful Anglican Church, however. Kent and East Anglia followed the Roman line under Canterbury. Wessex, too, inclined towards Rome, but its see at Dorchester was held by Bishop Birinus, who was still independent of Canterbury. Meanwhile, all areas directly under Northumbrian control belonged to the Iro-Celtic Church. The differences were structural rather than doctrinal. The loosely-knit monasticism of Ireland stood contrasted with an episcopal and highly centralized Church in the Roman mould.

16

Then, again, there were disputes over the method of calculating the date of Easter, which the Irish, so Bede tells us (*H.E.* III/25), computed 'after the Egyptian manner'. Finally, there were sundry minor but fiercely disputed points such as the question of tonsures. The Synod of Whitby, convened, under the aegis of King Oswio in autumn 663, was attended by Colman of Lindisfarne and Wilfrid of Ripon, who represented the Irish and Roman viewpoints respectively. It decided in favour of Rome, whereupon a number of dissenting Irish clerics returned to Ireland with Colman. With that, direct Irish ecclesiastical leadership in England came to an end.

However, by inviting Bishop Aidan and his Irish associates from Iona and assigning them the island of Lindisfarne, King Oswald had established close ties between Anglo-Saxon Northumbria and the rich spiritual world and imagery of Iro-Celtic culture. In conjunction with an abundance of Mediterranean traditions, this ultimately engendered a period of prime which derived sustenance from Celtic, Germanic, Insular Anglo-Saxon and Romano-Continental sources and had a great influence on High Medieval development. The sum total of this combination of factors is personified by the Venerable Bede (673–735) and exemplified by the *Lindisfarne Gospels*, a manuscript by the Northumbrian bishop Eadfrith (*c.* 700) and an extremely handsome illustration of this specifically Insular art-from. Moulded by the Celtic spirit in its script and ornamentation and fructified by the imagery of the North, it is distinguished from the earlier *Book of Durrow* and the later (Irish) *Book of Kells* by a more dispassionate approach. On the other hand, while using the same Vulgate text as the *Codex Amiatinus*, it follows Mediterranean traditions in its illuminated pages.

The products of Northumbria's late 7th- and early 8th-century prime not only travelled abroad but exerted a remarkable influence on the development of the High Middle Ages. It was symbolic of this that Abbot Ceolfrith of Jarrow should have set off proudly for Rome, intending to present the pope with a magnificent handwritten Bible produced in his own scriptorium—a Vulgate modelled with great stylistic purity on a South Italian exemplar. The abbot died en route at Langres in 716, the year in which Iona accepted the Roman Calendar, and the manuscript, now called the *Codex Amiatinus* after its site of discovery in a monastery on the Monte Amiata in Tuscany, eventually found its way into the Laurenziana in Florence.

But the spirit of Northumbria was disseminated by men as well as manuscripts. One of these was Willibrord, who did missionary work among the Frisians and founded the monastery of Echternach, where the *Echternach Evangeliar* was written, probably by a Northumbrian scribe. Another was Wynfrith of Wessex (675–755), who composed England's first Latin grammar, evangelized the Germans living between the North Sea and the Neckar under the name Bonifatius, founded Fulda, became Bishop of Mainz, and organized the Frankish Church in collaboration with King Pipin, the 'Patricius Romanorum'. The greatest of the 8th-century Anglo-Saxon scholars was Alcuin, who had been taught by the Irish monk Colgu at York and was conversant with Bede's 'Ecclesiastical History' as well as many other examples of his work. Having travelled abroad to further his education, he was invited by Charlemagne at Parma in 781 to reorganize the imperial scriptorium, a task which he carried out with the aid of the Irish monk Joseph and various scribes from Northumbria. As head of the court school, he helped to popularize Bede's works. Paulus Lombardus used Bede's theological and historical texts and Carolingian court poets conformed to his *De arte metrica*. In 814 the Irish scholar Dicuil wrote an astronomical treatise dedicated to Louis the Pious, and his *Liber de mensura orbis terrae*, written in 825, was 'the most important geographical work of the early Middle Ages' (Ludwig Bieler).

Such were the ways in which Irishmen and Anglo-Saxons of the court school and in the council of Charlemagne brought the faith and spirit of Ireland and Northumbria, coupled with an erudition derived from their study of classical literature, to the hub of Western Christendom. They were the fruits of a golden age in the British Isles, of a period which, though notable more for its personalities and their ideas and achievements, more for its manuscripts, paintings and skilled craftsmanship, than for its architecture, did evolve distinctive features in the latter field as well.

EXCURSUS ON THE ANGLO-SAXON HALL

The archetypal Anglo-Saxon church was a hall, not a basilica; not an open chamber divided into aisles by arcades, demanding movement and affording scope for various forms of activity; not a structure evolved by the receptive spirit of Athens and developed by the splendour-loving spirit of Rome; but a single enclosed and compact chamber with firmly defined boundaries. So far from being regarded as 'barbaric' in comparison with something more culturally advanced, it should be recognized as the product of a different mentality. True, the simpler structure was partly dictated by considerations of expense, but this element of modesty may itself be regarded as typical. Single-chambered churches were, of course, to be found in Mediterranean and Roman areas during the early period between the decline of Rome and the reformist prime of the 10th century, but other symptoms of differentiation based on a different spiritual approach are also in evidence. Thus the basilica was generally preferred in the former Roman towns on the Rhine-Danube axis, whereas the hall type predominated in the old Germanic region, e.g. in East Franconia.

The Anglo-Saxon church was born of various formative impulses: on a small scale, the hut built of sticks, wattle and plaster, and, on a larger scale, the hall constructed of massive baulks of timber, such as the one discovered on the site of the ancient Northumbrian royal seat at Old Yeavering in 1957, near another timber-framed building which may have been a heathen temple pressed into service as a Christian church. Bede (H.E. II/13) refers to one of these long rectangular wooden halls as the scene of the memorable conference held by King Edwin of Northumbria and his elders in the presence of Paulinus, who expounded the Christian faith to them. Before his baptism, Edwin had a wooden prayer-cell erected as a place of preparation. That small timber-framed ecclesiastical buildings were common in the early days of Anglo-Saxon Christianity is evidenced by written sources, but it can also be inferred from structural and formal echoes found in later stone buildings (e.g. Pl. 185). One out-of-the-way village even boasts an Anglo-Saxon stave-church of c. 1000 (Pl. 24), though its construction is already of an advanced nature.

During the early Anglo-Saxon period, stone buildings were the exception in a countryside which was mantled in vast forests. Since the indigenous population had no real experience of building in stone, only buildings of special importance were distinguished by stone construction. In 710, as Bede describes at first hand (H.E. V/21), the King of the Picts requested Abbot Ceolfrith of Jarrow to send him some trained builders capable of constructing a stone church 'in the Roman manner', as exemplified by the churches at Jarrow and Wearmouth. Shortly after his baptism, King Edwin, too, decreed 'that there be erected a larger and grander stone church which was to enclose the earlier small wooden oratory. The foundations were laid and a rectangular church built' (Bede, H.E. II/14). The principle of preserving a 'vetusta ecclesia' also plays a part in the structural history of Glastonbury. It is thought that two tendencies can be perceived in this: first, a wish to make the building grow into a family of churches, as it were, just as the early ecclesiastical buildings at Canterbury and Jarrow were each formed out of several distinct structures; and, secondly, the tendency of the 'hall' to be augmented by adjoining but independent chambers.

If we reflect on the markedly small size of early Anglo-Saxon places of worship, we find that hut and hall are joined by yet another important basic element in the development of the Anglo-Saxon hall, namely, the early Iro-Celtic stone oratory, whose austere design still radiates something of the simplicity of early Christianity. An English example of Irish influence can be seen in St Patrick's Chapel at Heysham (Lancs.). As time went by, the rectangular, cell-like oratory evolved into the Anglo-Saxon two-or three-celled church, which still had a place in Anglo-Norman architecture. This consisted in essence of rectangular chambers—

very small in the early phase—which were annexed to each other and linked by an arcade, extremely simple at first but more strongly emphasized in the advanced phase. St Kevin's Church at Glendalough *(Pl. 123)* is an archetypal illustration of the two-celled church. In a special Anglo-Saxon variant of this type of building, the lower storey of a massive tower forms the nave, and annexed to it is an inset square-ended chancel, as at Earls Barton *(Pl. 217)*.

There are further variants of the three-celled type, e.g. west cell nave chancel or west vestibule nave chancel, west tower-nave-chancel as at Barnack *(Pl. 201)*, or nave-crossing tower-chancel, in which the tower may form the main interior chamber as at Barton-upon-Humber *(Pl. 185)*. The three-celled church, with its west-east arrangement, may also be extended in a north-south direction by the addition of porticus to a central tower, or can even develop into a thoroughgoing cruciform church, as at Stow *(Pl. 189)*, thus displaying a formal affinity with East Mediterranean architecture. This cellular multiplication, if we may be permitted a biological analogy, is a process whose origins cannot be established, but the majority of examples came into being in the north, even after the Conquest.

As the archetype of Anglo-Saxon church architecture, the 'hall' occurs in two basic forms which allow of clear, though not exclusive, differentiation. One of these basic forms is the elongated rectangular nave with a slightly inset rectangular chancel. Two variants of this exist: a less extreme form modelled on Irish churches, and an elongated high-walled form reminiscent of the Germanic long-house, e.g. Escomb *(Pl. 172)*. During Anglo-Saxon times, the first basic form became disseminated mainly in the north of England and almost invariably in areas which had been evangelized by Irish monks. The extent of its dissemination on the Continent is also relatively clearly defined, especially where the 8th and 9th centuries are concerned. It embraced Flanders, Holland, the Lower Rhine and Westphalia—i.e. the original abode of the Anglo-Saxon tribes which migrated to England and the areas evangelized by Irish and Anglo-Saxon missionaries. The Iro-Saxon rectangular nave sometimes acquired lateral articulation in the shape of side-annexes, as at Bradford-on-Avon *(Pl. 72)*.

The second basic form of the original 'hall' occurred in the south of England, primarily in areas which had been evangelized by missionaries from Rome. This was a rectangular building with an east apse which was only slightly inset, if at all. No building of this type has survived intact, unfortunately, but some idea of it can be gained from the foundations of St Andrew's, a church built by King Ethelbert I of Kent in 604, the time of Augustine's mission (Bede, *H.E.* II/3), and identified beneath the façade of Rochester Cathedral. The proportions of the Kent type are better balanced than those of the Escomb type, which gives a rather tall and elongated impression. The more harmonious southern type is reminiscent of profane buildings of the Late Roman period.

The second form is distinguished by yet another noteworthy architectural feature: the nave and chancel are separated by a wall pierced by three narrow round-headed arches which sometimes vary slightly in width. Viewed in terms of formative influence, this was a modified application of the basilican triple-access scheme; structurally, it was a feature which can be identified both in Gaul and North Africa, and thus corroborates the existence of Mediterranean affinities which are also manifest stylistically. We might call it a 'classicizing' of the Iro-Germanic hall. This is particularly apparent in the case of Bradwell-juxta-Mare *(Pl. 239)*, an incomplete but readily interpretable building erected c. 653 by St Cedd of Lindisfarne, i.e. by a member of the Irish-orientated Church of Northumbria, which favoured the narrow, compact, rectangular type of building. The church at Bradwell is thus in the same tradition as the churches which Augustine commissioned half a century earlier, furthering their construction by importing stonemasons from the Continent. The latter used masonry instead of timber, unlike the Anglo-Saxons, and brought the indigenous 'hall' closer to the Roman conception of what a church should be.

The subsequent and increasingly diverse development of the Kentish type is exemplified by Reculver *(Pl. 19)*. The basic 'hall' design, with its triple arcade, apse and porticus (c. 669), was augmented during the 8th century by the addition of more side chambers and a west end. At this 'biological' stage in architectural development, central England produced the church at Brixworth *(Pl. 215)*, founded c. 670 by the monastery of Peterborough, which belonged to the southern group. The Synod of Whitby (663) had ended the predominance of the Iro-Celtic Church in the North, and Archbishop Theodore embarked, from Canterbury, on his Rome-orientated remodelling of the Anglo-Saxon Church. This vital transformation seems to have become crystallized at Brixworth, the most important 7th-century building in England. The interpretation that follows is based on the results of recent excavation.

The original layout conformed to the advanced Kentish type: rectangular nave—triple arcade—square, slightly inset presbytery—apse. In addition, there was a two-storeyed west end. Ranged about this nucleus were independent side-chambers which were later developed into aisles, presumably in the course of 'Latinization'. This completed the transformation of All Saints Brixworth from the advanced Kentish type into the basilican type. We are justified here in speaking of 'Britannia romanica', being in the period when Benedict Biscop and Wilfrid were active and the Venerable Bede had just been born.

It was Wilfrid, as far as we can ascertain, who built the first church of Anglo-Saxon times to be conceived as a basilica from the outset, namely, St Andrew's Hexham, which was probably intended to be a simplified version of Old St Peter's at Rome. Anglo-Saxon basilicas are extremely rare. One very pure specimen of an Anglo-Saxon basilica on the modest Kentish scale was All Saints Lydd (Kent, *post* 950). Its almost square ground-plan, comprising a three-bayed nave, two narrow aisles, west fore-building and slightly inset apse, can be inferred from the arches and ruined walls that are still visible. It should be noted that at Lydd, as at Brixworth, the clerestory windows are situated above the piers instead of above the arcade arches. In this sense, Worksop Priory *(Pl. 186)* revived an Anglo-Saxon tradition at the very end of the Romanesque period. The first English basilica with a Norman accent is Westminster Abbey, dedicated to St Peter by Edward the Confessor (1042–66).

It is remarkable how often Roman building materials, which were in plentiful supply, came to be used for buildings in the Roman tradition. The variable quality of the masonry in early buildings enables us to identify the preliminary handiwork of masterbuilders, probably of Continental origin, who had been trained in the construction of stonework and arches, whereas other sections clearly illustrate the efforts of native masons to imitate their example. Naturally enough, experience of building in stone increased as Anglo-Saxon architecture progressed.

Where no Roman materials were available, a wide variety of stone was used. In the south, walls were mainly of random masonry and rubble bound with mortar and reinforced with inset strips composed of large slabs of hewn stone *(Pl. 32)*. Sometimes, particularly near the Welsh border, these walls were also reinforced with stone slabs laid in horizontal herringbone courses. In the north, walls are usually of squared stone dressed with varying degrees of fineness, and strip-work is unnecessary. The walls of Anglo-Saxon buildings are, generally speaking, thinner than in Norman buildings of the same size, even though Anglo-Saxon architecture is proportionally taller. External corners and the edges of interior arches were reinforced, and simultaneously ornamented, by the insetting of large, carefully hewn slabs of stone laid either vertically or horizontally in a variety of arrangements. Long narrow cross-slabs are commoner in the south, whereas an alternation of massive horizontal and vertical slabs is more often found in the north *(Pl. 217, 173)*. Long-and-short work and pilaster strips are typical features of Anglo-Saxon architecture. However, although examples of long-and-short work can be found elsewhere, e.g. in Late Roman buildings in North Africa, pilaster strips, which were not uninfluenced by the timber-building techniques of very early Anglo-Saxon builders, are exclusive to towers in England.

Windows in early churches tend to be larger than in later ones, which have internal facing or, from the middle of the 10th century onwards, double facing. Seldom rectangular or circular, they are usually round- or triangle-headed and can appear singly or in pairs. Anglo-Saxon architecture displays an uncommon attachment to the triangle-headed doorway *(Pl. 233)* and window *(Pl. 97)*. The concave head of a small round-arched window would often be hewn out of a single block of stone. Fine voussoir-work does not occur until later on, and then only rarely. It is strange that, even where Roman arches have been imitated, a certain disregard for the radial arrangement of voussoirs can be observed. Anglo-Saxon architects did their best to make tower and chancel arches as massive as possible. The wide variations in constructional technique do not permit of chronological classification. Archaic-looking designs *(Pl. 202)* can be contemporaneous with Roman reminiscences *(Pl. 173)*, and classical formulations conceived entirely in stone *(Pl. 52)* with others which betray structural ideas based on timber-work *(Pl. 201)*. The emphasizing of interior arches in Anglo-Saxon buildings continued to make itself felt in Romanesque architecture of the post-Conquest period. Herein lie the origins of the elaborately enriched tower, crossing and chancel arches found in Insular Romanesque churches, especially those of small dimensions *(Pl. 6, 40)*.

Northumbria's prime (*c.* 700) was an early indication of what was to come. People were receptive to a synthesis of the heritages of North and South, East and West, the Mediterranean area, Scandinavia, Ireland, the Ancient World, and a Christianity which was conscious of its youthful vigour. Even during the dark age heralded by the Danish raids at the end of the 8th century, their awareness of belonging to the *Patrimonium Petri* never entirely waned. It was this which prompted King Burgred of Mercia to go to Rome when he was defeated by the Danes, just as earlier Anglo-Saxon kings had also made pilgrimages to Rome after abdicating for reasons of age, e.g. Offa of Essex, Caedwalla, and, in Bede's day, Ine of Mercia.

Alfred (849-901), a historical figure of outstanding importance, administered his royal birthright with great energy. Asser, his biographer, wrote: 'What shall I say of his innumerable campaigns against the heathen and his daily concern for his peoples? We have seen letters and gifts which he received from Elias, Patriarch of Jerusalem. What shall I say of the towns which he either restored or built where none existed before? What shall I say of the royal halls constructed of timber and stone at his behest? What of the royal buildings in stone which he ordered to be removed from their old sites and rebuilt in better places? But he stood alone, alone with the help of God.'

Alfred summoned builders from the Continent. His monastery at Athelney (Somerset), built to commemorate his victory over the Danes in 878 but only completed by his son Edward, betrayed Carolingian influence. Alfred intended it to provide the country with a new religious centre now that the monasteries of Lindisfarne, Jarrow, Wearmouth, Hexham, Peterborough and Ely had been destroyed by the Danes. He sent to Corvey in Westphalia for the Saxon monk Johannes and to Saint-Bertin in Flanders for Grimbald, who later became Abbot of Winchester. However, the preconditions for a new renascence were not yet forthcoming, which was why Alfred sought consolation in Boethius. No fresh creative activity could take place until about the middle of the 10th century, when political authority had been stabilized and religious discipline consolidated by reform.

While Alfred's successors embarked on the conquest of the Danelaw, the Normans established themselves in Gaul under Rollo. In 911, after making raids on Scotland and Ireland, the Norman leader had been granted territory round the lower reaches of the Seine by Charles the Simple in the hope that this would pacify him. As legitimate rulers of Neustria, Rollo and his successors proceeded to extend their sovereignty over Normandy, one of whose subsequent rulers, Duke William II, was destined to conquer England and become King William I.

By about the middle of the 10th century, Anglo-Saxon England had been reunified and Northumbria reintegrated. As Archbishop of Canterbury, Dunstan became the symbol of a religious and cultural revival in the island. Simultaneously, in 955, Otto the Great decisively worsted the Hungarians on the Lechfeld and thus paved the way for a new spiritual reunification of the West under the auspices of an emperor in the tradition of the Roman Empire. The great age of the Ottonians had begun. By contrast, the Papacy had reached its nadir with John XII, a totally depraved, arrogant and cynical youth who was so ill-educated that he could only speak the vernacular. For all that, new vistas had already opened up within the Church. This was the period when the Benedictine monks of Cluny in Burgundy were demanding and, by their example, actively promoting radical Church reform.

Conditions in the majority of monasteries, in England as elsewhere, were apalling during the late 9th century. Married lay abbots looked upon monastery estates as heritable family property. Monks, too, lived off monastery estates with their families, and orderly monastic life had almost ceased to exist. At the Synod of Trosly, near Laon, one of the pre-Cluny essays at reform, Archbishop Herivaeus of Rheims asked plaintively: 'How are the rules to be expounded by an abbot who tells me "I cannot read"?' The final century of the first Christian millennium, seen and dreaded as a terminal point in time, brought reform in its train—reform which was the product of many small beginnings and a slowly burgeoning desire for improvement on the part of bishops and a section of the nobility.

The monastic community of Cluny, founded in 910 by Duke William of Aquitaine, became the standard-bearer of the new movement. The great age of Romanesque dawned. Existing abbeys which wanted to join Cluny were incorporated in and subordinated to it, though they were often left in the care of their own abbots. The modified nature of Cluny's centralization also revealed itself in architectural design, which owed more to suggestion than to strict regulations of the sort later imposed by the Cistercians. Daughter monasteries were founded as priories, one of them at Lewes in Sussex. Spiritual revival was accompanied by a revival of interest in holy places, and bands of pilgrims trudged across Europe en route for distant monasteries and churches. Ideas spread by a process of exchange, and conceptions of the world became unified. Portrayals of God as the Pantocrator appeared on the tympana of church portals everywhere.

Cluny emitted a splendid aura. Its position in the heart of Latin Christendom and on the main north-south route, its internationalism and ideological unity, to use modern terms, and its genuine concern for the fundamentals of monastic and Christian life in general—all contributed to its success. Ignoring powerful opposition, especially from the feudal bishops, Cluny soon began to appoint bishops of its own and secured the co-operation of the Popes. The accession of Pope Gregory VII (Hildebrand of Soana) soon after the Conquest meant that the throne of St Peter was now occupied by a Cluniac whose ambition it was to realize St Augustine's City of God on earth. By that time, however, Cluny had already become too prosperous and powerful and too much involved in worldly matters, with the result that it was soon eclipsed by the new reforms of Cîteaux and Clairvaux.

Reformation in England—only indirectly influenced by Cluny, since other forces were more active there—took place in three stages: under Dunstan in the middle of the 10th century; under the Lotharingian bishops and abbots in the middle of the 11th century; and as a result of the monastic reorganization carried out by the Normans—partly from political motives—at the end of the same century.

Among the earliest 10th-century reformist movements, which were initially independent of Cluny and only became co-ordinated with it at a later stage, were those of Flanders and Lorraine. The *post*-919 Flemish reforms of Gerhard de Brogne, notably the model monasteries at Ghent, acquired such a reputation that Flemish monks were invited to reorganize the Norman abbeys of St-Wandrille, Mont-St-Michel and St-Ouen in Rouen. It was at Ghent that Dunstan, an Anglo-Saxon, became inspired by the idea of reform. Appointed Abbot of Glastonbury by Edward I in 943, he transmitted the impulse to England. With King Edgar's support, Dunstan resuscitated the abbeys of Malmesbury, Westminster, Bath, and Exeter. In 960, having previously held the sees of Worcester and London, he became Archbishop of Canterbury, thereby lending weight to his reformist activities throughout England. Dunstan was not only supreme pastor of his country and political and spiritual adviser to the kings of Wessex but also a liturgist of the first rank. (His order of service for royal coronations is still in use today.) He also promoted cultural activities of every kind. The consolidation of royal authority in England, which had brought increased trade and prosperity, together with the consolidation of the English Church and the resulting demand for ecclesiastical buildings and appurtenances, ushered in a new period of prime. The high-quality metal-work, carved ivory and fabrics produced by English manufactories became known throughout Europe under the name 'opus anglicanum'. Scriptoria began to operate once more. All the fruits of this outstanding artistic activity are classified as 'School of Winchester', after their principal source. There was a rebirth of scholarship, and interest in Anglo-Saxon history prompted the compilation of Old English literary works, which were handed down in codices of the late 10th century. Works by Fathers of the Church and classical authors were read and annotated, as were the works of Bede, Alcuin, Hrabanus Maurus and others.

Among those who assisted Dunstan in his ecclesiastical reforms were Ethelwold and Oswald, the latter a scion of a Danish family which had settled in England. It was through him that Cluny's influence made itself felt, since he had spent several years at Fleury, which had joined the Cluniac movement. As Bishop of Worcester in 962 and, subsequently, Archbishop of York, Oswald was always at pains to exploit what he had learned at Fleury, especially in monasteries of his own founding, such as Ramsey and Evesham. Ethelwold had recognized the course of his future career while a monk at Glastonbury during Dunstan's abbacy. As Bishop of Winchester, where he was active from 963 onwards, he introduced Dunstan's rules into the monasteries under his jurisdiction. He also maintained contact with the monasteries of Ghent and Fleury and injected new life into Peterborough, but his most important achievement, in all probability, was an Anglo-Saxon translation of the Benedictine Rules.

Of supreme importance to the Church and monasteries of England was the synod of all the bishops, abbots and abbesses in the country, convened c. 970 by King Edgar for the purpose of laying down a universal code of religious observance, the *Regularis Concordia Anglicae Nationis*. Monks from Ghent and Fleury attended, and the text was edited by Ethelwold. The *Regularis Concordia* shunned extreme solutions and took account of Old English monastic usages in so far as they accorded with the spirit of reform. Great importance was assigned to the Liturgy. Monks had to be able to spread themselves in church, and this seems to have been one of the reasons for the elongated chancels so typical of English cathedrals. Lotharingian ideas also played an undoubted part, and clerics from Lorraine were responsible for promoting a revival of the Anglican Church in the 11th century, after the second wave of Danish invasions.

The Danish raids continued for almost four decades, less in the Danelaw districts of East Anglia, York and Lincoln, which were now occupied by converted Danes, than in the south. Their object was not so much loot and plunder as Danegeld or 'protection money' paid in the gold and silver of which England had accumulated a great deal during the comparative calm of the 10th century. England was prosperous now. London was a focal point of resistance, true, but it cleverly exploited its status as a commercial centre. These difficult days marked the beginning of its rise in the world, which eventually brought it precedence over the royal capital, Winchester.

The Vikings were led by Sweyn Forkbeard, King of the Danes and a ferocious Christian warrior. His son Canute (1016–36), though brought up a pagan, had the strength and intelligence—as well as the political acumen—to effect a reconciliation of opposites after his accession to the throne. His reputation at death was that of an upright Christian, just lawgiver, and generous benefactor of churches and monasteries. Canute modelled himself on the two 'greats', Charlemagne and Alfred. He visited Rome, but as King of Denmark, Norway, England and the Hebrides, he ruled an empire which encompassed the North Sea. In consequence, despite his close contacts with Europe, he temporarily diverted England's gaze northwards. The reign of Edward the Confessor reversed this trend. It was the Normans, the Northerners who had become Romanized in Neustria, who complected the process and drew England wholly into the Romanesque orbit.

THE AGE OF TRANSITION

Edward (1042–66) was a son of the ill-starred Anglo-Saxon king Ethelred and his wife Emma, daughter of Richard I, Duke of Normandy. Their marriage had taken place at the instigation of the Pope, who was anxious to end the tension between the Anglo-Saxons and the Normans. The Danes forced the royal family to seek refuge at the Norman court, where Edward was brought up. He was a frequent and zealous visitor to Norman monasteries. Although regarded as an Anglo-Saxon by the Norman military aristocracy, Edward learnt to speak Norman and dressed like a Norman. And when, after a brief interlude, he succeeded Hardicanute as King of England, he came to court accompanied by a Norman entourage and a whole world of Norman ideas.

Edward had not been reared as a successor to the throne, and it was only an unexpected chain of circumstances which brought him to the fore. Canute's line had become extinct, and Edward was chosen in his capacity as a distant relative. He accepted his inheritance, although the spectre of legal uncertainty which had haunted England since the passing of Edgar and Dunstan—and which had really prompted the Danes to launch their renewed attacks on the island—must have loomed over him too. Edward despised the Danes and refused to have anything to do with his mother, who had married Canute. He was no warrior, but he issued edicts for the restoration and maintenance of public order which were still extolled in William's day as 'the good laws of Edward'. It had horrified him that his elder brother Alfred had been murdered at the command of Godwin, Earl of Wessex and the most powerful of the Anglo-Saxon nobles. Edward's long and vicissitudinous struggle with Godwin, who, with his sons, dominated the whole of England, made it impossible for the childless monarch to contemplate an Anglo-Saxon successor—even Harold Godwin, whom he had taken into his court entourage. Edward favoured William of Normandy, and William's bold and resolute moves after Edward's death show that he was fully aware of this.

By deciding on a Norman successor, Edward had come down on the side of authority and order. He admired the robust soldier and politician in William, a man who had imposed his will upon the political and ecclesiastical hierarchy of Normandy. Condemned by birth to a dual legacy of Anglo-Saxon and Norman blood, Edward was a far more complex character.

The Normans were intrepid fighters whose lust for conquest took them far—to southern Italy, Sicily, even the Holy Land. They were great organizers, too—the precision with which William solved the complexities of invading England proves that. They founded new states and were adept in exploiting others for their own ends, as witness their relations with the Pope. Their manners were those of war-lords, and their attendance at court was an act of homage. They were a young and virile people compared with the Anglo-Saxons. Anglo-Saxon noblemen, with their long hair, fine clothes and polished manners, struck them as effeminate. The Bayeux Tapestry clearly stresses the differences between the two sides. The Anglo-Saxons proved that they were also capable of hardship and great military achievement by their northward march against the Norwegians and their southward march against the Normans in 1066. They acquitted themselves brilliantly in the first engagement at Stamford but lost the second because they were rash and impatient. Camp life was not their milieu nor war their raison d'être. They were accustomed to luxury and devoted to more refined pleasures. They lived not in castles, like the Normans, but in residential halls like Harold's at Bosham, which also figures in the Bayeux Tapestry.

The Anglo-Saxons were the more cultured of the two peoples. This was partly because they had been settled in their island home far longer than the Northerners round the Seine, and partly because their Christian tradition was older and more diverse. The Normans had conquered their domain and quickly founded a unitary state without parallel elsewhere. The Anglo-Saxons had never really developed into a political unit. The suzerainty of the 'Bretwalda' remained largely formal, and all that linked the various kingdoms was a measure of popular fellow-feeling. Unification was only carried out under Sweyn's coercion and Canute's leadership. It was left to the Normans to impose centralization with a firm hand. Yet the Anglo-Saxons bore a cultural heritage which was alien to the Normans and impressed them as being older, more mature, less vital, perhaps—the rich heritage adumbrated by our allusions to the golden age of Northumbria, Alfred's greatness, and Dunstan's reforms.

The Normans sensed this inferiority and tried to offset it by an expenditure of material resources and military strength. The Anglo-Saxons were conscious of their cultural superiority and did not conceal the fact. Tension often made itself felt when well-educated Anglo-Saxon clerics were subordinated to less well-educated Normans. Edward, Archdeacon of London, planned to leave Norman-dominated Canterbury. Commenting on this in 1080, the Flemish monk Goscelin wrote: 'We are witnessing a time when the uneducated man derides and mocks the scholar.' History repeats itself after a fashion. Early in the 6th century the British bard Gildas had derided the pagan Anglo-Saxon invaders as 'dogs' and 'whelps of the barbarian pack', and it remained for Christianity to civilize them. In the 11th century, Anglo-Saxons and Normans met on a common religious plane, and the process of mutual adjustment—to which both parties contributed—fulfilled itself more rapidly. Church architecture, for instance, which was still wholly Norman during the first post-Conquest generation, had already been imprinted with Insular tradition by the time of the second, or post-1100 generation.

Little is known about architectural activity in England during the first half of the 11th century, although Archbishop Wulfstan decreed at the beginning of the century that one-third of all Church tithes should be devoted to the restoration of churches which had become dilapidated, whether as a result of Danish raids or through neglect. Ethelred's reign was not a time of new buildings. A vast sum had to be paid to the Danes in 1012, so no money remained for building purposes. Canute was no builder, either, despite his patronage of churches and monasteries. He was more concerned with the maintenance of order within his vast sphere of influence. Edward more or less voluntarily left responsibility for new building to Harold Godwin, later King Harold. The one project to which he devoted himself personally was the construction of the new abbey church of St Peter at Westminster. It was significant that he sited it on the outskirts of London, the international trading centre, rather than in Winchester, the ancient capital of the Anglo-Saxon kings.

Very little of Edward's one major building project has survived. It was modelled on Jumièges, whence came the alternation between compound and cylindrical piers, though the Benedictine triapsidal chancel was more closely related to the ground-plan of Bernay. The church had two west towers, a transept, and a crossing tower. The aisled nave boasted thirteen spans and was thus longer than any building in contemporary Normandy, let alone England. A most striking impression of its majestic appearance—beside which the little church at Bosham, also depicted, looks modest—can be gained from the Bayeux Tapestry. Westminster Abbey was begun at about the middle of the 11th century and consecrated on 28 December 1065, nine days before Edward died. His death unleashed events which not only led to the conquest of England but were to make the country burgeon anew.

THE NORMAN ERA

Harold Godwin, who had himself anointed King of England immediately after Edward's death, quickly subdued all internal opposition but had to contend with William's reaction to his move. His position was further prejudiced by the fact that, to Rome, Archbishop Stigand of Canterbury was a usurper who supported the Antipope, whereas William had secured Pope Alexander II's blessing on his projected invasion, almost as though it were a Crusade.

This was just one more example of the Duke of Normandy's political expertise. When his father Robert I died on a journey to the Holy Land in 1035, Normandy, which was still in process of consolidation, seemed likely to disintegrate as a result of internal struggles for power and external attacks on the part of Maine, Blois, Anjou, Brittany, and, in particular, the King of France. William was only eight years old at the time. Although designated his father's successor, he was a bastard offspring of Duke Robert's liaison with Arletta, a tanner's daughter. There is no doubt that one of the strongest motives underlying all William's actions, his seizure of the English crown included, was a wish to efface the stigma of illegitimacy. This was one of the reasons why he clung to his marriage with Matilda in defiance of the Pope's ban, which was probably issued on the grounds of consanguinity. Matilda was the daughter of Baldwin V, the powerful Duke of Flanders, and of Adela, daughter of the French king Robert II. In atonement for their enforced marriage, Matilda founded the nunnery of St Etienne and William the abbey of St Etienne, their respective burial-places in the town of Caen, which William had made capital of the dukedom.

William managed to survive his early years as duke by a combination of tenacity, luck, shrewdness, and cunning restraint. He proceeded to reinforce his position within the Norman nobility and among the rulers of Europe with diplomatic skill, displaying great determination and, when need arose, considerable severity towards his opponents. The main factors which emboldened him to make a bid for the English crown were three in number: first, his military successes against rebellious noblemen and, in 1057, against the French king; secondly, his establishment of a rigid political system supported by a new aristocracy which owed direct allegiance to his own person; and, thirdly, his vigorous sponsorship of Church reform in Normandy.

The Norman nobility was not yet fully crystallized, even in 1035, and this afforded William an opportunity—of which he soon took full advantage—to bind its members to him with posts at court and grants of land. This policy of identifying the nobility's interests with his own was one to which William adhered after his conquest of England. Among the youthful dignitaries with which the still youthful duke surrounded himself in increasing numbers were his two half-brothers, Robert of Mortain, who became one of the wealthiest landowners in England, and Odo, Bishop of Bayeux and later Earl of Kent, as well as William Fitz Osbern, later Earl of Hereford, and Roger de Montgomery. By appointing viscounts directly responsible to himself and enacting a law which reserved the maintenance of castles to the Crown, he centralized his new political regime and ensured that it was carefully supervised by a select body of administrators.

William also devoted his full attention to the Church. Being a realist to whom spiritual and temporal matters were conjoined, he recognized the importance of the Church as an ally in political ventures, which, in their turn, affected the realization of God's kingdom on earth. This was how, as standard-bearers of the Papacy, Normans under Robert Guiscard established fiefs in Apulia, Calabria and Sicily in 1061. It is notable that, immediately after his various victories, William marked each step in the construction of his state by initiating Church assemblies in his capacity as a defender of the faith. In October 1047, for example, personal feuds were declared to be at an end and 'divine peace' solemnly proclaimed by the Council of Caen. The Council of Lisieux, convened after the battle of Mortemer and attended by the papal legate, deposed Archbishop Mauger of Rouen, one of William's uncles, and, at William's instigation, replaced him with a less conservative reform bishop who had trained at Halberstadt. William's collaboration with the Church was founded on his almost friendly relations with Lanfranc, Prior of Bec.

Bec, a hermitage founded by Count Herluin and a handful of followers in 1039, occupied a special place among the many well-run monasteries of Normandy. In quest of communal solitude, Lanfranc of Pavia joined the monastery in 1042. Thanks to Lanfranc's activities as a teacher, Bec swiftly earned a reputation as one of the spiritual centres of Europe, and many a future English bishop was trained there. Ever on the lookout for shrewd minds to enlist in his service, William summoned Lanfranc to Caen in 1063 and made him Abbot of St Etienne. In 1070 he promoted him Archbishop of Canterbury. A pillar of the Church, Lanfranc was convinced of the necessity for reform, both in respect of the clergy and of those laymen who participated in Church affairs. He co-operated admirably with William, who trusted him, and, provided William's nominees were worthy of office, gave the king a free hand in the appointment of bishops and abbots—in sharp contrast to Anselm's attitude later on. Lanfranc pursued his activities in England until the anointing of William's successor-designate, William Rufus.

Anselm of Aosta entered Bec in 1060, drawn there by Lanfranc's reputation. Having become prior and abbot of the monastery, he succeeded Lanfranc as Archbishop of Canterbury in 1093, but fell out with William Rufus over investitures and was twice forced into exile in France and Italy. Two factors were reflected in this friction: the king's inferior personality and the archbishop's inferior political skill. Anselm was less a Church leader than a theologian, and one whose writings affected the spiritual climate, both during the Romanesque period and thereafter. 'Credo ut intelligam', he declared—'I believe that I may understand'. He exemplified the world of High Romanesque, which conceived of Christianity not only as an other-worldly doctrine but as a vital force permeating everything, however mundane. Regarded in this light, mundane activities became feats of divine endeavour.

Church reform in Normandy was essentially monastic, not episcopal. The concept of the feudal system and of central ducal authority was too ingrained in the new Norman aristocracy, whose leading families supplied most of the bishops. Odo of Bayeux, William's halfbrother, was typical of this intimate connection between ecclesiastical and political office—yet another factor which helped to buttress the political system. Without such collaboration, the building of a new ecclesiastical order in England would doubtless have been impossible. Thus, Normandy sowed what England was to reap. Only this attitude could have given birth to Durham, both as an idea and as an outward symbol. It was as though, in all his deliberations, ordinances and actions, William had banked on acquiring the English crown from the very first.

His preparations for invasion were marked by the same circumspection. The facts are known. The Bayeux Tapestry, over 230 feet long, provides us with an artistically condensed view—from the Norman angle—of the events leading up to the invasion, its planning, the equipping of the fleet, the crossing, the deployment of the armies, and the battle of 14 October 1066. Nowhere else in Europe is there anything to compare with this 'opus anglicanum'.

William's defeat of Harold's army was not in itself enough to subdue England. Years elapsed between Christmas Day 1066, when William II, Duke of Normandy, was crowned William I, King of England, and the final quelling of the sporadic rebellions led by Anglo-Saxon noblemen with the support of Danish invaders. Events in and around Peterborough, Ely and Durham speak plainly enough. Thirty-eight-year-old William may initially have hoped that his claims would be accepted by the English on the grounds of their legitimacy, but he was soon disillusioned. The Norman intruders long remained alien to the Anglo-Saxon nobility and high clergy, but the latter had to yield to superior force. William never felt at home in England, and it is significant that he soon abandoned his intention of learning the English language.

He did not abandon his principal aim, however. He, the bastard who had already made himself one of the greatest rulers in Europe, was determined to assert his status as King of England. Resistance was countered with brutal severity. It cannot be ignored that the primary effect of the Conquest was destruction, but this only increased the need for thorough reconstruction. William's experiences in Normandy stood him in good stead. He built strongholds—earth ramparts, ditches and palisades at first, then stone castles like the Tower of London. These fortifications were alien to the English and served as a warning to them. Manned by garrisons directly responsible to the king, they made it clear that all land belonged to the Crown.

To the Norman nobility, the conquest of England was a profitable venture. William arbitrarily distributed land among his vassals for services rendered. To the rural population, long reduced to the status of servants and tenants, the change of masters brought no undue change in living conditions. Their hardships remained the same, except that output had to be stepped up still further to meet increased property taxes. To the English nobility, especially the once influential senior nobility, the change was at once trenchant, oppressive, and humiliating. They were not only deprived of their landed property but ousted from all posts at court and replaced by Normans. William's measures were sweeping and ruthless. Government posts and their incumbents changed, but not, in so far as it served its purpose, the actual structure of government. The Chancellery was strengthened. 'Writs', or written edicts bearing the royal seal, were retained, though they were now drafted in Latin rather than English or even French. Language was a breach between victors and vanquished which took long to heal, and Latin, the language of the Church, was called upon to serve as an intermediary. Mediation had to be sought in the field of law, too. It says much for William that he enacted laws which took both Norman and English usages into account. The old district and local courts remained, but all were supervised by royal courts.

As the anointed Rex Anglorum, William was fully aware of his absolute powers. For himself, he claimed about one-fifth of all cultivable land, the metropolis of London, and vast game forests protected by special laws. Border areas such as Kent, Northumbria and Hereford were singled out for bestowal upon one or other of his intimates, who, as earls, represented the king and guaranteed his frontiers by maintaining castles and garrisons. Further grants of land went primarily to members of the youthful Norman aristocracy with whom William had grown up. In return, the recipients performed military service and remitted taxes, with the emphasis on the latter. Necessity, coupled with William's personal greed, ensured that these were high. It was characteristic of him and indicative of his political acumen that he should have decreed the compiling of a land register, or Domesday Book, in 1085. Royal officials travelled the country, estimating and recording the extent of all ecclesiastical and secular estates, together with their population, income and outgoings. It was a vast operation, but the king had the will and the man-power to carry it out. The report was completed within a year. Admittedly, William had little time to evaluate it and his sons showed little interest in it, but no contemporary book of a similar nature exists. It informs us that the population of William's kingdom, that is, exluding Scotland and Wales, totalled about one-and-a-half million, or roughly one human being to every twelve acres—a very low density when we reflect how many enormous churches were built during the Anglo-Norman period.

The Anglo-Saxon Church could undoubtedly boast an older and richer tradition than the Norman. This cultural superiority and independence rendered it particularly suspect to the Norman nobility, who, where church buildings had not been ransacked or burnt, saw them in their original form and found them alien. The manners and education of the high clergy were equally strange to them. William, who felt himself to be absolute master of the English Church, as of all else, instituted radical changes in ecclesiastical structure and personnel, wisely consulting Lanfranc in advance and often enlisting the support of Church synods. His authoritarian claims naturally brought him into conflict with Gregory VII, the reformist Pope. However, since William had conquered England with papal backing and had always joined the reformist Popes in advocating an improvement in the status of the clergy and a reform of ecclesiastical organization, Gregory was virtually hamstrung. Archbishop Anselm and Henry I later evolved a modus vivendi in the matter of appointments.

The death of the Archbishop of York in 1069 and the dismissal of Archbishop Stigand of Canterbury by the Council of Winchester in 1070 presented William with a welcome opportunity to reorganize the English Church. Old episcopal sees centred on small places were transferred to large towns such as Lincoln. Primacy was vested in the Archbishopric of Canterbury, to which Lanfranc was now appointed. The hierarchy was rigidly organized, from bishops, archdeacons and deacons down to parish priests. The training of the junior clergy, monks included, was to be improved. The rules of religious orders were to be observed, among them that of celibacy. Secularized canonical chapters were disbanded and many establishments handed over to the Benedictines. William regarded the monasteries as a consolidating factor. The tradition of cathedral abbeys such as Canterbury, Winchester, Worcester and Sherborne accorded with this notion and was therefore retained. Chief among the new additions were Norwich, Rochester and Durham. Elsewhere, as at Chichester, Hereford and York, well-run canonical chapters were introduced.

Above all, since the episcopacy was closely linked with the central authority of the Crown, English abbots and bishops were soon supplanted in all places of importance by Normans or, in rare instances, by Lorrainers. No fewer than twenty-eight abbots and five bishops were imported into England from the reform monasteries of Normandy during William's reign. This meant that the senior ranks of the clergy were virtually purged of Anglo-Saxons. By 1080 or thereabouts, Wulfstan of Worcester was the only bishop of Anglo-Saxon origin. The Norman bishops and abbots were, needless to say, a mixed bunch. Turold of Peterborough and Thurstan of Glastonbury were war-lords rather than shepherds of their flock, but this somewhat incongruous minority was far outweighed by figures such as Paul of Caen at St Albans or Serlo of Mont-Saint-Michel at Glastonbury. Nevertheless, all these princes of the Church were at one in their determination to erect worthy ecclesiastical edifices in honour of the Eternal Ruler.

NORMAN ARCHITECTURE

William founded Battle ('de bello') Abbey on the site of the battle near Hastings. This provides a clue to one important reason for the spate of architectural activity which broke out a few years after the Conquest: churches were founded as a form of atonement. The Romanesque concept of man was such that, even when waging a just war, he was felt to have become involved in something evil for which he must make due atonement. In 1070, with the approval of the papal legate, Norman bishops published an edict concerning the strict penances required, most of which could be commuted into endowments for ecclesiastical buildings. The Church itself made further contributions from its large revenues.

A more important reason for the many new ecclesiastical building projects was the Normans' conviction that existing Anglo-Saxon churches were unworthy of the Almighty. Again, many of them had been damaged and were suitable for use only as building material, while others, e.g. Rochester and Durham, were demolished to make room for larger and more massive houses of God. Last but not least, the Normans' pride impelled them to outdo the Anglo-Saxons on principle. As organizers and founders of states, the Normans erected strongholds for themselves and their God. Apulia, Sicily and the Holy Land demonstrate this too, but England does so more vividly. Not only had the Normans swiftly secured a new outlet for their boundless energy, but they now had at their disposal a country whose resources they could deploy as they thought fit. All their great abbeys and cathedrals were built within barely two generations—a phenomenon unique to the Romanesque period. It would be wrong to confine English Romanesque to the so-called Norman style alone, but there is no doubt that the Norman assumption of power brought it into full flower.

Some authorities suggest that it was the havoc wrought by the post-Carolingian migrations, coupled with a permanent sense of insecurity, which prompted architects to design buildings that could not easily be destroyed. This would explain the architectural concept of the solid, organic stone church—a concept which the Normans carried to extremes. While material considerations of this sort cannot entirely be dismissed, the reasons underlying changes in religious architecture are apt to be of a more spiritual nature. Religious architecture always expresses prevailing ideas of God and the world, hence the contrast between the Ravennine basilica and the Romanesque or Gothic cathedral. The Romanesque God was an absolute ruler whose vassals erected sacred strongholds and palaces to him on earth. That was why, as Christian warriors, the Normans built lofty and austere fortresses of God like St Etienne in Normandy and Durham in England.

Despite their individual differences, Anglo-Norman buildings do exhibit similarities. In the first place, all public buildings were larger than their Anglo-Saxon predecessors. Their layout was more complex and invariably basilican. Chancels fell into two main categories. Most of them belonged to the Benedictine or stepped triapsidal type exemplified by the churches at Caen, but others resembled Rouen and Jumièges in having an ambulatory and radiating chapels. Changes set in as early as 1100, and a preference for square-ended chancels soon manifested itself.

Another common feature was the tripartite division of walls into arcade, gallery and clerestory, with a wall-passage running along the massive walls at the height of the clerestory windows. The alternation between compound and simple square or rectangular piers, doubtless inspired by Jumièges, remained customary but fulfilled no more than an aesthetic function. This tendency to develop rhythmical intervals within the structure of walls brought with it a predilection for adorning piers and walls with engaged demi-shafts which rose to the ceiling as though intended to support vaults. The location of towers varied, but a preference for crossing and west towers can be discerned. The general lay-out was as follows: first a projecting west end, often strongly emphasized, leading to a crossing traversed by a transept, often with aisles of its own, and, finally, a more elaborately enriched chancel. All such buildings were distinguished by their grandeur of conception, by an austerity which did not wane until later years, and—certainly during the early phase and even thereafter—by a certain crudity of execution compared with that of French or Italian buildings.

Of the first generation of cathedrals, all of them begun before 1080, e.g. Lanfranc's Canterbury, William's Battle Abbey, Lincoln, Old Sarum and York, only small built-in remnants and traces of foundations can still be seen. The purest surviving impressions of Anglo-Norman architecture are provided by the nave at St Albans *(Pl. 26)* and the transept at Winchester *(Pl. 51)*, where the galleries leading to the upper east chapels have also survived, or by the later (begun 1088) priory at Blyth *(Pl. 187)*, which is closely related to Caen's St Etienne. St Albans exemplifies an early trend which affected all Anglo-Norman churches except those in the west of England. This was a predilection for extending the chancel by one or more bays and a marked tendency to elongate nave and aisles. English cathedrals are among the longest in the world, Ely *(Pl. 223)* and Norwich *(Pl. 249)* being pre-eminent in this respect. The fact that this tendency towards elongation does not occur in Normandy and is not present in the west of England, but gains strength in Anglo-Norman buildings with the growth of an individual style *c.* 1100, lends weight to the theory that it was an after-effect of the elongated Anglo-Saxon 'hall', whose disproportionate length was further exaggerated by the Norman conquerors.

The cathedrals of the first generation, built between 1080 and 1090 but after the consolidation of Church and State, e.g. Ely *(Pl. 221)*, Rochester *(Pl. 18)*, and Worcester, exhibit a trend towards greater structural subtlety. Gloucester *(Pl. 93)* represents an important member of the western group. Disregarding other idiosyncrasies, the chief characteristic of this group lies in the nave arcades, whose piers consist of uncompounded cylindrical columns of great height, the tribunes surmounting them being no more than a narrow band. The origins of this particular style are unknown, though some have ascribed it to Rhenish influence. Despite the individuality of this special group, it should be stressed that English Romanesque displays none of the strong regional differences discernible in France or Spain. Specific schools of architectural thought are equally hard to distinguish. Strong architectural personalities played their part in English Romanesque as elsewhere, of course—we have only to think of William of Sens and William the Englishman, who built the new choir at Canterbury—but, in general, the absolute unity of the Church and its administrators, the Norman bishops, was echoed by the basic homogeneity of its buildings.

The foundation-stone of Durham Cathedral *(Pl. 161)* was laid in 1093, the year in which Anselm of Canterbury embarked on *'Cur Deus homo?'*, his spiritual edifice. The cathedral was designed from the outset to be spanned by vaults. By 1133, during a new efflorescence under England's third Norman king, Henry I, the principal components of the vast structure were already completed. Its rib-vaulted chancel aisles, transept and nave made it the most up-to-date building of its time. The same efflorescence of English High Romanesque produced Norwich Cathedral *(Pl. 249)*, whose lucidly articulated interior brought two further characteristics of English Romanesque to full flower: seriality, achieved by a repetition of identical members; and an increasingly pronounced division of interior walls into a structural complex of arcades, galleries and clerestories which transformed what used to be massive fortresses of God into bright palaces erected in his honour.

The year 1110 marked the beginning of a second phase in English High Romanesque. Most large churches of earlier date were augmented with remarkable consistency, even though Durham's aura tempted builders to deviate. In the case of new chancels, however, novel architectural ideas were introduced, and there was a growing recourse to the square-ended type. Work also began on a second generation of new buildings, e.g. Hereford *(Pl. 108)*, Exeter *(Pl. 68)*, Southwell *(Pl. 194)*, Romsey, Leominster, and, above all, Peterborough *(Pl. 211)*. There was an increasing use of sculptural decoration, splendidly exemplified by Kilpeck *(Pl. 103)* and, later, Barfreston *(Pl. 1)*, by the Prior's Portal at Ely *(Pl. 228)*, and by a whole series of very typical fonts, mainly in areas near the Welsh border *(Pl. 99, 110)*. This upsurge in sculptural activity, which extended to capitals as well, stimulated architectural ornamentation in general, which had tended to be rare in buildings of the 11th century. In about 1110 there appeared a decorative feature which stemmed from the Anglo-Norman predilection for seriality and became a symptom of the late phase, namely, enlaced or intersected blind arches. These could cover entire interior walls *(Pl. 115)* or whole façades *(Pl. 244)*. A second decorative motif, which appeared soon afterwards, rapidly became an important distinguishing characteristic of late English Romanesque. This was the chevron or zigzag, a motif whose fecundity was such that it spread virtually everywhere—to string courses and friezes, jambs, archivolts and soffits, tower and chancel arches, windows and towers—and even travelled to Apulia and Sicily in the wake of the Normans. Less widely disseminated but no less important was the 'beak-head' *(Pl. 88)*, an individual and highly plastic English motif which emerged during the turbulent middle years of the 12th century and was robust enough to be developed to the verge of abstraction. In fact, many motifs degenerated into geometrical designs in the late phase towards the end of the century.

With the accession of Henry II (1154–89), the kingdom passed into the firmer hands of the Anjous. Thanks to a combination of luck, marriage and military success, Henry had become heir to four of the greatest European dynasties and could style himself 'King of the English, Duke of the Normans and Aquitainians, Count of the Angevins'. Normans and Anglo-Saxons became more closely fused at this period, and there was an admixture of new French blood as well. The Benedictines were joined by the Cistercians, whose arrival symptomized a new impulse within the Church and a new wave of internationalism. Preparations were made for a new Crusade in which Richard Cœur de Lion, King of England (d. 1199), took part and Emperor Frederick I (Barbarossa) lost his life.

Romanesque had attained fulfilment. A comparison between the positively classical articulation of the crossing tower at Norwich *(Pl. 253)* and the west end at Ely *(Pl. 222)*, completed *c.* 1200, illustrates the final stage. A transition to a new stylistic world was beginning because people's outlook on the world had changed. The arches at Malmesbury *(Pl. 78)* and Glastonbury *(Pl. 70)* and the superb doorway at Barfreston *(Pl. 1)* show that an age of greater humanity was dawning: the Gothic God was a heavenly father.

The Romanesque image of God, by contrast, was that of a Cosmic Creator, Ruler and Judge, omnipresent and eternal. He was a supreme reality in an unseen world, yet constantly and symbolically glorified by the whole of visible Creation. To Romanesque man, a realist without parallel and realistic, too, in his full understanding of the sinfulness of a world that had fallen as a result of original sin, manifest on earth as a thousandfold demonic temptation, the world presented a constant choice for or against the Almighty. It was in the service of this omnipotent god that hermits built their austere cells, that land-owners endowed chantry chapels, that monks erected churches, abbeys and cathedrals at the behest of bishops and abbots—all of them labouring at a common task. Cells and cathedrals alike represented oases of divine peace in a threatening world, places that were directed inwards at the reality of God on earth.

Romanesque gazed into the unseen, as Marcel Probé rightly says, but the unseen had to have a visible abode on earth. The Romanesque world was not a world hereafter. Unlike Gothic cathedrals, which soar heavenwards like some celestial Jerusalem, filled with mystic radiance, Romanesque cathedrals stand four-square on the earth, divine fortresses and palaces reared by the sweat of man's brow. Anselm of Canterbury asked why God had become man. To the people of the Romanesque period there was only one answer: if the words 'Thy Kingdom come' were to become reality, they must be realized here on earth, by restoring the divinity which the world had lost. King and bishop, monk and pilgrim—all laboured to that end. They could do so only because they believed in the promise of fulfilment in this world. To be edifices built by man in the service of this promise by the Eternal Ruler was the essential function of the churches and cathedrals of the Romanesque period.

THE PLATES

1 BARFRESTON (Kent): St. Nicholas

2, 3 BARFRESTON (Kent): St. Nicholas

4, 5 BARFRESTON (KENT): St. Nicholas

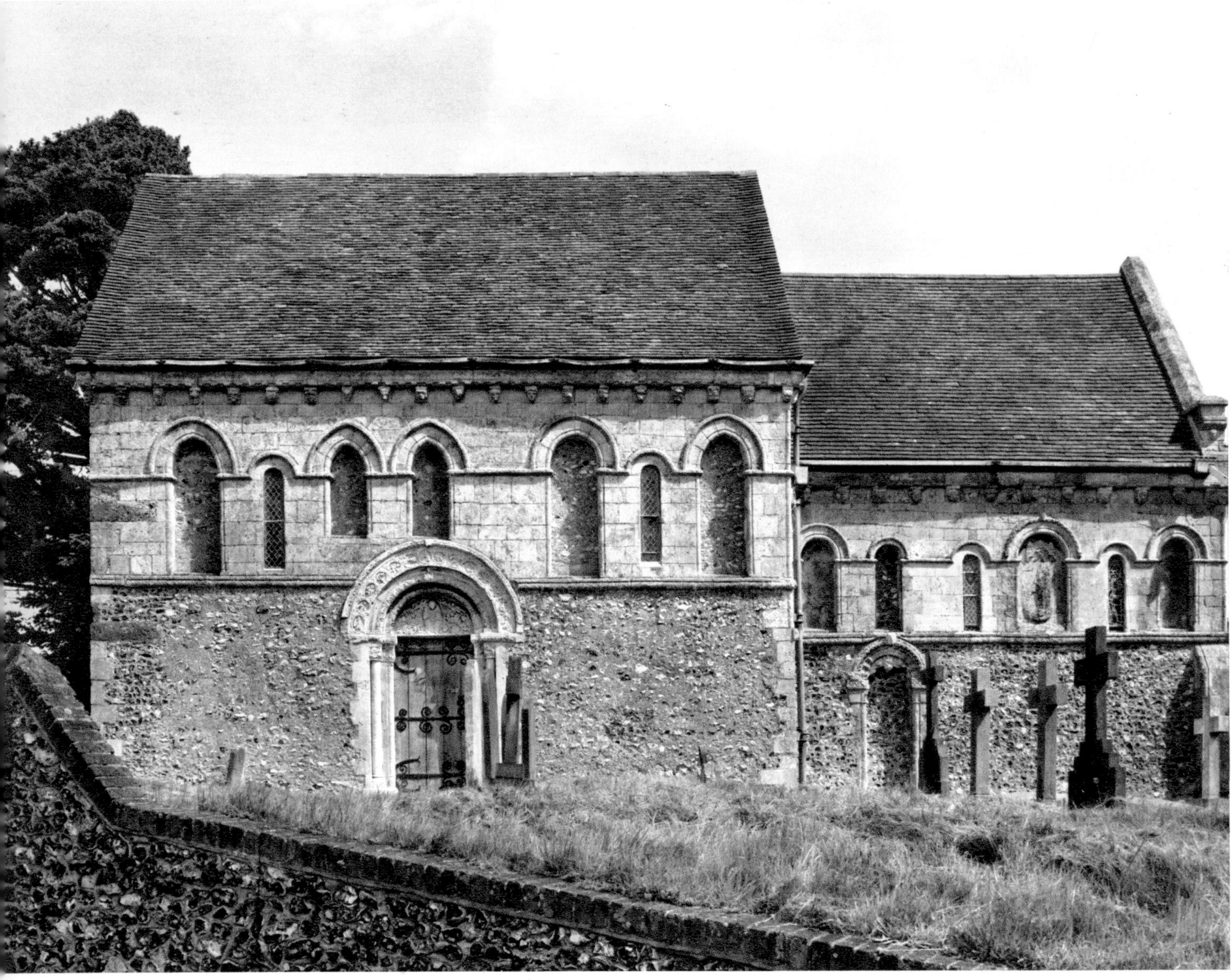

6 BARFRESTON (Kent): St. Nicholas

7 PATRIXBOURNE (Kent): St. Mary

8, 9 CANTERBURY (KENT): Cathedral

10, 11 CANTERBURY (KENT): Cathedral

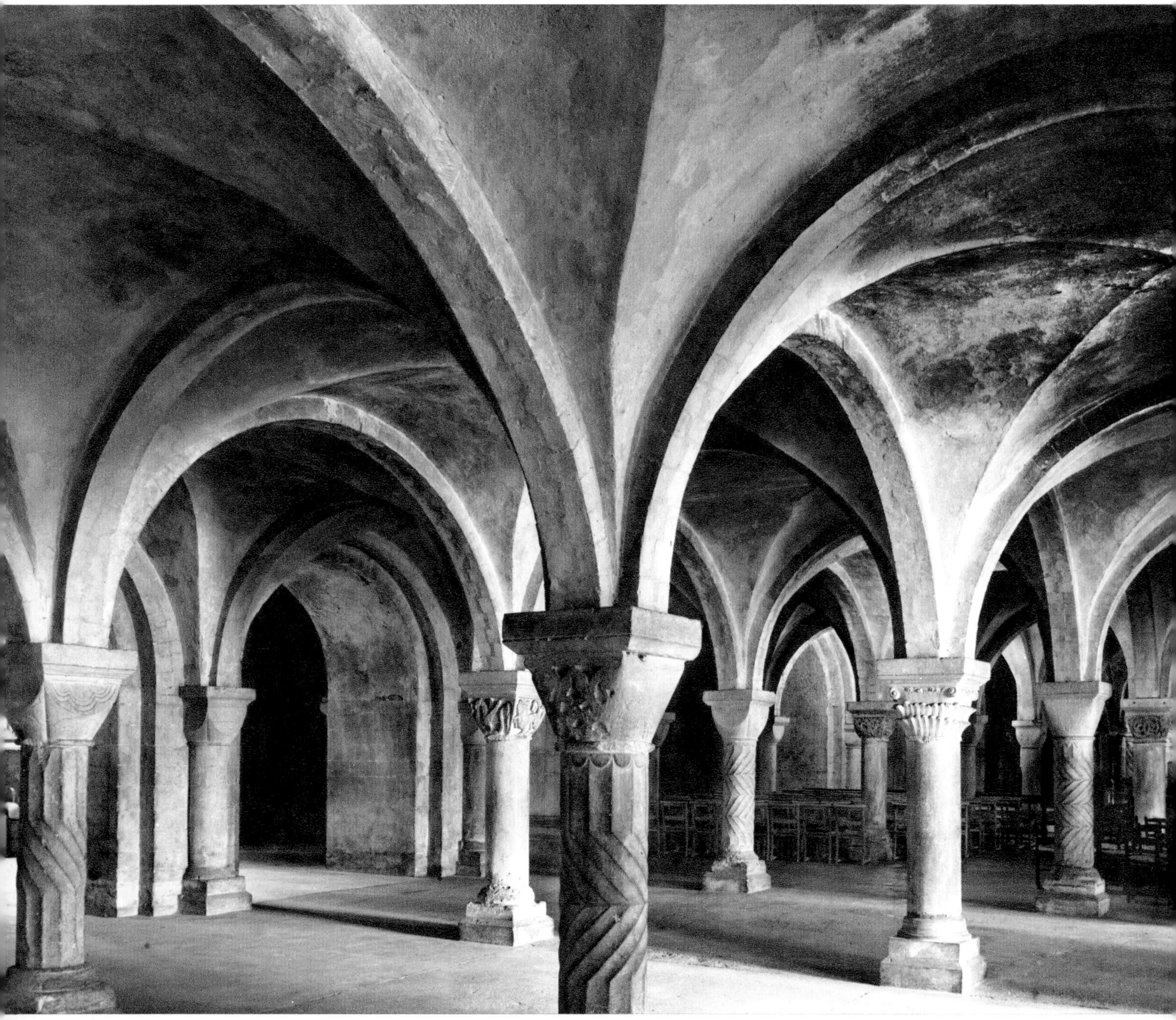

12, 13   CANTERBURY (KENT): Cathedral

14, 15   CANTERBURY (KENT): Cathedral

16 CANTERBURY (KENT): Cathedral

18   ROCHESTER (KENT) : Cathedral

19 RECULVER (KENT): St. Mary   20 ROCHESTER (KENT): Castle

23 LONDON : Tower   24 GREENSTED-IUXTA-ONGAR (Essex) : St. Andrew

25 WALTHAM ABBEY (Essex)   26 ST. ALBANS (Hertfordshire) : Abbey

27, 28 ST. ALBANS (Hertfordshire) : Abbey

29 ST. ALBANS (Hertfordshire) : Abbey   30 BROOKLAND (Kent) : St. Augustine

31, 32 WORTH (Sussex): St. Nicholas

33, 34 CLAYTON (Sussex): St. John the Ba[

35, 36 BRIGHTON (Sussex) : St. Nicholas

37 BISHOPSTONE (Sussex) : St. Andrew

38 STAPLEHURST (Kent)

39 OLD SHOREHAM (Sussex) : St. Nicholas

40 OLD SHOREHAM (Sussex): St. Nicholas

41 OLD SHOREHAM (Sussex) : St. Nicholas

42 NEW SHOREHAM (Sussex): St. Mary de Haura   43 SOMPTING (Sussex): St. Mary the Virgin

44, 45 CHICHESTER (Sussex): Cathedral

46, 47 CHICHESTER (Sussex): Cathedral

48-50 WINCHESTER (Hampshire) : Cathedral

51 WINCHESTER (Hampshire): Cathedral 52 BOSHAM (Sussex): Holy Trinity

53 SOMPTING (Sussex): St. Mary the Virgin

54 READING (Berkshire): Abbey

55, 56 WINCHESTER (Hampshire): St. Bartholomew

57 ROMSEY (HAMPSHIRE): Abbey

58, 59 ROMSEY (HAMPSHIRE): Abbey

60, 61 ROMSEY
(HAMPSHIRE): Abbey

62 ROMSEY (Hampshire): Abbey

63   KNOOK (WILTSHIRE): St. Margaret

66 CHRISTCHURCH (Hampshire): Priory   67 BERE REGIS (Dorset): St. John Baptist

70 GLASTONBURY (Somerset) : Abbey

71 GLASTONBURY (Somerset): Abbey

72　BRADFORD-ON-AVON (Wiltshire) : St. Laurence

73　AVEBURY (Wiltshire) : St. James

74, 75 **BRISTOL**
(Gloucestershire): Cathedral

78-80 MALMESBURY (Wiltshire) : Abbey

81 MALMESBURY (Wiltshire) : Abbey   82 DORCHESTER (Oxon) : St. Peter and St. Paul

83 LANGFORD (Oxon) : St. Matthew

84   LANGFORD (Oxon): St. Matthew

85, 86 IFFLEY (OXON): St. Mary the Virgin

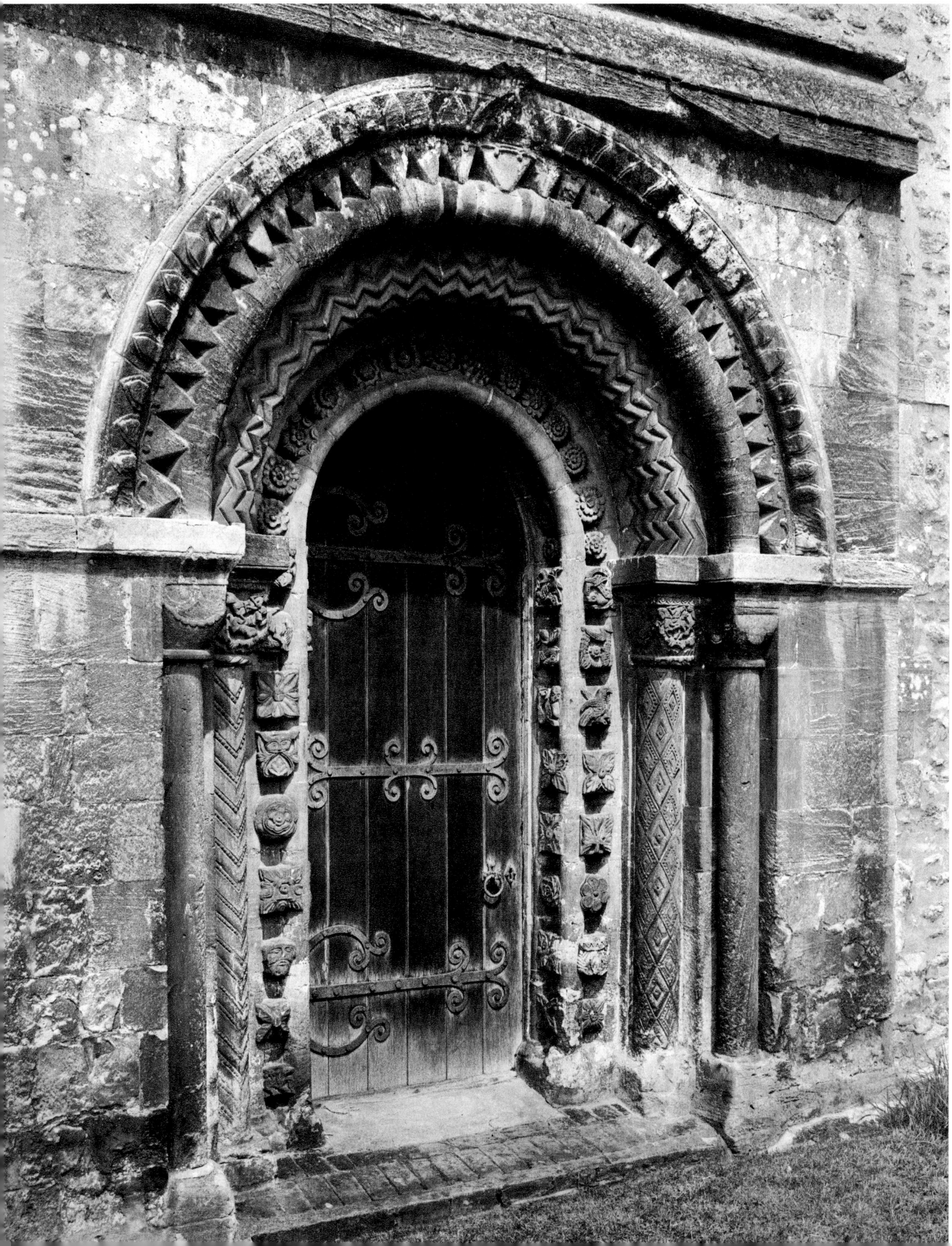

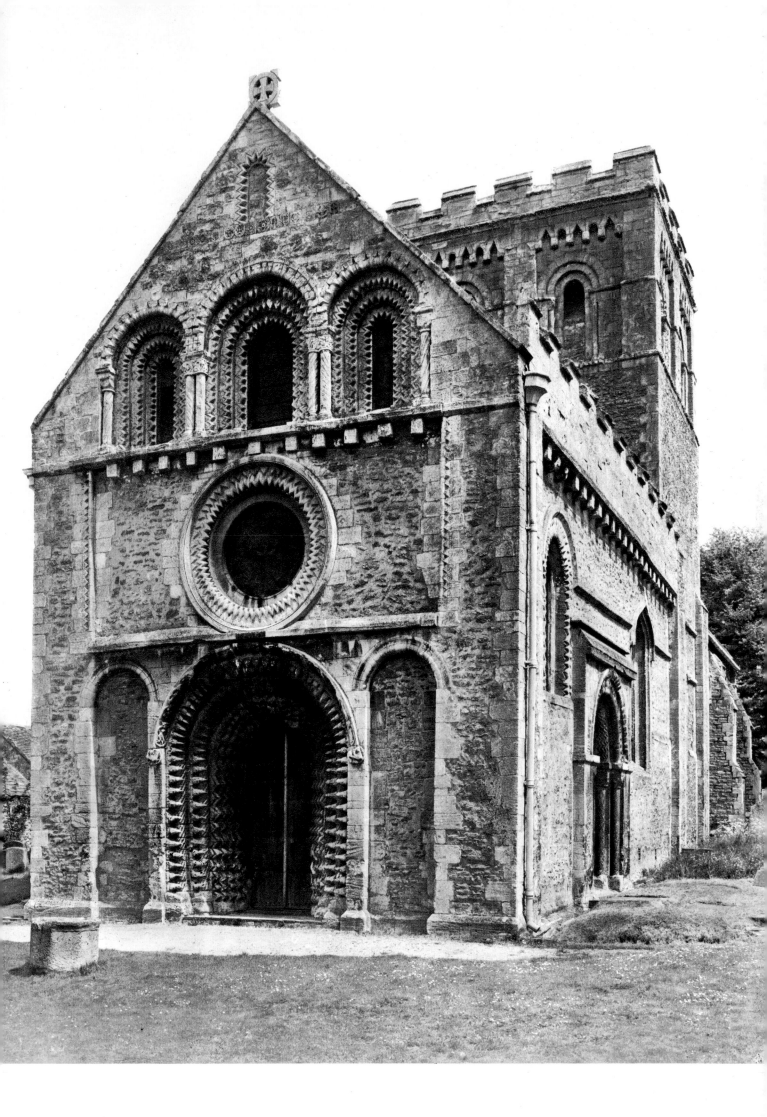

88 OXFORD (OXON): St. Peter's-in-the-East

89, 90 OXFORD (Oxon): St. Peter's-in-the-East

91, 92 GLOUCESTER (Gloucestershire) : Cathedral

93 GLOUCESTER
(GLOUCESTERSHIRE) :
Cathedral

95, 96   TEWKESBURY (Gloucestershire) : Abbey

99   CASTLE FROME (HEREFORDSHIRE): St. Michael and All Angels

102 WORCESTER (Worcestershire): Cathedral

103 KILPECK (HEREFORDSHIRE): St. Mary and St. David

104   KILPECK (Herefordshire): St. Mary and St. David

105 KILPECK (Herefordshire): St. Mary and St. David

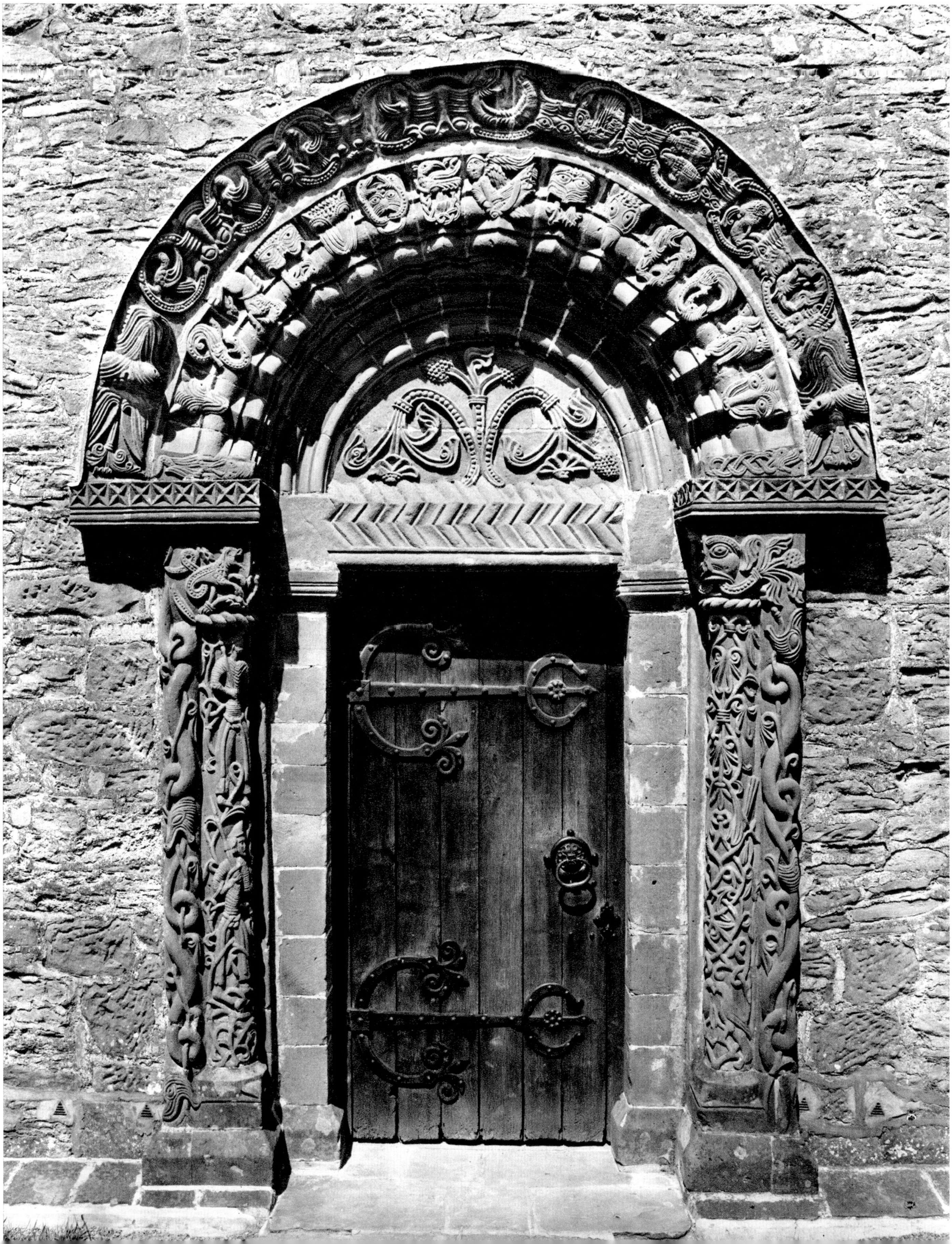

106, 107 KILPECK (Herefordshire):
St. Mary and St. David

110, 111   EARDISLEY (Herefordshire) : St. Mary Magdalene

112 ROWLSTONE (Herefordshire): St. Peter

113 STRETTON SUGWAS (Herefordshire): St. Mary Magdalene   114 LEOMINSTER (Herefordshire): Priory

115, 116   MUCH WENLOCK (Shropshire) : Priory

117, 118   MELBOURNE (Derbyshire): St. Michael and St. Mary

119 BREEDON-ON-THE-HILL (Leicestershire) : St. Mary and St. Hardulph

120 GOSFORTH (Cumberland)

121 RUTHWELL (Dumfriesshire)   122 GLENDALOUGH (Co. Wicklow)

123 GLENDALOUGH (Co. Wicklow): St. Kevin's Church

124 GLENDALOUGH (Co. Wicklow)

125 GLENDALOUGH
(Co. Wicklow):
St. Saviour's Priory

126 MOONE (Co. Kildare)

127 MOONE (Co. Kildare)

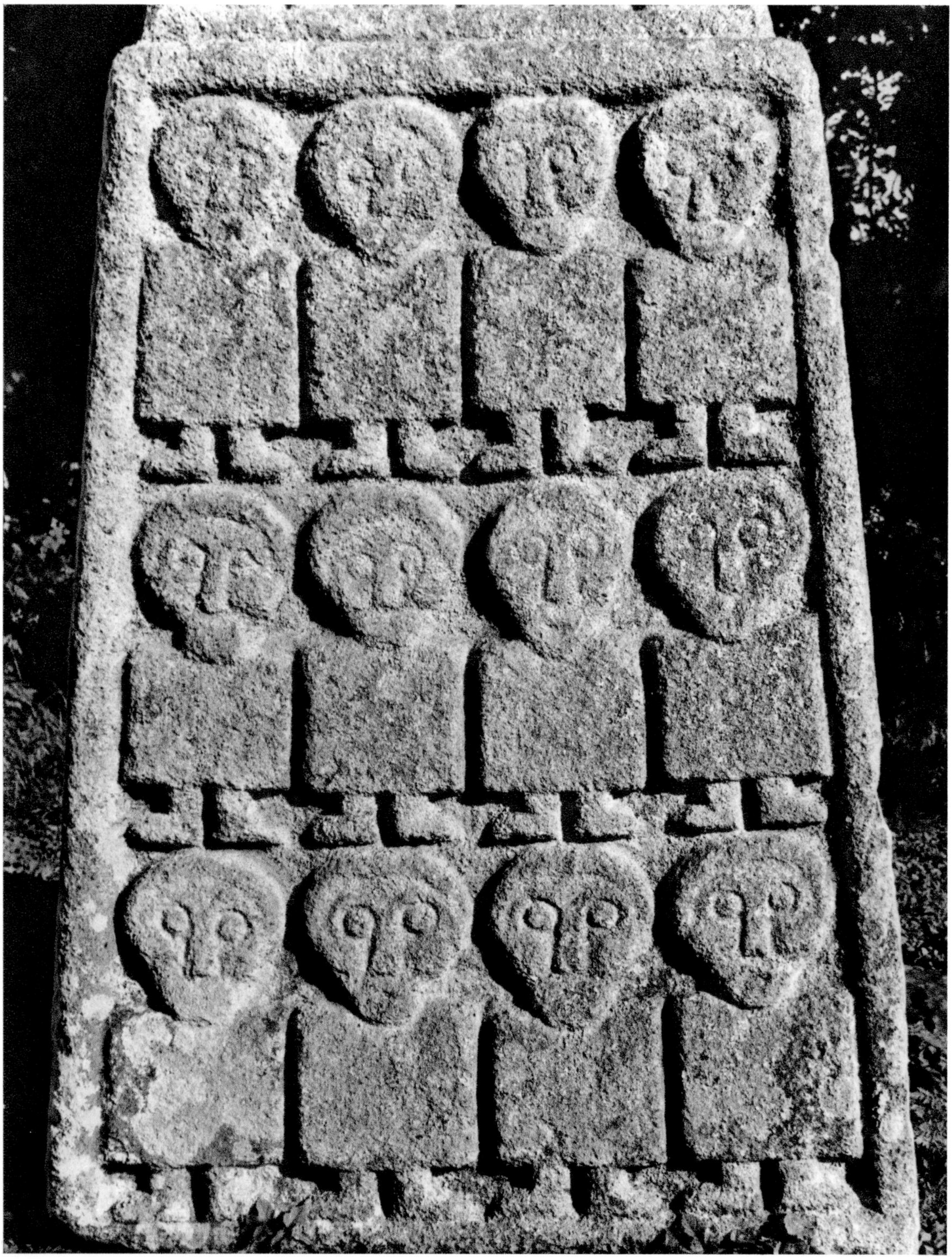

128 ARDFERT (Co. Kerry): St. Brendan's Cathedral

129 AHENNY (Co. Tipperary)

130 ARDMORE (Co. Waterford) : Cathedral

131, 132 CASHEL
(Co. Tipperary):
Cormac's Chapel

133 CASTLEDERMOT (Co. KILDARE)

134 CASTLEDERMOT (Co. KILDARE)

135 KILFENORA (Co. CLARE)

138 CLONFERT (Co. GALWAY): St. Brendan's Cathedral

139 CLONMACNOIS
(Co. Offaly)

140 CLONMACNOIS (Co. OFFALY) : O Rourke's Tower   141 CLONMACNOIS (Co. OFFALY) : Temple Finghin

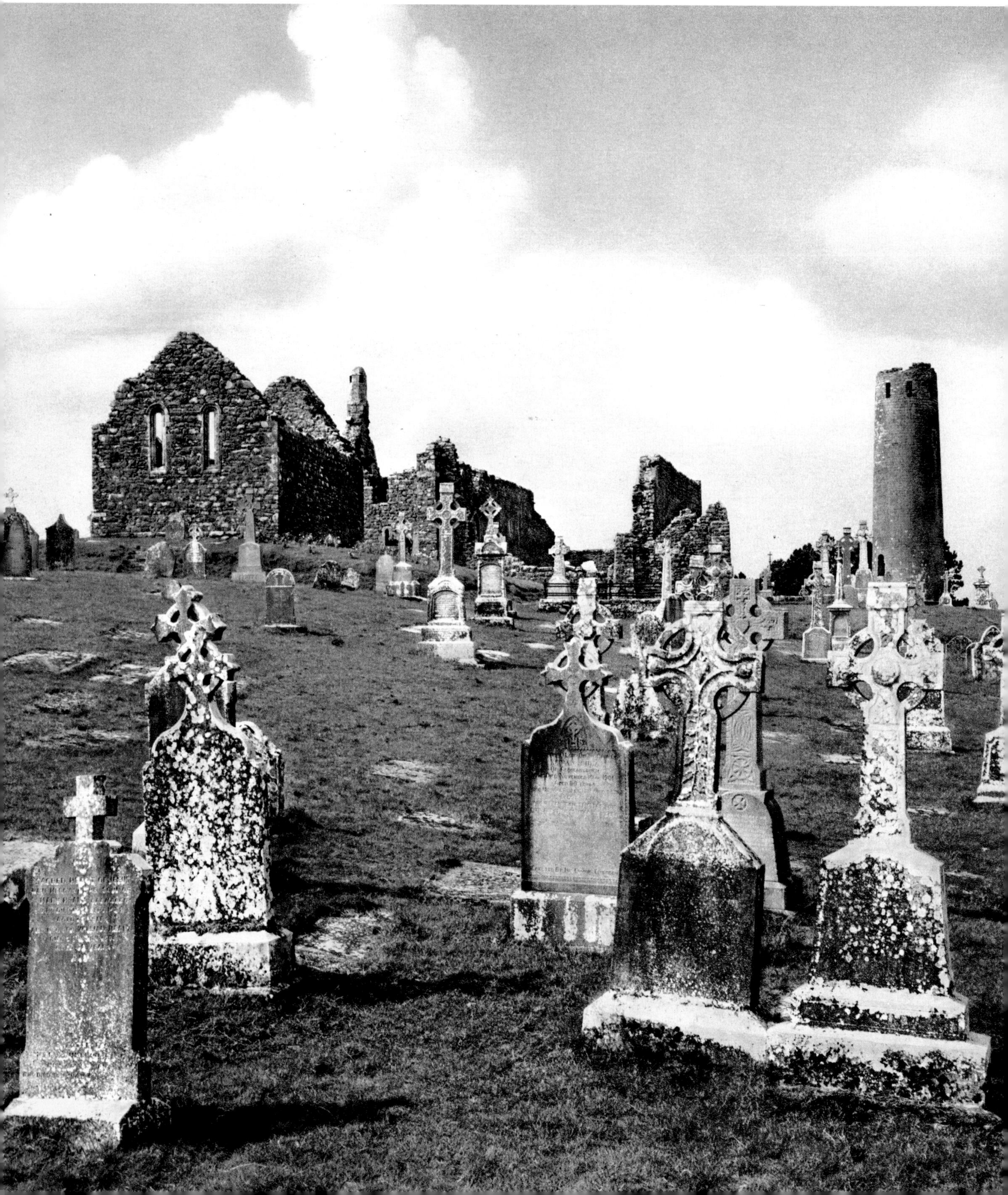

143 MELLIFONT (Co. Louth): Abbey

144 MONASTERBOICE
(Co. Louth)

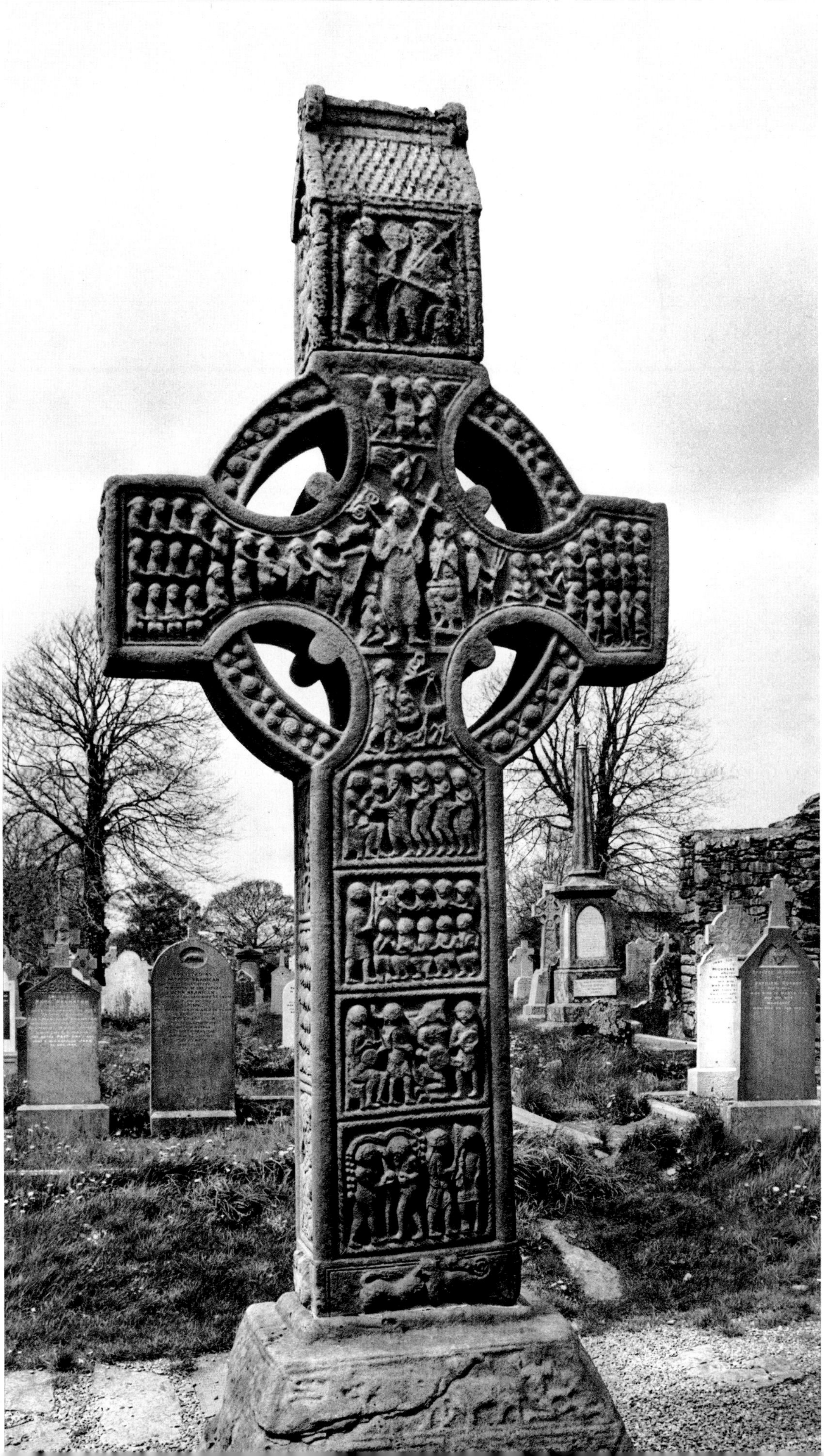

145 MONASTERBOICE
(Co. Louth)

146   MONASTERBOICE (Co. Louth)

147   JEDBURGH (Roxburghshire) : Abbey

148, 149 JEDBURGH (Roxburghshire): Abbey

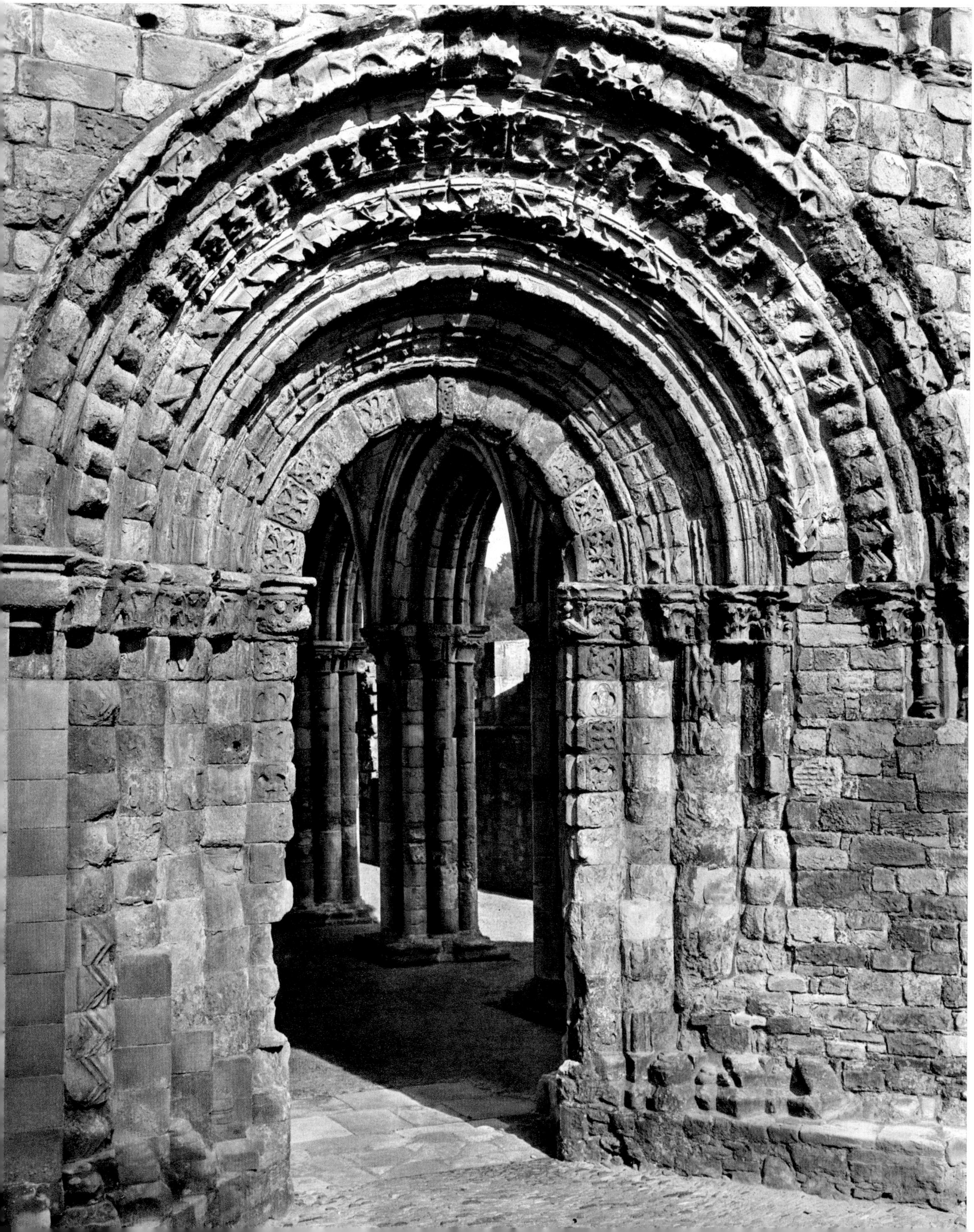

150 JEDBURGH (Roxburghshire): Abbey   151 KELSO (Roxburghshire): Abbey

152 KELSO (Roxburghshire): Abbey   153 DUMFERLINE (Fife): Abbey

154 DUMFERLINE (FIFE) : Abbey

155 LINDISFARNE (Northumberland): Abbey

158, 159 HEXHAM
(Northumberland) : Priory

160 DURHAM (Co. Durham): Cathedral

161, 162 DURHAM (Co. Durham): Cathedral

163 DURHAM (Co. DURHAM) : Cathedral

164 DURHAM (Co. DURHAM) : Cathedral

167 DURHAM (Co. Durham): Castle

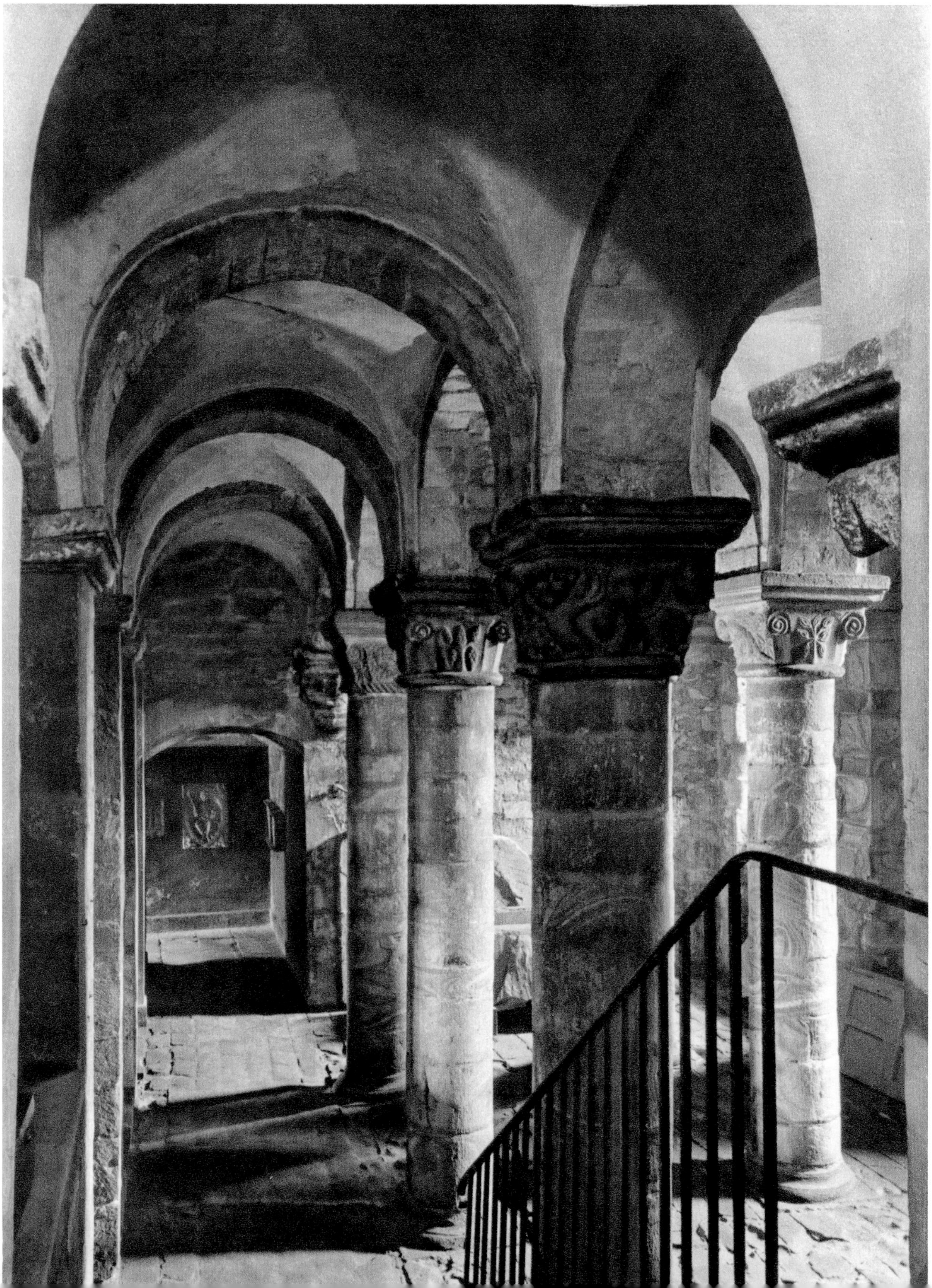

168   HOUGHTON-LE-SPRING (Co. Durham): St. Michael and All Angels

169   CHURCH KELLOE (Co. Durham): St. Helen

170 PITTINGTON (Co. Durham) : St. Lawrence

171 ST. ANDREW AUCKLAND (Co. DURHAM) : St. Andrew

172   ESCOMB (Co. Durham)

175 FOUNTAINS ABBEY
(YORKSHIRE)

176 FOUNTAINS ABBEY (Yorkshire)

177   FOUNTAINS ABBEY (Yorkshire)

178, 179 RIEVAULX ABBEY (Yorkshire)

180 STONEGRAVE (Yorkshire):
Holy Trinity

181-183 YORK (Yorkshire):
Cathedral

184 YORK (YORKSHIRE): Cathedral   185 BARTON-UPON-HUMBER (LINCOLNSHIRE): St. Peter

186 WORKSOP (Nottinghamshire) : Priory

187 BLYTH (Nottinghamshire) : Priory

188 BLYTH (Nottinghamshire): Priory   189 STOW (Lincolnshire): St. Mary

190, 191 LINCOL
(LINCOLNSHIRE):
Cathedral

192 LINCOLN (LINCOLNSHIRE)
Cathedral

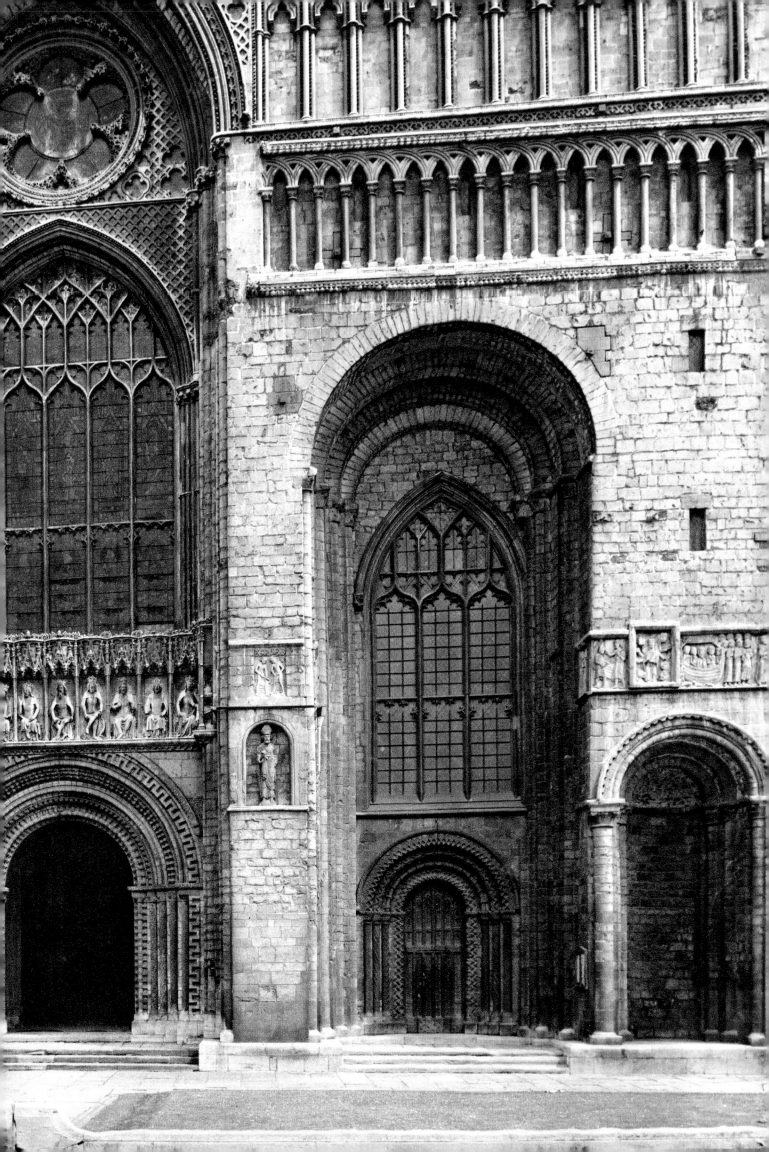

195, 196 SOUTHWELL (Nottinghamshire) : Minster

197, 198 SOUTHWELL (NOTTINGHAMSHIRE) : Minster

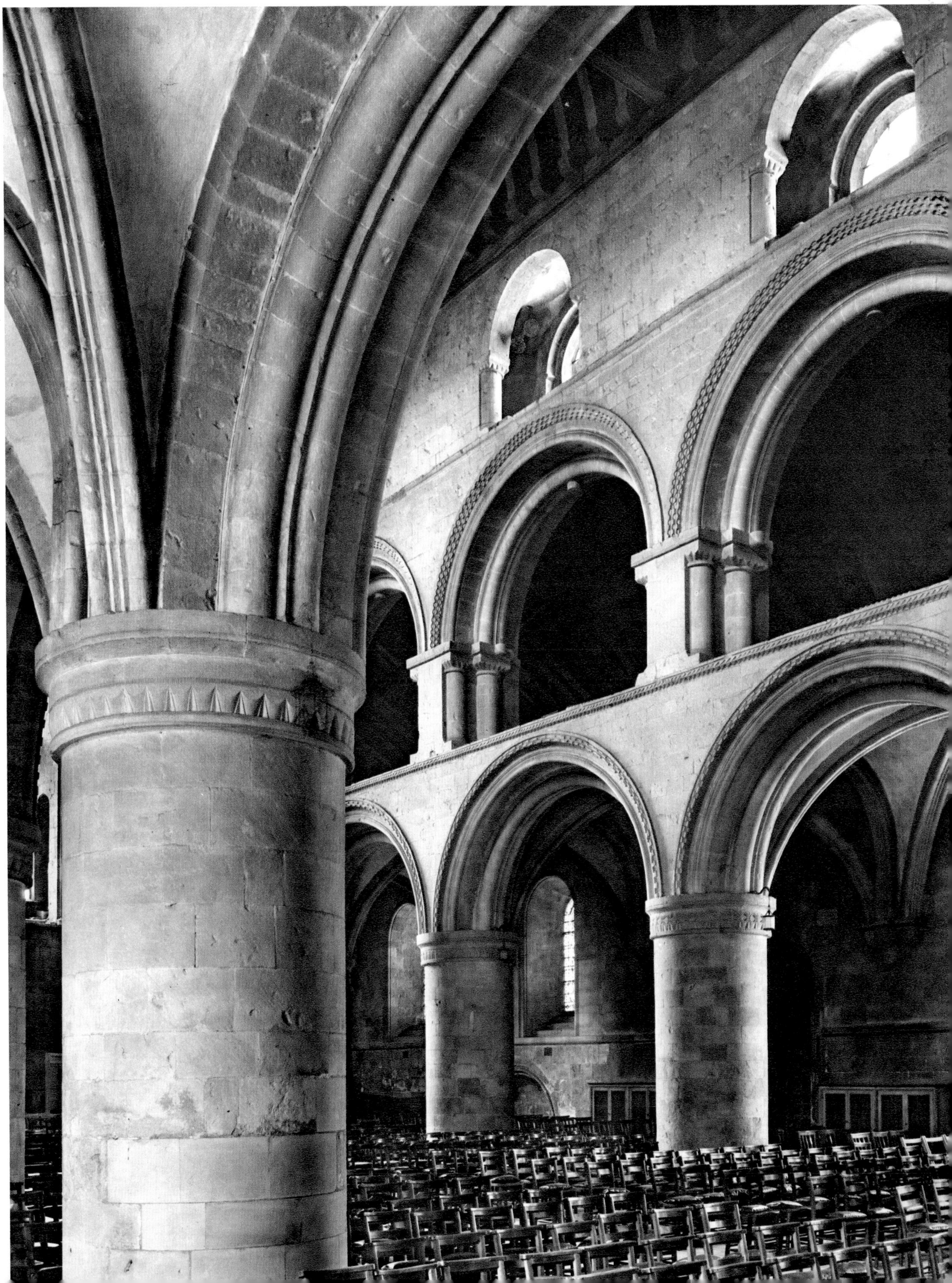

199 OAKHAM (Rutland): Castle   200 BARNACK (Northamptonshire): St. John Baptist

201 BARNACK (Northamptonshire): St. John Baptist

202 WITTERING (Northamptonshire): All Saints

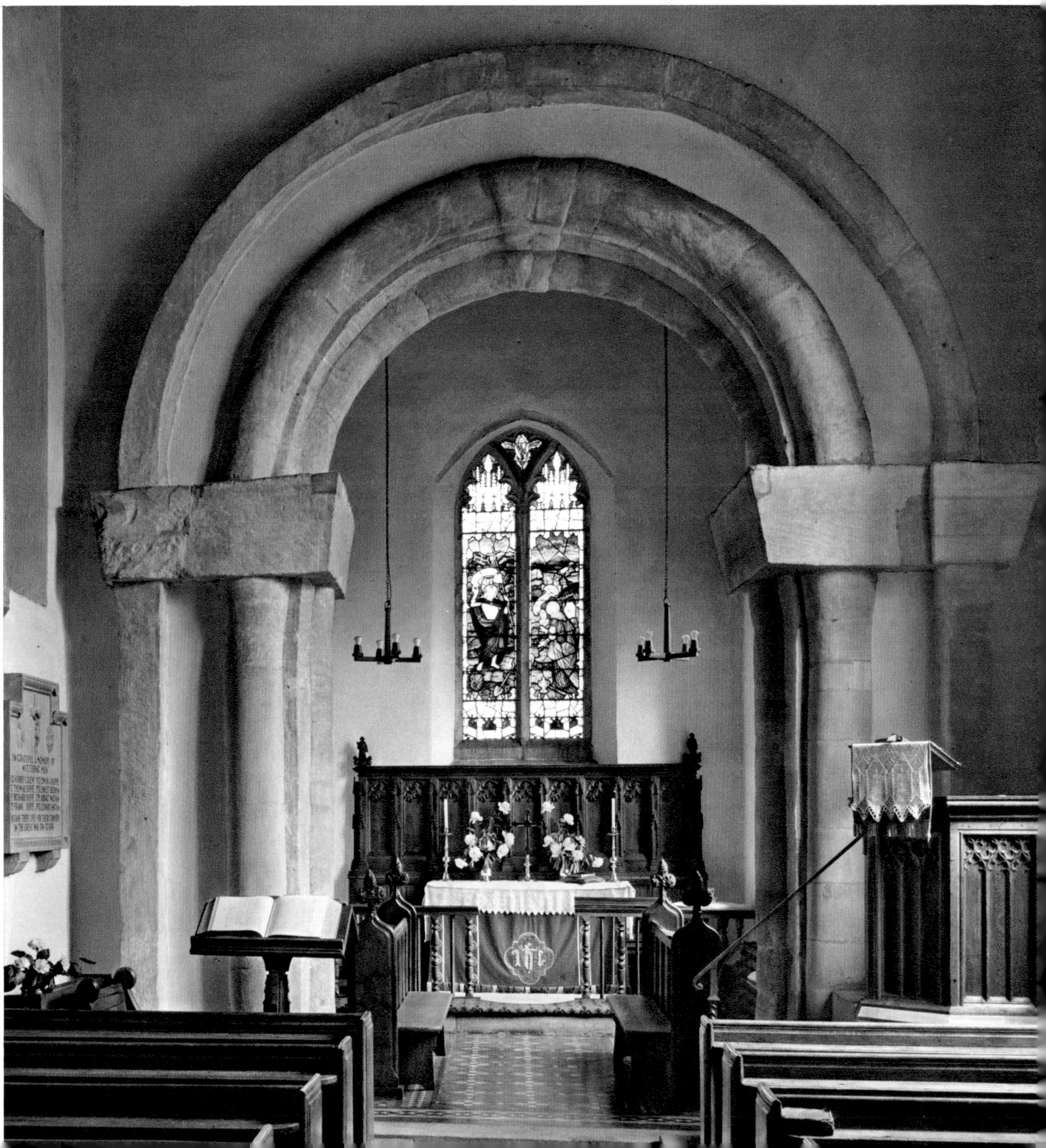

203 WITTERING
(Northamptonshire) : All Saints

204 NORTHAMPTON
(Northamptonshire) : St. Peter

205 NORTHAMPTON (NORTHAMPTONSHIRE): St. Peter   206 NORTHAMPTON (NORTHAMPTONSHIRE): St. Peter

207 NORTHAMPTON
(NORTHAMPTONSHIRE): St. Peter

208 CASTOR
(NORTHAMPTONSHIRE): St. Kynebu

209, 210 CASTOR (Northamptonshire) : St. Kyneburga

213 PETERBOROUGH (Northamptonshire): Cathedral   214 PITSFORD (Northamptonshire): All Saints

215 BRIXWORTH (NORTHAMPTONSHIRE): All Saints

216 BRIGSTOCK (NORTHAMPTONSHIRE): St. Andrew

217 EARLS BARTON
(Northamptonshire) :
All Saints

218 CLAPHAM
(Bedfordshire) :
St. Thomas of Canterbu

219, 220 CAMBRIDGE (CAMBRIDGESHIRE): Holy Sepulchre

221, 222 ELY (Cambridgeshire) : Cathedral

223, 224 ELY
(CAMBRIDGESHIRE) :
Cathedral

225, 226 ELY
(CAMBRIDGESHIRE)
Cathedral:

227 ELY (CAMBRIDGESHIRE): Cathedral

228   ELY (CAMBRIDGESHIRE) : Cathedral

229, 230   ELY (Cambridgeshire): Cathedral

231, 232 COLCHESTER (Essex): Priory

235 ORFORD
(SUFFOLK) : Castle

236 HELMSLEY
(YORKSHIRE) : Castle

237 IPSWICH
(Suffolk) : St. Peter

238 IPSWICH
(Suffolk) : St. Nicholas

242 HALES (Norfolk): St. Margaret   243 HADDISCOE (Norfolk): St. Mary

244   CASTLE ACRE (Norfolk): Priory   245   CASTLE RISING (Norfolk): Castle

246 CASTLE RISING (Norfolk): St. Lawrence   247 NORWICH (Norfolk): Cathedral

248, 249 NORWICH (NORFOLK) : Cathedral

250, 251 NORWICH
(Norfolk) : Cathedral

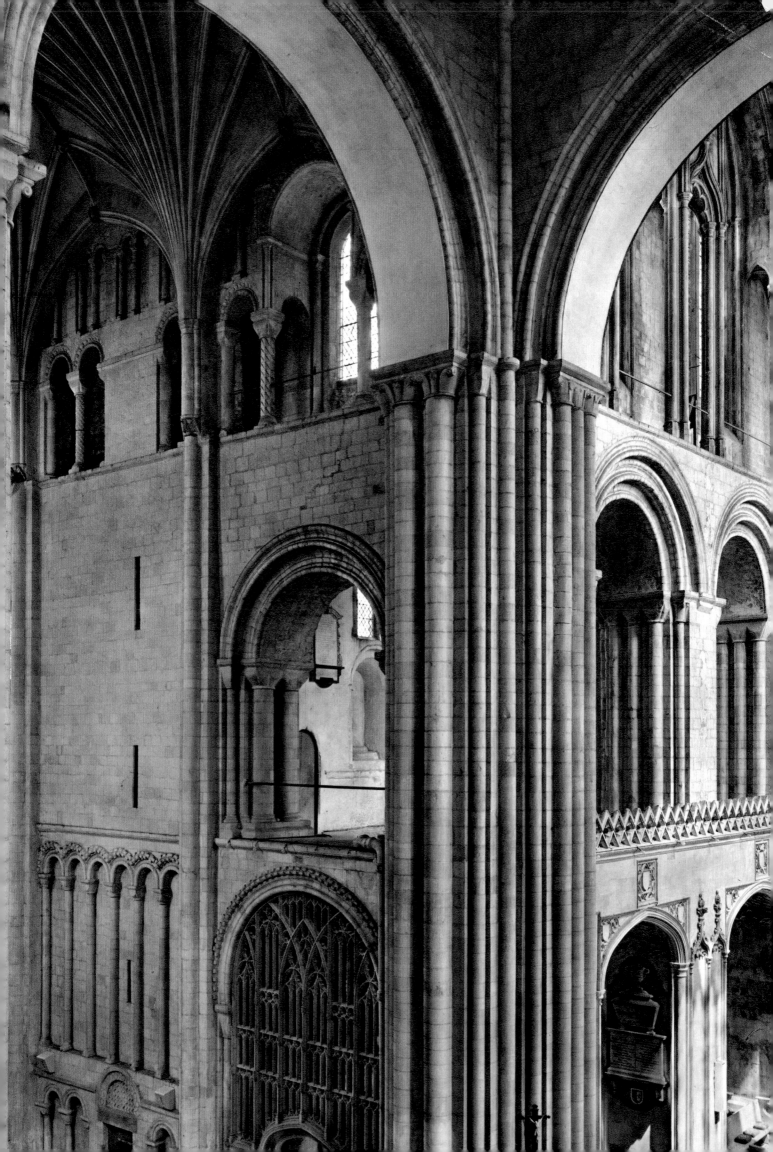

252, 253 NORWICH (NORFOLK): Cathedral

254 NORWICH (NORFOLK) : Cathedral

NOTES ON THE PLATES

The sequence of these Plates takes the form of a round trip. Starting in Kent, they traverse the south of England, the west coast, Ireland, the border abbeys of Scotland, and, finally, East Anglia. Their grouping accords with the old Anglo-Saxon tribal areas and kingdoms which continued to exert an influence on Norman Romanesque, though lines of demarcation are somewhat vague.

KENT AND SUSSEX

1-6 *Barfreston* (Kent) lies off the main road mid-way between Dover and Canterbury. The church of *St Nicholas* is one of the treasures of English Romanesque. Much of the *interior (Pl. 6)* was restored in 1840, and only drawings of the original wall-paintings survive. An elaborately ornamented chancel arch, remarkably high for such a small nave, spans the access to the modified chancel. The niches on either side probably used to be open. *The building as a whole (Pl. 4)* consists of an undivided rectangular nave and a slightly inset rectangular chancel, each with a saddleback roof and no tower, and measures 50 ft by 23 ft. The upper reaches of the flint walls were faced with slabs of finely hewn Caen stone, it being cheaper at the time to import stone by sea than to transport English stone overland. Improvements to the choir of Canterbury Cathedral may also have acted as a stimulus and example in this respect. Barfreston formed part of a Norman family estate. The unpretentious flint church was probably built at the end of the 11th century, after William the Conqueror had rewarded the services of Hugo de Port, a Constable of Dover Castle, by bestowing Barfreston Manor on him in 1079. A century elapsed before the church was faced with Caen stone and enhanced with rose windows, doorway carvings and other sculptural work. This decorative overlay, which paid deference to the small original windows but endowed the simple unaisled church with great visual charm, was probably undertaken on the occasion of an alliance between the de Ports, now resident in Kent, and a Norman family. In 1180 Adam de Port married Mabil d'Orval, and his family church was given a wedding-dress of its own.

In fact, the impression made by this church is at once festive and strange. The articulation of the *east face (Pl. 5)* is particularly emphatic. The plinth stage has a purely supporting function. The fenestration is symmetrically disposed, three narrow round-arched windows being linked by four rhythmical blind arches of niche-like aspect. The gable is bounded at the foot by a heavy string course elaborately decorated with interlace, flanked by two lions guardant, and supported by corbels carved to resemble heads. The figures let into the gable-end are obviously fragments of an earlier ensemble: the eagle of St John, a dragon, medallions representing a lion and griffin, Martin of Tours in the left-hand niche, and in the right-hand niche (probably) a fragment of the figure of God which once, as a print of 1773 shows, occupied the space above the rose window. Thus the theme of the gable was probably associated with the Last Judgement. Rose windows were seldom located in the east face and are more commonly found in the west front or transept, but this rose or wheel window is what lends the whole gable-end its peculiarly majestic appearance. Eight spokes in the form of cylindrical shafts link the hub with the outer ring, which is richly adorned with foliage and beasts of various shapes. The rose window, too, must have been associated with some pronouncement, now obscure but once explicit, on the inexorable progress of the world and every individual towards a day of final reckoning.

The fenestration stages of the north face and *south face (Pl. 4)* are essentially similar in arrangement. They are bounded at the foot by a string course and at the head by a frieze resting on figured corbels, but vary in the rhythmical disposition of their blind arches. Those on the north and south sides of the chancel are round-arched, whereas the early pointed arches in the nave have an affinity with the choir of Canterbury Cathedral. One further point to note: the external articulation of St-Eutrope at Saintes exerted a wide-ranging influence on the pilgrim route to Santiago. Commonly found in the churches of Saintonge and extending into Gironde, the bold horizontal string courses and their mode of continuation round the outer window arches may well have inspired those who designed the exterior walls at Barfreston.

There are doorways on both sides of the nave, the arched recesses above them being curtailed in each case. The north doorway was accorded very simple treatment, whereas the *south doorway (Pl. 3)* is one of the most elaborate in England. The basic design is straightforward: jambs with nook-shafts, capitals and abaci, a lintel-less tympanum, two archivolts, an arched surround, and a hood-mould. Engraved sun-dials without gnomons can be discerned on the outer jambs, placed there as aids to punctual attendance at church services.

The *tympanum (Pl. 1)* portrays a Majestas Domini. Christ sits enthroned in a mandorla, or almond-shaped glory, with his left hand holding the Book of the Law open on his knee and his right hand raised in benediction. From the mandorla sprouts some branch-work whose loops are filled with vine-leaves and figures: left and right of centre, two angels with scrolls; outside them, two Old Testament prefigurations of Redemption in the shape of Solomon and Sheba, portrayed not as Sol and Luna—a common convention—but as king and queen; above them, the heads of a man and a woman—possibly Sol and Luna; and, at the top, two angels supporting the mandorla. So much for the celestial domain. Below it, on either side of Christ's feet, lies the world with its temptations and perils depicted in fourfold guise: temptation as a winged siren, seduction as a naiad, deception as a sphinx, and evil itself as a griffin. Doorways of this kind were programmatic, and aids to their interpretation must be sought not only in the Scriptures but in well-known works by contemporary preachers, e.g. the *Psychomachia* by Prudentius and the *Physiologus* and the bestiaries based on it. Their message is seldom specific. Instead, they portray universal themes such as the conflict between good and evil, in which mankind is deeply embroiled and will remain so until the end of the world, when God comes to preside over the Last Judgement. Thus, though the capitals are adorned with beasts and centaurs, symbols of evil and deformation by evil respectively, knightly champions of righteousness can be seen on the right, together with the watchful lion reputed by the *Physiologus* to sleep with its eyes open.

The *innermost order (Pl. 2)* is adorned with leaf-work, while the central band of ornamentation depicts the world of illusion in twelve medallions: a fop playing a trio with a hare and a monkey; a bear, the medieval personification of the Devil, playing the harp like David while a female dancer turns somersaults; two more bears, one of them scouring a honeycomb with his tongue and the other holding a drinking-horn; an actor; love-scenes; huntsmen and the chase; a priest mounted on a palfrey; and a monkey riding a she-goat. In the centre of these worldly caricatures is an archbishop with his hands raised in admonition. The round arch immediately beneath the hood-mould depicts—apart from the warriors at either end—nine figures from daily life—a lady, some musicians, a cellarer, a master armourer, an agricultural labourer with his spade, a woodworker with his axe—and, finally, next to two unidentifiable figures, Samson subduing a ferocious lion. The programme thus ranges from the superficialities of the world to the central figure of God himself. The south doorway is a remarkable example of Late Romanesque sculpture, and is related in this respect to the portals of Malmesbury *(Pl. 78)* and the Lady Chapel at Glastonbury. It is perhaps the finest product of the Kentish school of stonemasonry which flourished during the third quarter of the 12th century. The west door of Rochester Cathedral *(Pl. 18)* was a forerunner.

7 *South doorway of St Mary's Patrixbourne* (Kent). The village lies about three miles east of Canterbury. The church dates from the late 12th century and probably occupies the site of a smaller predecessor. A massive central tower juts above its long nave. This sculptured doorway is on the south side. It may be attributed to the Kentish school but its technique is flatter than Barfreston, simpler than Rochester, and far more Insular in general. A shallow gabled surround encloses the arch and a niche containing a Lamb of God in relief. The doorway itself is of three orders with inset shafts, and the round arches are adorned with geometrized birds' heads, zigzag, foliage, and beasts of various kinds. The tympanum bears a Majestas surrounded by angels and other figures while the lintel has leaves, branchwork, and enlaced serpents.

8-17 *Canterbury Cathedral* (Kent). The advent of Augustine and his Benedictine companions in 597 introduced England to a Christianity which was linked with Rome and founded on the reputation of the Roman Church. This is why Bede includes the text of Pope Gregory's 'apostolic letter' in his history of the English Church (*H.E.* I/23). Having secured permission to preach the Gospel from King Ethelbert of Kent, Augustine led his companions, armed with crosses and icons of Christ, into the royal capital of Cantawarabyrig, where he founded the first episcopal see in England.

A very modest Christian church, St Martin's, already existed there and still does, though with many alterations. After being baptized by Augustine, King Ethelbert bestowed property on the Benedictines in the city where the cathedral now stands. In addition to restoring various churches and erecting new ones, Augustine founded the abbey church of SS. Peter and Paul—now St Augustine's Abbey—outside the city. It was still under construction when he died in 604. The early history of Canterbury Cathedral itself has never been fully elucidated. Whether newly built or merely restored, as Bede reports (*H.E.* I/33), the episcopal church was furnished by Pope Gregory (*H.E.* I/29) with sumptuous vestments and altar-cloths, precious relics and books. Archbishop Odo restored this centre of religious life *c.* 950, but it was destroyed by fire a year after the Conquest.

William took vigorous action where Canterbury was concerned. The cathedral was ordered to be rebuilt and Archbishop Stigand, who had usurped the archiepiscopal see, removed from office and replaced. William's choice of successor was Lanfranc, the Lombardic Abbot of St Etienne in Caen and a mature personality. Brought to Canterbury almost under duress, Lanfranc was consecrated archbishop within sight of the ruined cathedral in 1070. He tackled his task with decision, building a new monastery for 150 monks and inaugurating work on the cathedral which has since grown, through the centuries, into the architectural complex we know today. Canterbury Cathedral owes its principal features to Romanesque and Early and Late Gothic. Its beauty derives, not from unity, but from a diversity which grew out of a single faith. It is a visible embodiment of ecclesiastical and royal history.

Lanfranc's aisled nave, transept and triapsidal chancel were augmented by his successor, Anselm (1093–1114), who commissioned his prior, Ernulph (1096–1107), to add to the chancel. The choir was extended far to the east, two stairway towers and an east transept with two small east apses built on to it, and the east end enlarged by the addition of an ambulatory and two tangential chapels. Lanfranc's crypt was extended beneath the chancel. Ernulph's successor, Conrad (1108–26), continued and completed this work after Anselm's death. The consecration took place in 1130. Although changes have since been made, notably to the interior facing, most of these improvements still survive (choir walls, east transept and stair-towers, chancel chapels, crypt, etc.).

Pl. 8 provides an *exterior view of the north chancel chapel*, St Andrew's, and its remarkably large window. Adjoining it on the right is the vestry or treasury annexed to it (except for the Gothic upper storey) by Prior Wilpert (1151–67) in Late Romanesque style. The differentiation of the three original storeys by means of varied round arches is particularly handsome. A man of great drive and energy, Wilpert also improved the water supply by installing a system of lead pipes and made additions to an existing water-tower. He likewise built a guest-house for pilgrims (now part of King's School) whose façade and covered steps *(Pl. 17)* display an unusual degree of architectural vigour.

View from the north aisle of the choir, looking westwards across the north arm of the east transept (Pl. 9). This shows alterations to Anselm's interior. Anselm was responsible for the large round arches between the aisle and the transept, which bear the zigzag motif first identifiable in England shortly before 1110. To the north of them are the slender shafts of Purbeck stone added by William of Sens as supports for new vaulting after 1175, as well as the pointed arches of the triforium-type blind arcading which he superimposed on the interior of Anselm's transept, retaining the Romanesque windows in conformity with the Transitional style then in force.

Lanfranc's and Anselm's cathedral was the scene of a dramatic incident which, if only because it exerted an architectural influence, must be mentioned here: the murder of Thomas Becket. Chancellor to Henry II from 1155 onwards, Becket was consecrated Archbishop of Canterbury in 1162. He held office for eight years, six of which he spent in exile in France, at Sens and Pontigny, because of a dispute with the king over jurisdiction in cases involving clerics. Hopes of agreement rose in 1170, and Becket returned to Canterbury, but dissension broke out once more. Four of the king's knights and their escort pursued the archbishop through the cloister into the north arm of the west transept and murdered him on the threshold of the choir. He was canonized by Pope Alexander III only three years later, and his shrine at Canterbury became a renowned place of pilgrimage.

In 1174, four years after the archbishop's assassination, a great fire severely damaged Ernulph's and Conrad's choir. In 1175 the great French master-builder William of Sens took charge of the work of reconstruction. On his orders, stone from the quarries of Caen was transported by ship to Fordwich, not far from Canterbury itself. He refaced the walls of Anselm's choir, which were still intact, introducing many Gothic architectural features into England for the first time. However, his activities were cut short in 1178, when he fell from some scaffolding. His successor, William the Englishmen, completed the half-finished work in a harmonious fashion. Between them, the two Williams were responsible for the vaulting in the choir and east transept (1179), the new, lengthened apse, which extended eastwards from the original square-ended chancel, and, finally, the circular east chapel which houses Becket's shrine, known as the Corona or Becket's Crown and vaulted in 1184. Anselm's crypt was further enlarged to provide the necessary substructure. Between 1378 and 1411 the Romanesque nave was replaced by the noble Gothic structure which still stands today, and the majestic crossing tower followed c. 1500.

Anselm's crypt (Pl. 10) is aisled. It has an ambulatory and chapels located beneath the arms of the east transept, the tangential chapels and apse. The ornamentation of the cylindrical columns alternates between shaft and capital. Carefully executed groined vaults are inserted between transverse arches. Crypts of this type, which ran beneath the entire east end of a church, were more common in England c. 1100 than on the Continent (Winchester, begun 1079; Worcester, begun 1084; Gloucester, begun 1089). They can be found at Rouen early in the 11th century and later at Bari, where work on the massive Norman church of S. Nicola began in 1087.

Isolated capitals in Anselm's crypt date from Lanfranc's time, or the first phase of Norman Romanesque, e.g. the palmetted capital in the southernmost range (visible in

Pl. 10). The others, dating from the more advanced second phase, were produced between 1115 and 1125, under Prior Conrad. They were enriched and accentuated either with foliate scroll-work and corner-masks *(Pl. 15)* or with scenes taken from the realm of the *Physiologus* and the bestiaries, scenes similar to those found in contemporary illuminated manuscripts produced by the Canterbury scriptorium. They illustrate the lusts and passions of mankind. The she-devil with splayed thighs *(Pl. 13)* is related to the Sheila-na-gig of Ireland. Another naked she-devil mounted on a griffin *(Pl. 14)*, two-headed and with a peacock's tail protruding from between her legs, represents a warning against Luxuria. In St Gabriel's Chapel *(Pl. 11)*, beneath Anselm's capitals, can be seen a trio of devils *(Pl. 12)* reminiscent of Barfreston. The workmanship of these capitals is as excellent as their state of preservation. They embrace a wide variety of themes, among them a griffin and serpent *(Pl. 16)* attributable—or so one is tempted to speculate—to a stonemason who may have been familiar with Tuscan as well as French sculpture.

18   The *west doorway of St Andrew's Cathedral, Rochester* (Kent), betrays strong French influence. The knotted shafts are indigenous to East Anglia and date from a preliminary phase *c.* 1130, but the rest was executed after the middle of the 12th century. The tympanum bears a Majestas in a mandorla supported by standing angels and surrounded by symbols of the Evangelists. Seated Apostles occupy the lintel. The five arches are adorned with foliate scroll-work, some of it inhabited, which recalls doorways in Poitou and Charente. Echoes of St-Denis and Chartres (Portail Royal) are provided by the two attenuated figures on the jambs, which, like the earlier tympanum at Barfreston, portray Solomon and the Queen of Sheba. It is as though Rochester's status as a sea-port, which brought it into direct contact with the Continent, had enabled French influence to manifest itself there in a largely unadulterated form.

19   *St Mary, Reculver* (Kent) seen from the south-east. The Anglo-Saxon Chronicle records that in 669 King Egbert of Kent gave the village of Reculver, situated in the district of Regulbium, a former Roman camp on the northern coast of Kent, to his priest Bassa, instructing him to build a church there. This building, still identifiable by its foundations, followed the pattern typical of early Kentish churches: a rectangular nave, an apsidal chancel of the same width, and rectangular north and south chambers leading off the chancel. Nave and apsidal chancel were separated by three round-arched bays. Reculver belonged to the monks of Christ Church Canterbury during the 10th century. The church, which

figures in the Domesday Book, was enlarged, but the sea gradually eroded it. In 1805 the nave and chancel were demolished and the materials used to construct a new church further inland. Only the two Late Romanesque towers and intervening west wall were preserved and reinforced. In company with various foundation walls, these provide the visitor with a remarkable spectacle and the off-shore sailor—now as for centuries past—with a conspicuous landmark known as 'the Twins'.

20   *Rochester Castle* (Kent) seen from the north-west. At the point where the Medway widens into a harbour and ancient thoroughfares led across a ford which was later spanned by a bridge, both Romans and Anglo-Saxons established strong garrisons to guard the passage. Speedy action was called for after the Conquest, and the first Norman stronghold was probably a rampart-and-palisade affair located on the site of its Roman and Anglo-Saxon predecessors. Then, in the reign of Henry I (1100–35), probably through the agency of William of Corbeuil and concurrently with the castles of Corfe and Sherborne in Dorset and the castle and fortifications of Canterbury, work began on Rochester's own massive castle. It is a grim-looking edifice with a ground-plan 70 ft square and four corner-towers each 100 ft high. The northern access was guarded by a projecting tower. Now a ruin, the building belonged to the second generation of Norman castles, whose interiors were subdivided with greater variety.

21–23   *The Tower of London: St John's Chapel and south face.* The Normans built castles before they built churches. William quickly followed up his conquest of England by erecting strongholds designed to secure his centralized control over the country. The rapidly constructed rampart-and-ditch type (palisade, fosse, and earthen bank) was soon replaced by fortifications built of stone, including a few defensive towers in that material. Shortly after 1066 work began on the Tower, which was sited on a hill below London on the north bank of the Thames, i.e. within the compass of the old Roman walls. Blocks of stone were brought by ship from Caen, and the stone tower, which must have greatly impressed contemporary Londoners, grew at a slow but steady pace. The building, whose exterior coating of lime earned it the name 'White Tower', was completed in 1097. Primarily intended to be a symbol of authority, *the Tower (Pl. 23)* takes the form of a massive three-storeyed cube measuring 108 × 118 ft. It is exceeded in size only by Colchester Castle. The four corners are picked out as follows: in the west by two square towers, in the north-east by a round tower, and in the south-east by the salient of the chapel apse (the caps on the towers are later additions). The average thickness of the walls is 10 ft at base but less higher up, and their strength is augmented at regular intervals by buttresses. The original entrance was at first-floor height on the south side, via a flight of steps which led into a fore-building. Inside are spiral stairs of the sort which provided access to church galleries.

In addition to being a fortress with a military function, the Tower was also a royal residence. The storeys were subdivided by interior walls into dwelling-chambers of various sizes, each separated from the stairs by a sort of ante-room. The lowest level of the building contains brick vaults, the first floor rooms of various kinds, the second floor the main hall, a chamber of State and the chapel, and the third floor further chambers of State and the gallery of the chapel, which thus occupies two floors. Round the upper storey, within the thickness of the walls, runs a wall-passage of the type found in Norman cathedrals.

The *chapel (Pl. 21)* measures 60 × 33 ft. Virtually unaltered since it was built, it is one of the finest examples of Early Norman architecture in England. The general impression is massive, stern, and austere, and the masonry exhibits neat workmanship. The chapel has two aisles which converge into an ambulatory behind the chancel. Disposed round the altar, which is set forward, are twelve cylindrical masonry piers which may be symbolically associated with the twelve Disciples. The simple, unmodelled arcade proceeds from two responds in the west wall, and the arches remain round-headed until they reach the ambulatory, where they become narrower and more stilted. The monumental nature of the whole is also conveyed by the capitals—cushion capitals and simple scalloped capitals, one with a volute motif and others with a leaf at each corner and a St Anthony's cross in the centre of each face.

The gallery's square masonry piers repose directly on the unmodelled round arches beneath them and are devoid of capitals. *The aisles (Pl. 22)* are spanned by groined vaults, the galleries by barrel-vaults, and the nave—a rare phenomenon for England—by another barrel-vault.

24 *St Andrew's, Greensted-juxta-Ongar* (Essex). The nave of this small and secluded church provides the only surviving example of a timber-built church dating from pre-Norman times, probably shortly after 1000. Its walls consist of oak logs split in half, joined with wooden pegs, and fitted into an oak plinth with their cut sides facing inwards. The present substructure dates from the restoration of 1848, the brick chancel is early 16th-century, two of the dormer windows in the 19th-century roof are of Tudor vintage, and the wooden tower, a typical Essex feature, is new.

25 View of *the nave of Waltham Abbey* (Sussex). The origins of the church of the Holy Cross and St Lawrence are shrouded in legend, and few facts are known. It was built by order of King Harold and consecrated in 1060. From here, so it is said, Harold rode out to die in battle against William the Conqueror. 1177 saw the founding of an Augustinian abbey for men. Practically everything has since disappeared, and the present church is only a remnant, if a magnificent one. The wall arrangement followed the Norman cathedral pattern: a tripartite division into arcade, gallery, and clerestory. The alternation between simple cylindrical piers and piers with engaged shafts rising to the (restored) ceiling is reminiscent of Durham *(Pl. 163)*, just as the enrichment of the piers may also hail from Durham, which first displayed examples of it *c.* 1095. The gallery openings are not divided, although the inset demi-shafts suggest that this was the original intention. The aisles were once spanned by stone vaults, but these were removed to relieve undue strain, so that the gallery arches now open directly into the aisles themselves. In front of the clerestory windows, with their triplet arches, runs a wall-passage. The nave was probably begun from the west end early in the 12th century, the chancel of Harold's church (1060) being left as it was. However, the old chancel was finally demolished when the last and easternmost bays had been completed *c.* 1150.

26-29 *St Albans* (Hertfordshire) did not become a diocesan church, and, thus, a cathedral, until 1877. Thanks to Henry VIII's monastic dissolutions and the curtailment of building activity, it became an over-sized parish church in 1555 and remained so for more than three centuries thereafter. During the Middle Ages, however, the Abbot of St Albans was the premier abbot of England. Adrian IV (1154–59), the only English Pope in history, singled the monastery out for special mention in a bull entitled *Incomprehensibilis*. The first monastic foundation can be traced back to King Offa II of Mercia in the 8th century, but the hill overlooking the important Roman town of Verulamium had probably been occupied by a church since the time of Constantine. It was there, in about 300, that the first English martyr, Alban, probably a Briton in the Roman service, was beheaded in the course of Diocletian's persecution of the Christians.

We do not know what Offa's church or its predecessor looked like. The present building was started by Abbot Paul of Caen (1077–88). It had an aisled nave, a transept with stepped apses in the east, a separated crossing with a tower, and an apsidal chancel. As building materials, Paul of Caen ordered Roman bricks and tiles from Verulamium. The massive edifice was consecrated in

1115. Sections of the nave and transept and the huge *crossing tower (Pl. 29)* are all that survive today.

The massive *north wall of the nave (Pl. 26)* affords the best impression of St Albans' interior as it was in early Norman times. Our westwards-facing view shows four-and-a-half of the six surviving bays built by Paul of Caen. The masonry piers are rectangular and stepped to conform with the recessed arches and pilasters. (The pier on the right was altered subsequently.) The painting on the white washed arcade arches is Romanesque (restored), and the piers themselves are adorned with figurative scenes of the 13th and 14th centuries. The massive arches of the second storey are almost as wide as those of the arcade, and unarticulated save for their slightly modelled round arches, but their sills and jambs are splayed. They are blind arches, since they lead into the roof of the north aisle. Their original condition has never been ascertained. Used they to be open to the sky, so that, in conjunction with the clerestory windows, they provided the nave with illumination from a second tier of openings? That would have been unusual, to say the least. Right at the top are a series of tall clerestory windows and a wall-passage. The general impression is one of bulk and severity. The subdued strength of this wall arrangement relates it in spirit to the façade of St Etienne at Caen.

Bolder altogether, with its broad and lofty crossing arches, is the *open crossing tower (Pl. 28)*, the crowning glory of Paul of Caen's original building. On the left, a view of the chancel; on the right, part of the south transept. Above each of the tripartite crossing arches, which are painted and consist of rubble and Roman tiles, runs an arcade of double arches screening a wall-passage. This form of wall articulation is more elaborate, therefore, than that of the nave. The restored ceiling (16th-century) is about 100 ft from the ground.

Pl. 27 gives a *view from the south aisle looking eastwards* across the south transept into the south aisle of the chancel. Above can be seen part of the south transept's triforium, which is both architecturally and historically informative. The front of the double arches has been left unfaced, clearly revealing the Roman brick used in the construction of wall and arches. The arches are properly vaulted and the filling laid herring-bone fashion. The cushion capitals are Norman, whereas the two central shafts were taken from a pre-Norman building and re-used. They are turned in Barnack stone of the sort found in Anglo-Saxon buildings such as St Peter with St Cuthbert Monkwearmouth (Co. Durham).

30 The *font in St Augustine's, Brookland* (Kent) must hail from an earlier building. It is 12th-century work, whereas the small aisled church in Romney Marsh was not built until 1250 or thereabouts. England, which was

a leading producer of lead during the Middle Ages, has over thirty lead fonts, sixteen of them Romanesque. They were popular for a time, but their popularity waned because they were so fragile. This particular font is encircled by a two-tiered arcade, each tier consisting of twenty bays and each arch bearing an explanatory legend. In the top tier are signs of the zodiac—visible here, from left to right: Virgo, Libra, Scorpio and Sagittarius—and beneath them scenes associated with the months of the year: a reaper with sickle in August, a thresher with flail in September, wine-pressing in October, and a swineherd knocking down acorns for fodder in November. These scenes were applied with moulds. Since twelve arches were not enough to cover the full circumference of the font, its maker duplicated the eight months from March to October. The band of cable-moulding at the top is interrupted by three moulded impressions of the Resurrection. The engraving displays sound craftsmanship rather than artistry, but fonts of this type were designed to edify and divert contemporary worshippers rather than appeal to their aesthetic sense.

31-32 The little church of *St Nicholas, Worth* (Sussex) underwent restoration in 1871. In the course of this, the *apsidal chancel (Pl. 32)* was largely rebuilt, though in accordance with the original design and dimensions. There is a distinct contrast between the almost pedantic workmanship of the apse's exterior and the *original masonry (Pl. 31)*. However, the church provides an instructive example of a mid-11th-century Anglo-Saxon church which has retained its original ground-plan intact. The only incongruous feature is the tower, which was built in 1871 and looks, appropriately, like a foreign body. The layout of the church was cruciform, the lateral arm consisting of two chapels connected with the nave by arches. The chancel is almost as wide as the nave and culminates in an apse lit by three small round-arched windows—a rare 11th-century feature. The exterior of the nave and chancel, but not of the chapels, is encircled below window-level by a string course from which pilaster strips descend at regular intervals. They project only slightly from the wall but are deeply embedded in it. Thus, their primary purpose is functional rather than decorative. Still preserved in the north face of the nave are a pair of typical Anglo-Saxon two-light windows with genuine round arches and squat shafts set between base and impost block in the centre of the thickness of the wall. *(Pl. 31* illustrates the single example in the south face.)

33-34 *Wall-paintings in St John the Baptist, Clayton* (Sussex). Overlooked by the Downs, this unaisled church stands beside the old Roman road about six miles outside Brighton. It was built shortly after 1000 and belonged to the Cluniac priory of Lewes from 1076 onwards. The chancel was extended during the 12th century. Considering all that has happened to the church—the addition of side-chapels (later demolished), alterations to windows, and modifications to the exterior and interior—one can only marvel that so much of its original appearance survives. This is due principally to two special features: the Anglo-Saxon chancel arch, and the wall-paintings. The chancel arch is unusual. It consists of three semicircular shafts which rise from hewn stone bases on either side, leaving the edges of the wall visible, and converge to form a round-headed arch.

The wall-paintings were laid bare during restoration work in 1893. Extremely careful cleaning and fixing undertaken in 1964 has restored as much of their original freshness as still survives. Together with the paintings at Hardham (Sussex), they may be ascribed to the school of Lewes Priory. Whether or not the suggested dating of 1080 is accepted, they are among the finest c. 1100 wall-paintings in England, and the absence of comparable examples invests them with special importance. The lower of the two tiers has almost entirely disappeared, but one can still make out a Weighing of Souls and, on either side of the chancel arch, St Peter receiving the Key and St Paul the Book. A band of loose scrolls separates the two tiers, and the upper tier is bounded at the head by a well-executed band of Greek key which indicates a date of origin in the early 12th century. The technique is linear but rhythmically dramatic. The basic theme is the Last Judgement. Christ, adopting a fine, vigorous pose, is seated on a stepped throne inside the mandorla, flanked by elegant angels. Apostles stand on either side, deep in animated conversation.

These paintings were executed in fresco technique. The mineral pigments do not possess the depth of Catalonian frescos but are deeper than many French examples. Certain aspects of pose and physiognomy do, nevertheless, recall the frescos at Brinay (Cher). That Continental influences helped to mould English wall-painting at this period is evidenced by the frescos at Kempley (Gloucestershire).

35-36 The *parish church of St Nicholas in Brighton* (Sussex) contains a stone font dedicated to the patron saint of seafarers and probably imported from France. It is an admirable example of 12th-century Norman workmanship. Restrained and symmetrical in style, the drum-shaped font is bounded at the foot by a band of floral ornaments and at the head by a band of horizontal lozenges carved in angled relief. The central band is devoted to a representation of the Last Supper.

The *shipboard scene (Pl. 36)* runs from right to left. It illustrates a legendary attempt at revenge by the goddess Diana, who, furious that her temple has been burnt at Nicholas' instigation, tries to talk a female pilgrim into burning his church at Myra. Nicholas, on the left, gives orders that the vessel containing the incendiary oil should be thrown into the sea. The figures on either side of the ship and its reefed sail combine to form an excellently balanced composition. Nicholas of Myra (4th century), who had been a favourite saint of the Eastern Church since the 9th century, won particular esteem in the West during the 11th and 12th centuries. In 1087 his relics at Myra were seized and brought back to Norman Bari, where the famous church of S. Nicola was built to house them. The *Last Supper (Pl. 35)* shows Christ and six of his disciples seated at a laid table. The sculptor tackled the problems of high relief with remarkable success. Christ, with a cruciform nimbus, beard and moustache, has raised the two fingers of his right hand in a characteristic gesture of benediction. The disciples wear caps but no haloes. Only four of them are bearded, but all sport luxuriant moustaches.

37 *South doorway of St Andrew's, Bishopstone* (Sussex). Modest as this quiet village church in the Downs appears today, its history and design are of great importance. The Bishop of Chichester had a seat here late in the 11th century. The present building is the product of numerous alterations and additions, the north aisle and chancel being Late Romanesque (Transitional) c. 1200. The earliest building, to which we may ascribe the present vestibule, originated c. 800. This consisted of a rectangular nave, a square-ended chancel, and, with their narrower sides abutting on the nave to north and south, two rectangular chambers known as 'porticus', which may have been used as chapels. The entrance to the original church was in the west. When the west tower was added, the door between the nave and south porticus was enlarged to form a portal, the outer wall pierced, a simple rustic Romanesque gabled doorway built in, and the Anglo-Saxon side-chamber transformed into a vestibule. The north porticus disappeared when the north aisle was built. In our photograph, which clearly illustrates the contrast in stonework, can be seen a sun-dial. Although inscribed with the name 'Eadric' and reputed to be Anglo-Saxon, it is made of Caen stone and does not date from the same period as the vestibule. Was it the work of a local Anglo-Saxon stonemason who collaborated in the building of early Norman cathedrals?

38 The *south doorway of All Saints, Staplehurst* (Kent) provides an example of an 11th-century oak door complete with iron fittings. It was transferred to its present site from some unidentified building of earlier date. The wrought-iron fittings, which are incomplete, may have been modelled on book illuminations or metal-work. They were more than merely ornamental, without doubt, but their purport remains obscure. The motifs include fishes and snakes, a bird's head reminiscent of designs in the wooden church in the Norwegian village of Urnes, a winged sea-monster, a ship(?), a crescent moon, and two crosses, one of them inside a circle. Pictorial symbols on church doors—the threshold between the perils of the outside world and the Kingdom of God—undoubtedly combined apotropaic motifs designed to ward off misfortune with Christian motifs inspired not only by bestiaries and the lamentations of Job but also, perhaps, by the fantastic stories which returning pilgrims and Crusaders used to bring home from across the seas.

39-41 *Crossing tower and crossing of St Nicholas, Old Shoreham* (Sussex). Three phases of construction can be discerned in this small unaisled cruciform church: very late Anglo-Saxon, 12th-century Norman, and 13th-century Gothic. The *exterior view from the south-east (Pl. 39)* shows the square-ended Gothic chancel. The massive crossing tower and transept date from the late 12th century. Since the flints employed elsewhere in the building did not lend themselves to neat corners, these were finished off with ashlar quoins. Surmounting the plain plinth-storey is a belfry-stage with magnificent round arches of three orders, the outer pair on each face being blind and the central one open, with twin sub-arches supported by a cylindrical shaft with a cushion capital. The highest stage is inset and adorned with two œils-de-bœuf on each face. The Norman church had two transeptal apses and an extended apsidal chancel, all demolished as a result of Gothic improvements.

The westward view along the narrow nave, past the crossing, and into the luminous *chancel (Pl. 40)* derives its fascination from a distinct contrast between different periods: Norman massivity and strength, and Gothic subtlety. The west arch is still spanned by a carved Norman beam, an extremely rare phenomenon. The crossing arches, almost too bulky for such a small church, share the same basic composition but differ in the extent of their ornamentation. The crossing and chancel arches visible from the nave are the most elaborate. The west crossing arch, consisting of two orders supported by quarter- and half-shafts with scalloped capitals, partly carved in low relief, has a flat inner rib, roll-moulding adorned with a spiral beaded trail, a band of double zigzag, a cat's head at its vertex, and a small meditative figure on the south side. The *crossing (Pl. 41)* displays a variety of ornamental motifs, notably the band of zigzag, which suggests a date of origin in the first half of the 12th century. By far the most richly decorated is the

chancel arch, which, apart from being bordered by an outer band resembling a necklace, has an inner band of zigzag on its roll-moulded soffit. We do not know the motives for such elaboration in a small church, but Shoreham was an important harbour at the time of building.

42 *St Mary de Haura, New Shoreham* (Sussex) resembles an abbey or cathedral but was never more than a parish church, and, as such, a piece of self-assertion on the part of a prosperous community of ship-builders and merchants. This being so, it heralds a trend towards ecclesiastical architecture on the grand scale, a trend which ultimately found full expression in High Gothic. What survives is only part of a larger whole. Our view from the south-west shows the dominant crossing tower (plinth-storey Norman, upper stages Transitional, with twin round arches surmounted by slightly stilted arches with pointed heads), the high-shouldered transept, and the one surviving bay of the original nave, which used to be a six-bayed structure flanked by aisles. The blocked arches leading to the transept and nave can still be seen. Constructed of Caen stone during the early decades of the 12th century, this proud edifice once possessed two transeptal apses and a round-ended chancel, but even that failed to satisfy the local community. Between 1185 and 1210 they demolished the Norman chancel and annexed a new chancel to the transept in budding Gothic style, then the height of modernity. An upper stage was added to the crossing tower at the same time. The building suffered during the 17th century as a result of naval warfare and civil disorder, and at the end of the same century the Norman nave was demolished with the exception of what survives today. In addition, the arcades and west wall were blocked up and a Norman portal and Late Gothic (Perpendicular) window somewhat clumsily inserted.

43 *The tower of St Mary the Virgin, Sompting* (Sussex), seen from the west. This long narrow church is an augmented 12th-century building, and stands on the site of an earlier church of which only the tower has survived. It is the tower which constitutes Sompting's claim to fame. All its architectural and sculptural characteristics point to a date of origin early in the 11th century, and the church figures in the Domesday Book. The ground-plan of the tower is square (internal measurement roughly 15 ft) and the flint-and-mortar walls are 27 ins thick. There are four storeys. At ground-level, beneath a 15th-century window, a 15th-century portal takes the place of the original entrance. Inside, providing an east access to the nave, is a massive archway with roll-moulded arches, demi-shafts at the sides, thin abaci, and capitals. The latter are among the best-preserved sculptural works of the Anglo-Saxon period. This applies both to the shaft capitals with their three rows of still-leaf and to the non-projecting capitals above the edges of the wall, which are carved in relief with robust volute-type motifs whose spirals resemble crosiers and enclose what look like clusters of berries *(Pl. 53)*. Their air of burgeoning life is enhanced by the shoot visible between the two curved motifs.

The tower doorway and arch are offset towards the south. The next two storeys have small lights on the north and south sides, either round-arched or furnished with typical Anglo-Saxon triangle-heads. The belfry-stage has two largish apertures in each face, triangle-headed on the east and west sides and double-arched with an inset shaft on the north and south. The tower is capped by a shingled pyramidal roof set on four gables, a so-called *Rhenish helm* of the sort that occurs in German Romanesque (approximate height of stone gable-ends: 60 ft; of apex: 75 ft). It is the only early example of such a roof in England, though it is just possible that it was converted to its present striking shape when the tower was repaired in 1762. Typically Anglo-Saxon are the hewn stone quoins at the corners, which give way, from the ornamented string course downwards, to stone pilasters (cf. Worth). Running down the centre of each face from the gable consoles to the string course are semicircular shafts, interrupted below the belfry-stage by figured capitals.

44-47 *Chichester Cathedral* (Sussex), *sculptures and south wall of the nave*. In the course of the diocesan reorganization ushered in by the Conquest, a see was established at Chichester, the erstwhile Roman town of Noviomagus and South Saxon Cissecaster. A bishop had previously resided in the near-by coastal town of Selsey, where St Wilfrid landed after fleeing from Northumbria in the 7th century. The last vestiges of Selsey's monastery and early church have been engulfed by the sea, but there is a theory that both the magnificent stone carvings in Chichester Cathedral were brought there from Selsey.

After the see had been transferred, Bishop Ralph de Luffa started work on the cathedral, a conventional aisled church of eight bays, with two west towers, a transept, a crossing tower, and an apsidal chancel which, in accordance with the tendency towards enlargement among Norman churches in England, was allotted three bays of its own. In *the nave (Pl. 47)*, a new wall of Caen stone with new arcade arches supported by shafts of dark Purbeck stone (cf. William of Sens at Canterbury) was superimposed on the original Norman walls, which were left intact. The whole of the clerestory stage was redone as well, the slightly pointed arches on either side

of the stilted round-arched windows introducing a new element characteristic of the Transitional style. Triple demi-shafts run all the way up the wall to meet the ribbed vaults, whose lateral thrust is absorbed by the reinforced walls and external buttresses. The cathedral thus testifies to the interaction of Late Romanesque and Early Gothic. It was consecrated in 1199.

In the south aisle of the choir are two four-foot-high panels: *Christ's meeting with Mary and Martha* and *The raising of Lazarus*. We do not know their original location. There is no evidence of any Lazarus patrociny, as at Autun, so they may have been votive panels associated with some incident on a pilgrimage or Crusade. Put together from limestone slabs, the 'panels' were found behind the choir-stalls in 1829. They suffered during the move, and there is some doubt about their reassembly, particularly in respect of Christ's raised hand in the *Lazarus scene (Pl. 45)*. Pieces are missing, too (note the palmettes and areas of patching). The stone, which hails from Caen, still bears traces of original pigment. The recessed eye-sockets used to be inlaid with glass paste, glass chips, or lead.

Though suggested by certain archaisms, a pre-1066 dating would seem to be incorrect, and it is more likely that the carvings originated during the second quarter of the 12th century. The scenes are no longer conceived in vacuo and have begun to detach themselves from their background. It is probable that they still represent divine and dramatic intervention of the 'theatrum mundi' type, but signs of natural observation can already be seen, e.g. in the grave-diggers, one of whom is clenching his teeth with exertion. Despite this piece of scenic individuality, the general tone is still 'exemplary'. Figures are not yet accorded their true proportions, and the medieval law of 'spiritual perspective', under which relative dimensions were governed by intrinsic significance, still holds good: Christ, being the principal figure, is also the largest. Both panels are instinct with profound solemnity. In the *Mary and Martha scene (Pl. 46)*, Christ strides along with heavy tread, deep in thought. His disciples, oblivious of their surroundings, follow him. It is this focus on the divine which invests the work with its extraordinary power. The figures of the two women are necessarily of secondary importance. The basic mood of the Lazarus scene is one of profound and unrelieved sorrow. Not a single face registers astonishment at God's miraculous mastery over death. The faces of *the mourning women (Pl. 44)* wear an expression of grief which could only have been conjured up in stone by a sculptor of great ability and one who belonged to a mature period.

Neither panel is the work of an early phase. The arcade behind the battlements in the Mary and Martha panel, for instance, is observed with such spatial precision

285

that it could only be the product of a well-developed visual sense. Certain archaisms, e.g. in the kneeling woman, may be attributable to clumsiness of execution, for the two panels are not the work of a single man. They are closely related and were probably produced in the same atelier, but by two different masters. The head of the ambulant Christ differs from that of the benedictory Christ, despite certain similarities, and the great master who carved the mourning women is not identical with the sculptor of the kneeling woman. Where strength of composition is concerned, however, the Martha and Mary master surpasses his colleague. We do not know the name of either artist, nor has it so far been possible to attribute any other works to them. In fact, no genuinely related monumental work of this period has yet been identified, the closest approximation being the *Externsteine* at Horn in Westphalia, which were probably executed in 1115. What is certain is that the authors of these two panels, who must be numbered among the finest sculptors of their day, had assimilated both French and Scandinavian influences. All these factors help to make the carvings at Chichester part of a magnificent Occidental tradition.

WESSEX

48-51 The core of *Holy Trinity, Winchester Cathedral* (Hampshire), is the Norman church built by Bishop Walkelyn. However, it has been so extensively built over and refaced that only isolated Romanesque components are still visible today, e.g. the crypt and the *transept and crossing tower (Pl. 50)*. The latter collapsed early in the 12th century and had to be rebuilt on top of reinforced crossing piers.

As the residence of the King of Wessex, Winchester first became a see in the 7th century. In the latter half of the 10th century, after the Viking invasions, the existing cathedral church was rebuilt and extended, only to be demolished by the Normans. Walkelyn, the monk from Rouen who was installed as bishop and abbot of Winchester in 1070, in place of Stigand, the last Anglo-Saxon bishop, wanted a new building of his own. He erected it on a new site: an aisled church with a transept and crossing tower, apsidal chancel with ambulatory and east chapel, and a crypt, complete with chapel, running beneath the entire chancel. This proud edifice was consecrated in 1093 and the remains of St Swithun (d. 862), bishop and patron of Winchester, reinterred in it. More work was carried out a century later, and further alterations were made in the course of the centuries, some of them substantial. The crossing tower acquired its fan-vaulted ceiling as late as the 17th century.

The many changes undergone by the fabric make it all the more remarkable that the transept should have preserved its Romanesque character—the south arm with additions and the *north arm (Pl. 51)* virtually untouched. Both arms of the transept have aisles, like the nave, and are invested with solemn majesty by their horizontal tiers of single and double round-headed arches supported by cylindrical shafts with cushion capitals. Undeveloped wall-shafts denote a modification of the original architectural plan. The north transept at Winchester is the sole surviving example in which the gallery extends bridge-fashion across the north wall, like the tribunes of Normandy. It was via the north transept that pilgrims entered the church on their way to the shrine of St Swithun. The walled-up pilgrim's door can still be seen today. This magnificent wing of the cathedral conveys the proud ambition of the first Norman abbot-bishop, in his capacity as the Conqueror's representative, to erect a condign house of God in the capital of the English kings—a city which was recognized as such by William himself and which, together with London, retained its royal prerogatives for a long time to come. William Rufus, son of William the Conqueror, was laid to rest here with due ceremony.

Winchester's wide-ranging associations are illustrated by a *black marble font (Pl. 48, 49)* which stands in the north aisle. This font and six more of its type, all situated in places near the coast, were imported into England from Flanders, and others can be found in Flanders itself. Having a straightforward liturgical function to perform and being unrelated to individual churches, fonts were often 'mass-produced' in workshops near suitable quarries and then shipped to their destination. This was how, c. 1160, the quarries of Tournai came to supply a number of similar fonts, square in shape but recessed to form a circular basin and supported by a central column and four corner-posts. A band of zigzag and foliage runs round the lip of this basin, and the four corners of the upper side display leaf-work and a Tree of Life. Two of the sides (roughly 33 ins long) bear circular medallions composed of interlace and filled with doves, grapes, and lions. The other two sides are occupied by scenes from the life of St Nicholas.

Set in Asia Minor, stories about this miracle-working Bishop of Myra gained a wide audience through the agency of Crusaders and of merchants involved in the growing trade with the countries of the Near East, including the Norman Principality of Antioch. Their maritime and feudal associations accorded perfectly with the spirit of the Norman 12th century. What was more, the episodic nature of the legend of St Nicholas—one of the first to be incorporated by Jacobus de Voragine in his *Legenda Aurea* (c. 1270)—must soon have provided material for morality plays. This dramatic tradition was very much alive at Winchester, as a Resurrection play from Bishop Ethelwold's *Liber Consuetudinum* indicates. The well-established nature of the tradition is also attested by another play from Winchester, the *Ludus super iconia Sancti Nicolai*. The Winchester font originated during a period of brisk intellectual activity. Giraldus Cambrensis (1147–1216), the son of a Norman and a Welshwoman, was producing brilliant treatises, letters, speeches, and topographical works, as well as a collection of quotations from other authors which he entitled *Gemma*. Also pursuing literary activities at this time, as secretary to Archbishop Theobald of Canterbury, was John of Salisbury, an intimate of the English Pope Adrian IV, a friend of Thomas Becket, and, ultimately, Bishop of Chartres.

The see of Winchester was currently held by Henry of Blois, an astute and wealthy nobleman who may, thanks to his connections, have commissioned the font from Tournai. In comparison with the Brighton font *(Pl. 35, 36)*, there is something exalted about these scenes and their mode of portrayal. In the first *(Pl. 49)*, St Nicholas saves the three marriageable daughters of an impoverished nobleman from prostitution by presenting them with three golden globes. On the extreme left stands an elegantly clad youth with a falcon on his wrist. He is waiting, though whether for the hand of one of the girls or her physical submission cannot be determined. In the second scene *(Pl. 48)*, a drowned youth is resuscitated by the saint's intervention. The figures of his noble parents are expressively treated, and the hull of the ship with the animal's head on the prow recalls the vessels in the Bayeux Tapestry. Genuine observation is apparent in the portrayal of the helmsman, who clasps the grotesquely adorned tiller under his right arm-pit. Both these scenes are distinguished by an air of grave dignity. The figures are deployed in stern and solemn rows, as though the action were unfolding on a shallow stage in the foreground. Narrative accuracy did not cramp the stonemason's freedom of execution. Particularly instructive is the portrayal of Myra Cathedral, with its tiers of arcades, tiled roofs, and crosses. The sculptor was such a stickler for accuracy that he carefully provided the portal with metal fittings and a lock.

52 *Chancel arch at Holy Trinity, Bosham* (Sussex). This small but historically and archaeologically important church overlooks one of the many small bays on the coast between Chichester and Portsmouth. Bede *(H.E. IV/3)* records that the Irish monk Dicuil and five or six companions—a Christian outpost in a heathen land—were living there in poverty and humility, surrounded by sea and forest, when St Wilfrid started to evangelize the South Saxons in 681. (Bede refers to the place as Bosanham.) Bosham's church and royal hall figure proudly at the beginning of the Bayeux Tapestry, which shows Harold and a companion kneeling before the church under the caption 'Bosham Ecclesia'. One striking feature of the scene, which is not, of course, a 'photographic' reproduction, is a large and clearly delineated round arch. Being a royal chapel with a rich estate attached, Bosham was listed in the Domesday Book.

No part of the present church can be dated earlier than the 11th century. The imposing chancel arch (over 22 ft high and 11½ ft wide) is of special architectural interest. Three shafts rise from bases on either side, matched by a round arch of three orders resting on capitals. The frontal shaft and the two subsidiary shafts which project from the right-angled recesses are of a piece with the edges of the wall itself, but the depth to which the elaborately contoured blocks are embedded in the wall varies. The shafts repose on a two-part base—one part annular and the other circular and moulded—and a square plinth. The capitals are bell-shaped, and the massive impost blocks let into the wall above them help to sustain the weight of the heavy chancel arch. The arch itself consists of voussoirs, roll-moulded to conform with the shafts but with the inner arch constructed separately from the outer ones, whose voussoirs extend the full depth of the wall so that the thrust and tension of the stones provides mutual reinforcement. England possesses other large chancel arches of the Late Anglo-Saxon period, e.g. Wittering *(Pl. 202)*, but none finer than the one at Bosham. It may genuinely be regarded as an epitome of the royal architecture of its day.

53 *Capital at Sompting* see note on *Pl. 43*

54 *Capital at Reading* (Berkshire). This abbey was founded by Henry I and administered by monks from Cluny, though it never became one of the genuine reform monasteries. The charter of 1125, which is preserved in a 13th-century copy, indicates that the abbey was sumptuously furnished. It used to be one of England's premier abbeys, but little remains of it today owing to the ravages caused by the dissolution of 1539. Nevertheless, the abbatial seal and the cloister capitals bear witness to its artistic standing. Compared with the somewhat earlier capitals at Canterbury *(Pl. 12–16)*, the Reading capitals, executed *c.* 1130–40, seem more severe and slightly more schematic, though of excellent craftsmanship. They are also closer in conception to the Insular style. Ornaments are employed in such a way as to encase every surface and, basket-fashion, to accentuate the cubic shape of the entire capital.

55-56 *Capitals formerly in Hyde Abbey, near Winchester* (Hampshire). This abbey, once situated a little to the north of Winchester, was dissolved in 1538. It was burnt down during the course of its vicissitudinous history (in 1141) but later rebuilt even more elaborately than before. All that survives of it now is a 16th-century gateway and several capitals of outstanding artistic and art-historical importance, now modestly arrayed on the window-ledges of the little parish church of St Bartholomew. These have been dated immediately before the fire, but their intaglio carving displays a mastery unequalled by other work of the same period. The Canterbury capitals of *c.* 1120 are linked with the Hyde capitals by affinities in decorative motifs, but the stonemason of Hyde Abbey went further. He belonged to a later generation and was nearer the phase which arrived *c.* 1170, when a new verism in outward form declared itself.

All the Hyde capitals are developments of the same fundamentally circular shape and have beaded borders which often overlap the sides. Some of the circles are filled with lobate leaves which culminate in human figures. There is something frivolous about such com-positions, for all their naturalistic accuracy, something incongruously modern—something surrealistic, even, about the face of one of the capitals *(Pl. 55)*, on which two small heads protrude abruptly from the enveloping foliage and confront each other across the stem of a third leafy shoot. The inspiration for this derived from illu-minated manuscripts, but what is remarkable is the three-dimensional treatment and the inclusion of interior shapes. The whole composition was brilliantly carved from stone and the drilled eye-sockets were probably inlaid with lead or glass. This positively scenic interplay of convex and concave, light and shade, is expressive of a late phase of artistic development, which is why the writer favours a dating in the third quarter of the 12th century. This would mean that the capitals were executed after the fire, probably as late as the reign of Henry II. There is, however, something un-English in their intaglio technique. The winged lion-griffin *(Pl. 56)* occupies a space determined by its own shape. The va-rious planes—anterior wing, body and raised tail, poste-rior wing—are clearly differentiated. The motif itself derives from the Sassanid world of imagery, but the execution is Mediterranean. Very similar carvings exist in at least two churches in Saintonge, that point of interaction between England and the Mediterranean world. It is not beyond the bounds of possibility that the masters of Hyde summoned stonemasons from France to refurbish the abbey after the fire.

57-62 *Romsey Abbey* (Hampshire) still bears witness to the solemn majesty of the former Benedictine nunnery. Its foundation may be ascribed to the middle of the 10th century, but a number of alterations and additions were made thereafter. The question thus arises whether the large *Crucifix hewn from three blocks of stone (Pl. 62)*, sit-uated immediately outside the south door but on the west wall of the south transept, should be attributed to the original Anglo-Saxon fabric or the first Norman phase. Opinions are very divided on this point. Christ, somewhat less than life-size, stands erect with both feet resting on the suppedaneum, arms horizontally extended and hands outspread. His raised head is turned slightly to the right and his eyes are open in the conventional Romanesque pose known as *Christus dominans*, or Christ victorious over death. Comparison with neigh-bouring Anglo-Saxon portrayals and, in particular, with Langford *(Pl. 83)* discloses that Romsey's Christ on the Cross was carved with a far greater understanding of human anatomy. Christ's sole garment is a carefully draped loincloth which clings heavily to his skin and allows the contours of his thighs to emerge with clarity. The torso and lower part of the legs are so subtly mod-elled that one might almost think they belonged to a living, breathing body, and the head is turned on the neck as if in spontaneous response to a summons. None of these features seems to be consistent with Anglo-Saxon technique and observation, and the figure is more likely to be of Norman origin. It should probably be dated *c.* 1100 and may conceivably have been brought back from the First Crusade (1096–9). Its original site is unknown.

Architectural evidence points to 1120 as the year in which work on the present church began. The basic Romanesque fabric of the building is excellently pre-served. The aisled nave is seven bays long. The transept, which is dominated by a low central tower above the crossing, has an apsidal *east chapel (Pl. 58)* on each arm. A splendidly enriched string course runs round the chancel and transept, adorned with a wealth of diverse heads and masks. The chancel is also aisled, and the choir has piers of fundamentally rectangular design with engaged shafts on the inside. These rise to the top of the clerestory, which exhibits the usual three-part orchestration and is equipped with a wall-passage. More engaged demi-shafts support roll-moulded arches resting on simple cushion capitals. The arches are elaborately enriched on the wall side with bold zigzag patterns of the kind favoured during the decades in question. The gallery openings are invested with rhythmical emphasis by an inset cylindrical shaft supporting two open arches and surmounted by an apical colonnette which rises from the spandrel between the arches.

The *crossing (Pl. 59)* impresses one by its very simplicity. Four massive compound piers support triple-stepped crossing arches devoid of architectural ornamentation, but this merely renders the masonry more imposing.

Round the first stage of the tower runs a gallery pierced on the interior by a double-arched arcade. The monastic and ascetic atmosphere of this unadulteratedly Romanesque building is tempered by the sumptuous Gothic windows (Decorated, latter half of the 13th century) at the east end of the chancel, where the double arches leading to the retrochoir form an exception to the general rule.

Chancel, transept, crossing, and one bay of the nave were completed in 1140, and represent a homogeneous unit. The nave was intended to have plain cylindrical piers (see *north-west view from the crossing, Pl. 61*), but a stylistic change occurred during the architectural interregnum that set in after 1140. In 1150, when work on the nave was resumed, the builders pursued a different policy. The outcome was an increased emphasis on verticals and a concomitant refinement of structural members. The year 1180 saw the completion of three more bays, by now in Late Norman style, and between 1230 and 1250, after another interlude, the nave was finished off in Early Gothic style. The *view of the south transept (Pl. 60)*, showing the massive tribune opening and the flattened roll-moulded arch above the entrance to the south transept, gives an idea of the increasingly 'sinewy' treatment accorded the series of vaults. Our view of the nave from the crossing does the same for the articulation of the walls. The differences between individual bays are expressive of a lively determination to keep abreast of stylistic changes at every stage of construction. Naturally enough, frank experimentation also took place. This is evident in the treatment of the arcade arches and in the variations between the inset gallery arches. A comparison between the gallery opening in the south transept and its counterpart in the north transept (cf. *Pl. 60* and *61*) brings out this contrast very strongly. The gallery arches in the chancel follow the second, more advanced pattern. As building progressed, they were remodelled, decorated, or left plain, adorned with fillets or filled in so as to form lunettes. The height of the arches remained constant, however. They rose to below the clerestory, drawing aisles and gallery into the same scheme of things.

It is surprising, in view of the lively and progressive nature of its architecture, that this building should grant such little prominence to sculptural work and that some of what it does possess in the way of genuine sculpture should display such a complete contrast in quality. Two figured capitals, each in a conspicuous position, not only fail to accord with the quality of the building but represent an iconographic and stylistic enigma. One of them is situated in the north aisle of the choir and the other, also a cushion capital, in a similar position on the leading pier in the south aisle of the choir *(Pl. 57)*. The narrow west face depicts a seated man holding a V-shaped scroll,

similar except for the position of his legs to the figure which occupies the east face (illustrated here). However, while the head on the south-east corner bears a grinning mask—a figurative perversion of the volute capital—the south-west corner is emphasized by the affronted figure of a standing angel. A king is approaching him carrying a cone-shaped object. Behind the king sits a third figure, facing the mask and supporting the V-shaped scroll which runs beneath it. Inscribed on the scroll is the legend 'Robertus me fecit'. Although no interpretation has yet emerged, this may refer to some religious bequest. Both capitals are probably by the same hand. Their general character is archaic and far less advanced than that of the main fabric. The abbey's structural history suggests a dating *c.* 1135-40.

63 Former *south doorway of St Margaret's, Knook* (Wiltshire). This small church was drastically restored—indeed, virtually rebuilt—in 1876, so that all dating must be undertaken with extreme caution. If the original relationship of breadth to height has been retained, it would indicate a date of construction *c.* 1100 rather than prior to 1066. The same would apply to the subdued but inherently fine south doorway, now walled up. The original arch is still visible from the inside, but it contains no stones which run right through the wall in the Anglo-Saxon manner. Outside, the structure projects a length of approximately two hands. The gable is flattish. The inset Norman shafts support small capitals and a roll-moulded round arch with a flat border. The tympanum displays some extremely shallow engraved scroll-work entwined round two mythical beasts. The motif is probably Anglo-Saxon—comparable examples can be found in manuscripts of the early 11th century—but the whole composition is so symmetrical, neat and well-balanced that it strikes one as a deliberate revival of *c.* 1100—a post-1066 product of the Saxo-Norman overlap.

64 The *Norman House at Christchurch* (Hampshire) is a ruined mid-12th-century mansion situated within the castle walls. A large proportion of the masonry has been restored. Very few Romanesque dwelling-houses proper have survived in England because most of the smaller buildings consisted of timber. Only stone houses had any appreciable chance of survival, but they, too, were extended, rebuilt and generally adapted to changes in living conditions as time went by. The Norman House at Christchurch formed part of a castle. Harold's hall, which can be seen beside Bosham church in the Bayeux Tapestry, gives us a rough idea of what such buildings were like. The ground floor, devoted to household offices, was surmounted by an upper storey with larger windows. Outside steps provided access to the house. The rafters were exposed. A large fireplace was let into the thick walls and the smoke led off through a chimney. Protruding flues did not become customary until the latter half of the 12th century. One side of the hall, which was in the region of 65ft long, may have been cut off by a wooden partition for use as sleeping quarters. Opposite, in the southeast corner, a stone annexe above a ditch served as a latrine—a considerable luxury in those days.

65-66 *Christchurch Priory* (Hampshire) was begun by Bishop Ralph Flambard, who became Bishop of Durham in 1099. It was conceived on a grand scale, with aisles, a west tower, a transept, and an aisled, square-ended chancel which was extended by the addition of a Lady Chapel. Flambard was to build on an even grander scale at Durham. Christchurch Priory had a chancel three bays long and was thus an elongated church of the Chichester type. Both arms of the transept were traversed by galleries, as at Winchester *(Pl. 51)* or Jumièges in Normandy.

The exterior walls of the *north transept (Pl. 65)* still display the enlaced blind arches which once ran round the entire church. Also visible are other blind arches, spandrels with squamiform ornamentation, and a stair-tower with diagonal trellis-work, similar to that of St Etienne at Beauvais but bulkier. The whole wing must have been a magnificent sight before the large Gothic (Decorated) window was inserted and the walls were modified.

Disregarding the excessively deep ribbed vaults, which impair its spaciousness, *the interior (Pl. 66)* presents a homogeneous appearance. The walls of the nave conform to the Romanesque system of arcade, triforium and clerestory with wall-passage, each storey being slightly shallower than the one beneath. This enhances the horizontal effect and conflicts yet again with the Gothicizing vaults. An exposed roof would create a far purer impression.

67 The *font in St John the Baptist Bere, Regis* (Dorset) dates from the first half of the 12th century. Its decoration consists of enlaced arcading and a band of six-petalled stellate flowers, all executed in a simple rustic style. The base is a later addition and falsifies the general effect. The intersected-arch motif was commonly used on fonts as well as buildings during the 12th century, and can be found in a number of places.

68 *Exeter Cathedral* (Devon) is the sole surviving example of a variant to be found nowhere else in England: its north and south towers are situated above the

arms of the transept. Our photograph shows the south tower, which is more elaborately enriched than its companion in the north. The south face is interrupted by the large Gothic (Decorated) window of the south transept. The battlements and pointed corner-turrets are later additions. The four corners of the tower are picked out and reinforced with pilaster-like projections, those on the nave side being narrower than those on the outside. Above the otherwise plain plinth-storey rise three intermediate stages of varying design, each separated by a string course. The first stage has ten tall narrow lesenes linked by shallow round-headed arches. The second stage has some very similar but rather taller blind arches, one of wider span to accommodate the round-arched central window and the others, grouped in two sets of three, compressed into the spaces between the central arch and the corner-projections. Surmounting these arches are circular recesses resembling œils-de-bœuf. The third stage has another ten tall and shallow blind arches of uniform width but is pierced by two narrow windows, so disposed that they are separated from each other by one complete arch and from the corner-projections by another two. One can discern an ability on the part of the builders to incorporate subtle rhythmical effects in their work. They brought it to a climax and relieved its inherent tension by furnishing the belfry-stage with three large round-arched windows and an alternation of broad and narrow blind arches.

Exeter Cathedral was begun *c.* 1110 by Bishop William Warelwast, a nephew of William the Conqueror, on the site of a modest Anglo-Saxon church. It was consecrated in 1133, but work continued until about 1200. Apart from some masonry and the two magnificent towers, nothing of the earliest Norman phase has survived. The cathedral was transformed from the 13th century onward, and its interior now represents the very embodiment of 'sinewy' Gothic.

69 The *west doorway of St Germans* (Cornwall) radiates a kind of elemental strength. The portal projects about a yard from the wall. The surround is divided into seven orders, four inset nook-shafts with capitals alternating with three bands of continuous zigzag which run round the archivolts and down to plinth-level. Jambs and arches are separated by stepped abaci. What must once have testified to fine workmanship has long since acquired the appearance of eroded mineral through exposure to the elements. This work is instinct with the spirit of the North, not with the balanced moderation of the Mediterranean. The huge archivolts frame a comparatively small doorway. Such is the impression of weight that the arches seem to sag in the middle and the sides to bow outwards. This contrasts with the greater verticality of Anglo-Saxon porches like those at Bishopstone, Escomb (Pl. 172) or Monkwearmouth (Co. Durham). The incorporation of such a doorway in a church of the latter half of the 12th century was meant to make it look more imposing. This one recalls the less ambitious arched doorway at Clonmacnois (Co. Offaly). The Celtic cross above St Germans' gable, restored during the renovations of 1888–94 but re-erected in the ancient manner, is a reminder of its Iro-Celtic origins, which probably date far back into the 7th century.

70–71 *Lady Chapel, Glastonbury Abbey* (Somerset). The abbey's reputation is rooted in its history rather than its architecture. Only remnants of the once extensive monastic buildings still survive—magnificent remnants, admittedly, but all save the Lady Chapel date from between the Early Gothic period and the beginning of the Renaissance. Remarkably enough, the Lady Chapel is the best preserved of all, almost as though veneration for the 'vetusta ecclesia' which it represents had exercised an enduring effect. Perhaps the most celebrated of all English monasteries, Glastonbury is linked by legend with the evangelization of England by Joseph of Arimathea and also with the burial of King Arthur. Modern research, based on careful excavation, has elicited the following facts. Glastonbury was very probably an Iro-Celtic foundation—understandably so, in view of its proximity to the Severn estuary. Archaeologists have unearthed the substructure of a church built during the reign of Ine, King of Wessex (688–726), but the earliest 'vetusta ecclesia' is said to date from the 2nd century. Dunstan, the great reviver of English monasticism after the depredations inflicted by Viking raids, made various alterations and additions during his tenure of the abbacy of Glastonbury (940–57). These were all demolished and replaced by the Normans, who are reported by the Anglo-Saxon Chronicle to have acted with especial vigour under Abbot Thurstan. Only the 'vetusta ecclesia', being a centre of pilgrimage, was left standing, but this too was destroyed by the disastrous fire of 1184.

Very soon after this fire, a new church—the present Lady Chapel—was built of warm yellow Doulting stone on the site of the ancient pilgrimage cell. Consecrated as early as 1186, it splendidly exemplifies the final phase of English Romanesque. With its rectangular ground-plan, four interior bays, gabled roof (collapsed), four small corner-towers (of which only two still stand), and richly articulated walls, it must once have resembled an ornate reliquary—an impression chromatically heightened by the fact that capitals of blue-green lias were superimposed on the yellow ashlar walls for added effect.

The plinth is encompassed by enlaced blind arches resting on projecting cylindrical shafts. This sequence is broken at the corners of the building by the thicker masonry below the corner-towers and on the long walls by three buttresses, the latter being only as high as the thrust of the (collapsed) vaulted roof demanded. Similar enlaced blind arcades run round the foot of the interior. The arches themselves are moulded, and protruding from them are the teeth of a chevron motif—a very late and already 'mannered' form of English Romanesque ornamentation. Shafts and arches are separated by the delicate crocket capitals popular in the early Gothic period.

The *north doorway (Pl. 71)*, like its southern counterpart, is still remarkably Romanesque. A slightly projecting gabled surround separates the surface of the doorway from the arcaded wall. There are five orders, only the second and fourth being furnished with capitals and shafts. The remaining three run straight down to the bases, turning into moulded jambs on the way. The innermost order of the north doorway is devoid of carving, whereas that of the south door is ornamented. The south doorway's second and fourth archivolts are not decorated, by contrast, and the span between capital and capital is blank except for two medallions on the second, clearly executed in situ. One depicts the creation of Eve and the other the Fall. It is not known why the work was never completed.

72 *St Lawrence's, Bradford-on-Avon* (Wiltshire). One can only assume that the reason why this remarkable church has remained virtually unaltered for so many centuries is that the small monastic community which it served had already ceased to exist by the time of the Conquest. It was used first as a graveyard lich-house, then as a barn, then as dwelling-place and school-room. Ever since 1859, however, when Canon W. H. Jones publicized the true significance of the building after his attention had been drawn to it by a reference in William of Malmesbury's *Gesta Pontificum*, interest in this remarkable example of Early Anglo-Saxon architecture has steadily mounted.

Additions and non-original features include, on the one hand, the whole of the west wall with its blind arcading incomprehensibly pierced by windows—the product of restoration work in 1875—and, on the other, the missing south porticus, whose former position is marked by the gabled outline and two projecting buttresses. The ground-plan of the church is clearly defined. It consisted of a rectangular nave, a slightly inset rectangular chancel, and a north and south porticus. The north porticus was probably extended to form a vestibule, and both porticus were located in the middle of the nave walls, though the outer doors appear to be off-centre. Each chamber had one window only—another reason why the restorer's windows are so spurious. Originally splayed on the inside only, they were later—probably at the beginning of the 11th century—remodelled into double-splays. The average thickness of the hewn stone walls is 2 ft 6 ins. Most of the stoutly constructed masonry dates from early in the 8th century, when this church was commissioned for a monastic settlement by St Aldhelm, who, under the tuition of an Irish monk named Maeldubh, became England's first real scholar. The tall and narrow proportions are very typical. The height of the nave walls (26 ft 3 ins) slightly exceeds their length (25 ft 6 ins) and is roughly double their breadth (13 ft). The height of the chancel is even more disproportionate, and the chancel arch must be one of the narrowest ever: although 9 ft 9 ins high, it is only 3 ft 6 ins wide. The other accesses are slightly narrower still, but less tall. They are properly arched with voussoirs in the Anglo-Saxon manner, the blocks of stone—some of them huge—running the full depth of the wall. The jambs, constructed of vertical slabs of stone, converge slightly towards the top, and a single heavy slab embedded deeply in the wall fulfils the double function of capital and abacus. The arcade arches are slightly stilted, and bands of very archaic roll-moulded ornamentation occur at various points.

The roof and sections of the upper walls were restored during the 10th century, and the walls articulated with blind arcading at the same time. The windows were also modified and the lower reaches of the walls endowed with a certain rhythm by cutting back the stonework except at the corners and in the centre to form pilaster strips. Small as the church appears from outside, the interior gives a monumental impression.

73 The *stone font in St James's, Avebury* (Wiltshire), a church which was extensively restored in the 19th century, possesses considerable artistic merit. Its barrel-shaped design is consistent with the latter half of the 11th century, but the enlaced blind arches on its lower half, which can only have originated at the time of Conrad's work on the choir at Canterbury, point to the beginning of the 12th century. However, the fact that memories of Anglo-Saxon motifs and pictorial ideas were still alive can be inferred from the foliate scroll-work in the upper decorative zone, loosely interwoven though it is. The scroll-work sprouts from beside a somewhat clumsily carved figure in a pleated cassock, a typically Norman form of clerical attire (half-visible on the left). The man holds a crosier in his hand and probably represents a bishop officiating at a baptism, because he is flanked by two serpents—symbols

of the Devil—which lie at his feet as though in submission. These small winged serpents, with their delicately enriched bodies and elegantly looped tails, show what the stonemason could accomplish when he kept to the beaten track of his imagination. The arches and their increasingly popular 12th-century cushion capitals look misshapen by comparison.

74-77 In the south transept of *Bristol Cathedral* is a carved stone slab about 7 ft high, clearly incomplete and customarily dated *c.* 1050. This sculpture *(Pl. 74)* comprises two levels: the background, which is deeply recessed, and the figures superimposed on it. The latter have little plasticity, the folds of drapery being hardly more than grooves, yet there are some distinctly perspectival features as well, e.g. the oblique figure in the bottom left corner, the gradated arrangement of the small figures on the right, and, above all, the ambulant figure of Christ, portrayed three-quarter-face with one hand raised in benediction. The scene depicted is Christ's descent into Limbo as decribed in the Acts of Peter, an apocryphal account written in the 5th century. Grasping a cruciform sceptre in his left hand, Christ uses his right to bless the naked man who strains to reach him. He strides almost light-footedly over the writhing figure on the ground—Satan, whom the abyss of Hell (bottom right) has spewed forth. The Lord 'put forth his hand and made the sign of the Cross over Adam' and all the others who were awaiting Redemption in Hell, and ascended from Hell once more, 'holding Adam's right hand the while'. The same theme is depicted on the Norman font at Eardisley *(Pl. 111)*.

Comparison with the Chichester reliefs *(Pl. 45, 46)* at once discloses that the Bristol carving is less advanced, although one cannot overlook certain similarities in power of expression, notably where Christ's face is concerned. Even though the profiled portrayal of Satan has its parallels in the mid-11th-century book illumination of the Winchester school, attention should be paid to Christ's realistically observed mode of walking, freely executed gesture of benediction, and three-quarter-face pose. Consideration of these factors suggests a *post-1066* dating. The author is inclined to ascribe this work to a native stonemason who managed to reconcile Anglo-Saxon tradition with new influences of Norman origin. It may, therefore, have originated in the last quarter of the 11th century. Its background is unknown, but it was undoubtedly brought to the cathedral from elsewhere.

The first major monastic settlement in the area was founded at Westbury-upon-Trym, north-west of Bristol. Though unimportant in Roman and Anglo-Saxon times, Bristol grew rapidly after the Conquest and was credited by the Domesday Book with roughly the same wealth and reputation as York. It became a see in 1542. Prior to that time the church and its annexes served an Augustinian abbey which was not founded until 1142. Bristol's finest feature is undoubtedly its Gothic choir (1298–1330), but the chapter-house is no less remarkable in its way. It dates from that late phase in Norman architecture when, sensible of their technical ability and material resources, builders and clients were extending themselves to the limit.

The chapter-house adjoins the south transept and is approached from the east range of the cloister by way of a *vestibule (Pl. 75)*. This is three bays wide and two deep. The piers, which are fundamentally square with engaged demi-shafts, support squat scalloped capitals and heavy ribbed vaults. The arches have bands of bead-moulding and the walls are articulated with plain and very shallow blind arches devoid of capitals. The vestibule is low-ceilinged to accomodate the dormitory above it. It makes an extremely austere impression, and its restraint is in dramatic contrast to the lofty *chapter-house (Pl. 76)*, which is astylar and elaborately enriched. The chapter-house is a rectangular oriented chamber 30 ft long and—like the vestibule—16 ft wide. The east wall and three stepped windows were restored after 1831. Other isolated features have also been restored, but faithfully so.

The fascination of the room derives from a contrast between limpid proportions and an extremely varied wall articulation. The low plinth forms a continuous seat, and the continuous blind arches above it served as recessed niches for members of the chapter. The roll-moulded arcading forms an integral part of the wall, and uprights flow straight into arches without any intervening capitals. Grooves are all that separate the arches from the projecting surface of the wall above them. Blind arcading of this sort is typical of Late Romanesque churches in the west of England and Bristol in particular. The bottom section of the wall, whose height was dictated by the human frame, is bounded at the head by a cable-moulded frieze. The wall above is more elaborate, having enlaced blind arches whose three-quarter shafts again form part of the wall and are alternately plain and spiral-beaded. The capitals assume various forms—scalloped, scaled, foliated, volute—and the beaded cable-moulding of the arches is surmounted by an expanse of diamond band-work. The individual arches are enlaced at their points of intersection. Visible on the left is the beginning of the *transverse arch (Pl. 77)* which divides the chamber into two bays. Adorned with roll-moulding and opposed bands of zigzag, this reposes on squat scalloped capitals supported by demi-shafts. The latter extend downwards only as far as the cable-moulded frieze, which they transfix with a pointed dowel. The

cross-ribs take the form of opposed bands of zigzag, the resulting rhombs being filled with stellate flowers. The enrichment of the walls attains its climax in the lunettes, which are covered with zigzag and continuous trellis-work. The bands forming the latter are grooved at the edges only. They ascend diagonally and then—usually after describing two right angles, though variations occur at the head—return to the foot, where they set off again in a contrary direction. The stonemasons gave them a blunt or angular finish according to where they met the enlaced blind arches—a piece of licence which implies great self-assurance on their part. The wall articulation of Bristol's Late Norman chapter-house is an extreme example of abstract wall decoration. As so often with the products of a late stylistic phase, one is irresistibly reminded of goldsmith's work. Echoes of similarly stratified fillings on Celtic crosses of the 12th century cannot be ignored either, but, be that as it may, the Bristol chapter-house is a magnificent piece of work and one that could only have originated in England.

MERCIA

78-81 What survives of *Malmesbury Abbey* (Wiltshire)—a truncated nave, half the west front, one wall of the south transept, no tower or chancel—is merely the residue of a once large and magnificent monastic complex. One feature of major artistic importance does survive in the south doorway, a chef d'œuvre of late English Romanesque, though the monastic settlement was undoubtedly an Irish foundation.

The Anglo-Saxon Chronicle records that the abbey suffered several fires, the last major one in 1042. There are various reports of extensions and improvements during the ensuing Norman period, but no tangible evidence of these has survived. It may be assumed that the abbey was severely damaged during the wars of succession which began in 1135 and continued for the next twenty years or so. Norman sovereignty proper came to an end with the death of William the Conqueror's grandson in 1154. Shortly afterwards, still in the same year, Henry II's coronation marked the beginning of rule by the Angevins, the royal Plantagenet line. Henry II—Thomas Becket's friend and adversary—reigned until 1189. His sovereignty extended not only to England and, later, Ireland, but also to large areas of France.

Malmesbury Abbey was entirely rebuilt during the reign of Henry II, almost as though the memory of times past was to be effaced by a completely fresh start. The chancel was probably completed in 1163, to be followed in 1175 by the nave. Setting aside the Gothicized clerestory and vaults, the impression made by the wall system of the *aisled interior (Pl. 81)* is wholly Romanesque. The stilting and slight pointing of the arcade arches already occurs in French Romanesque (Autun), for structural as well as aesthetic reasons. The masonry piers are squat, robust and cylindrical, but their Late Romanesque flavour derives more from their articulation than anything else. They are surmounted by shallow multi-scalloped capitals, and the abacus of the pier on the right displays palmettes. No longer purely static and functional, the moulding of the arcade arches has acquired a formal validity of its own. Above the arches are hood-moulds which could only have served a useful purpose on an outside wall. Adorned with billets, these have broad animal masks at the vertex and stops in the shape of animal heads which might have come from an Irish manuscript. The tradition itself is Anglo-Saxon, as Deerhurst *(Pl. 98)* shows, and it is characteristic of a late stylistic phase that it should hark back to its beginnings. Triple wall-shafts rise from the capitals of the drum-piers on the nave side and fan out into ribbed vaults at the foot of the clerestory. The Norman tradition of an upper wall-passage was maintained. The gallery openings consist of groups of four round arches on cylindrical shafts with scalloped capitals of varying form, each group being spanned by a round arch with deeply recessed zigzag set at right angles to the wall surface.

The south porch was built on to the third west bay of the south transept. The cloister and monastery buildings lay to the north of the abbey. The sculptural composition of the porch, which forms an almost square vestibule (ribbed vaulting 1905), contributes to Malmesbury's high reputation in the field of English Romanesque. No similar porch exists, nor, we may assume, has ever existed anywhere else in England. This is remarkable enough in itself. Sculptured areas include the broad outer arch, the side lunettes, and the tripartite inner doorway, whose tympanum portrays Christ in a mandorla supported by two angels.

The *outer entrance of the south porch (Pl. 78)* has no tympanum. The jambs run directly into the arch without interruption, a circumstance which the sculptor exploited in the interests of narrative continuity and of the sculptural execution of his pictorial medallions. The composition of the doorway is unified by the fact that the continuous orders of the jambs-cum-arches are arranged in pairs, flat orders alternating with convex. The two innermost orders—a geometrical chain of lozenges and a floral band—are purely ornamental. In the latter, the thin 'climber' from which the enlaced shoots spring forms the inner edge of the order itself—

a decidedly late-phase motif. In the three outer pairs of orders, narrow floral bands of varying design alternate with beaded trails which intersect to form medallions— circular or oval according to the nature of each curve. These loops, seventy-eight in all, contain figure sculpture. On the jambs can be seen mythical beasts, figures (singly or in pairs), and—possibly, as at Barfreston *(Pl. 2)* or Brookland—zodiacal signs and Labours of the Months. Some figures are still identifiable, e.g. the acrobat at the foot of our picture.

The archivolts bear scenes from the Old and New Testaments and from Prudentius' *Psychomachia*. A 10th-century copy of this account of the conflict between Vice and Virtue was in Malmesbury's library at the time in question. Starting with the fourth medallion from the bottom and proceeding in ascending order, the medallions in the third order from the right of our photograph depict the Creation of Adam, the Creation of Eve, God's Warning, the Fall, and Adam and Eve hiding. The equivalent medallions in the fifth order depict God conversing with Noah, the building of the Ark, Noah in the Ark, the sacrifice of Isaac, and Abraham with the ram. In the seventh order: Annunciation, Nativity, Annunciation to the Shepherds, Adoration, and Presentation in the Temple. Old and New Testament scenes were thus arranged as a concordance, although no very distinct sequence could be attained—despite the obvious expansion of the outer medallions—because of the radial discrepancy between the orders. Moreover, the stonemason carved his scenes in situ, after the stone voussoirs were in place. He did not sculpt them radially on the centre of the doorway or tangentially in accordance with the curve of the arch, but was guided by the natural pull of gravity, so that the pictorial medallions in the outer order lean away, as it were (cf. the Presentation in the Temple)—a piece of licence in which only a late-phase sculptor could have indulged. It can also be seen that the figures occasionally overlap their borders so that the medallions provide them with a sort of scenic depth. The figures themselves are elongated, delicate and long-legged, their movements loose-limbed and elegant. The doorway was undoubtedly inspired by English miniatures of the mid-12th century, as the decorative treatment of the whole arch clearly conveys. The above-mentioned features, all characteristic of a waning stylistic phase, help to date the porch at Malmesbury in the decade 1175–85 and thus bring it close in time to the doorway of the Lady Chapel at Glastonbury *(Pl. 71)*.

This poses the problem of when to date the tympanum of the inner portal and the two splendid *figured lunettes (Pl. 79 and 80)* above the four-arched blind arcades in the side walls of the porch. The fully sculptured porch—

a characteristic of France, or, to be more precise, south-west France—does not occur anywhere else in England. Yet the tympanum itself, though certainly no stranger to French influence, betrays an Insular touch, e.g. in the way in which the point of the mandorla bites into the zigzag frame, or in the bizarrely inclined head of the angelic figure on Christ's right. In the lunettes, this inclination of the head recurs in two of the Apostles (each of the fourth from the inside), giving them the appearance of having to duck to avoid the angels soaring over them in the direction of Christ (on the tympanum). It is also a means of isolating them, for the pairs of Apostles on either side have turned to each other as though wishing to communicate their astonishment, while the figures nearest the doorway, Peter with his key *(Pl. 80)* and Paul *(Pl. 79)*, gaze at the manifestation of Christ on the tympanum. An abundance of contrast can also be observed in the figures' hands, in their subtly varied postures, in the position of their feet, and, last but not least, in their robes. Comparison with the Blessed Ones on the sculptured frieze in the centre of the west front at Lincoln *(Pl. 192)* is not only instructive but discloses that the seated Apostles of Malmesbury are a later and astonishingly advanced development of the same English style.

As to their authorship and date, the carvings originated in the reign of Henry II, whose personal origins may help to explain their strong French associations. The south porch was probably the last piece of work to be carried out on the rebuilt abbey, somewhere in the region of 1180. It is not all by the same hand. The tympanum and lunettes were executed by an older and more considerable artist who endeavoured to combine native Insular tradition with novel ideas from France. That is why these qualitatively high-ranking works seem to be imbued with a surprising and archaic restraint. Features of lesser importance, such as the outer garments and arches, were carried out at the same time or slightly later, though in a more modern spirit, by a younger but no less gifted master. His medallion figures, which make a more animated, elegant, modern, and, at the same time, frivolous impression, are closer to the end of a stylistic and historical era.

82   Only the *font in the former abbey church of Dorchester* (Oxfordshire) has preserved its pristine splendour. It is less tall than the one at Brookland *(Pl. 30)* but resembles it in shape (cylindrical) and material (lead). The base and lip are bordered with floral bands, and the main surface area is filled with an arcade of slightly flattened, moulded round arches reposing on cushion capitals with abaci and spiral shafts, all in medium relief. Each archway is occupied by a figure sitting on

a roughly indicated bench with its feet resting on the lower floral band, which acts as a sort of step and gives a slightly three-dimensional effect. A comparable font can be seen at Walton-on-the-Hill (Surrey), and both may be attributed to the decade 1170–80. All the figures wear haloes, so the supposition that they represent the Disciples seems plausible, especially as Peter and his key can be identified. Another of the figures holds a sceptre and may have been intended to represent Christ, but this is doubtful because his halo resembles all the others and displays no inscribed cross. Each man holds a book in one hand, the other being either raised or extended towards the book. The general assumption is that the figures represent the Disciples—presumably minus Judas, since there are only eleven of them. If Christ were present, which of the others would have been excluded as well?

83-84   *Crucifixion scenes, St Matthew's, Langford* (Oxfordshire). Apart from an Anglo-Saxon tower and sundial, St Matthew's most noteworthy features are the two large stone carvings of the Crucifixion. They are not in situ, having been transferred to the walls of the south porch which was built on to the Norman aisle. One is mounted in the east wall and the other in the gable-end. Hewn from large blocks of stone, the Crucifixion on the east wall *(Pl. 83)* is located far too close to the eaves, but it looks magnificent despite its fragmentary condition. Undoubtedly, the hand of God must once have been visible above it, as in the Romsey Crucifixion *(Pl. 62)*, with which it has already been compared. The Langford Christ wears an alb, the long belted and pleated robe worn by priests. The missing head must have been very erect, and the feet probably rested on a suppedaneum, which is also missing. The arms are horizontally extended, but the taut sleeves invest them with a slight curve which attains a dramatic and sculptural climax in the long attentuated hands. These are superimposed on vertical stone blocks, and droop slightly. The stone blocks were incorporated for structural reasons because they facilitated the remarkable intaglio treatment of the sleeves and a more three-dimensional development of the hands themselves. The work would seem to be attributable to the Anglo-Saxon period and probably dates from the second quarter of the 11th century.

Controversy surrounds the appraisal and dating of the Crucifixion group *(Pl. 84)*, a smaller work mounted in the hewn stone gable-end. Assessment of it is rendered more difficult by an error in assembly which has distorted its original appearance. In the first place, one is put off by the niche, whose shape detracts from the internal movement of the piece. Moreover, the figures of the Virgin and St John were transposed when the group was removed to its present site. The Virgin, who, as Christ's mother, always stands on his right, now stands on his left, whereas John, whose proper place is on Christ's left, now appears where the Virgin should be. Because of this transposition, they now look outwards instead of inwards at Christ. One is tempted to ask whether, in view of the incorrect thumb-position of Christ's right hand, the blocks of stone incorporating the arms and hands may not also have been transposed; in other words, whether the arms should not be inclined upwards so that Christ hangs suspended from the Cross. For all that, the hands may have been deliberately distorted in order to heighten the appearance of twisted agony, for this work, too, is characterized by great dramatic force. An example of the 'Man of Sorrows'— Christus patiens, not dominans, like the other Langford Christ—used to be in St Mary's Breamore (Hampshire) during Anglo-Saxon times. This would suggest a date of origin in the first half of the 11th century for this group as well. On the other hand, the presence of two subsidiary figures casts doubt on such an early dating, and the author would prefer to date the group later than the other Langford Christ.

85-87 *Parish church of St Mary the Virgin, Iffley* (Oxfordshire). This benefice was created at the beginning of the 'new order' ushered in by Henry II's reign, when, after a period of turmoil, new churches arose which were stamped by the self-assured spirit of the English Church under Archbishop Thomas Becket (1162–70). St Mary's is one of a group of small but elaborately enriched Late Romanesque English churches. All of them came into being between 1160 and 1180, the period when St Nicholas Barfreston *(Pl. 1–6)* acquired its rich facing.

The parish church at Iffley has undergone many changes in the course of the years, but restoration work undertaken at various times in the 19th century has largely re-created the original Norman fabric—often skilfully but not always so. The gable cross and the battlements on the tower are romantic additions. Above all, the pointed-arched window inserted in the *west front (Pl. 86)* during the Late Gothic period was replaced in 1858 by the rose window visible today. Although based on traces of the original window, this is larger than it should be, with the result that the balance of the façade has been impaired (cf. Barfreston, *Pl. 5*). The façade, which is still imposing, is tripartite in its horizontal and vertical articulation. The ground, central and gable stages are separated by string courses, and a flat band of ornamentation traverses the wall beneath the small gable window, now blocked up. Prominent among

the vertical members are the corner buttresses, which were skilfully wedded to blind arches at porch level. The surrounds of the large gable windows have three recessed orders and are decorated with continuous zigzag. In front of them, flush with the wall, is a three-light arcade with figured capitals and spiral-fluted shafts. The curves of the arches display radially arranged beak-heads. This ornamental motif is used to even greater effect on the west doorway beneath.

The sculptural ornamentation of the *south porch (Pl. 85)*, which was probably executed before its companion in the west, is worthy of special note. Much of it has been restored, but with painstaking accuracy. The doorway, which stands out against the rubble walls of the church by reason of its ashlar-work surround, has a chamfered cornice and extended abaci. There are three orders. The first, set beneath a hood-mould ornamented with leaf-tongues, is roll-moulded and adorned with beak-heads so stylized that only their triangular shape and eye-nodes identify them as such. The second order is also roll-moulded but has a chevron motif. Both these round arches repose on abaci, figured cushion capitals, and cylindrical shafts, the outer pair smooth and the inner pair decorated with chevrons (left) and lozenges (right). The carving becomes noticeably more elaborate towards the interior. The innermost order has no capitals and is studded with leaves, flowers, birds, beasts, masks and heads. This is another late stylistic feature and typical of the west of England.

The same inward crescendo is apparent in the capitals. The outer pair take the form of a couped quatrefoil (right) and a lunette (left), and the side of the latter also depicts beasts in combat. Both capitals appear to have been carved in situ. The inner capital on the right depicts a battle between mounted men. On the left, carved in the crisp manner typical of Iffley, a centaur armed with a bow rides over a tumbled lamb, symbolizing the overthrow of meekness and innocence by the animal passions of man. This male centaur proffers a fruit to his wife (round the corner). The *she-centaur (Pl. 87)*, also armed with a bow (damaged) is giving suck to her offspring while on the move. The moral of the capital—evil breeds evil—would have been abundantly clear to any 12th-century Christian.

88-90 *St Peter's-in-the-East, Oxford*. This quiet church, which stands in a secluded position among college buildings of later date, is only one of Oxford's renowned architectural treasures. The existing Norman church was endowed by Robert D'Oilly in 1140 and probably completed c. 1150. It consists of a nave, chancel, and crypt. It may also be assumed that a tower was erected, but not a central tower as at Iffley. One noteworthy feature is the *south door (Pl. 88),* though it bears traces of restoration work undertaken during the last century.

The archivolts are adorned in a positively programmatic manner with three of the most durable Insular motifs: saltire cross, beak-head, and chevron. The last two are only found at scattered points on the Continent. The saltire cross lends itself to the most varied treatment. It can be enclosed by a rectangle, square or circle, assume the shape of a star or flower—even acquire a double outline and transform itself into four triangles. This ornament, which has an eminently decorative effect when ranged in multiple series, derives from the field of metal-work—goldsmith's work in particular—and appears on chased buckles and clasps. Intersecting lines with dots in intervening spaces constitute a basic form of rhythmical decoration, but the origins of the motif are unknown.

The chevron or zigzag band, by contrast, was the main ornamental motif used in England during the High and Late Romanesque periods. The theory that it derived from the oblique strokes of the timber-builder's axe seems untenable, since it would inevitably occur somewhere in the transition of Anglo-Saxon architecture from timber to stone, e.g. on the towers at Barton-upon-Humber *(Pl. 185)* or Earls Barton *(Pl. 217).* However, it was an Anglo-Norman motif which made an abrupt appearance *c.* 1110 and was not used on the Continent until later. Although England developed the chevron band, the inspiration probably came from outside. The origins of the motif are still shrouded in obscurity, but it may have been an echo of Islamic architecture, notably of the jagged indentations in door-lintels and voussoirs.

The strangest of these three typically Insular ornaments is the beak-head, so called because it consists of an affronted bird's head with its beak clamped round the roll-moulding of an archivolt. Always furnished with a pair of huge eyes, these heads became variously transmuted and distorted (cf. the pure stylization in *Pl. 85),* transformed themselves into dogs' heads, lions' heads, wild beasts of every description, and beak-less demons whose tongues loll from their open jaws and—as the third head from the left clearly illustrates—wrap themselves round the roll-moulding. This motif occurs mainly on the doorways of small churches, but not exclusively so, for variants of the 'tongue-head' can be found on the portal at Lincoln (*c.* 1140), at Southwell, Peterborough, and elsewhere. The beak-head spread through England during the second quarter of the 12th century, though its dissemination was extremely uneven. It very seldom occurs in the south-east, i.e. in Surrey, Kent, and Essex. Although one cannot dismiss the theory that beak-heads are of Scandinavian origin

and derive from the art of wood-carving (via ships' prows and Norse stave-churches), the extent of their dissemination does not coincide with the Danelaw, or that part of England which was under Danish jurisdiction. The inspiration for the development of this typically Insular motif probably stemmed from several different sources. It cannot be doubted that demonic ideas of pagan Scandinavian origin played their part, and impressions brought back by pilgrims may also have contributed. Insular artists then reattired the demonic-cum-apotropaic features of such imagery in North European guise.

The *crypt* of St Peter's *(Pl. 89),* seen here from the east, is a rectangular chamber measuring approximately 36 ft by 20 ft. In the east is a small altar niche, and in the west a barrel-vaulted sarcophagus chamber situated between the original steps leading from the nave. The crypt is divided into three bays of equal height and has groined vaults separated by transverse arches. The cushion capitals vary in elaboration, some of them being figured, e.g. with a double-lion above a Tree of Life, a serpent, and a Samson-and-the-Lion scene. The west side of one such capital *(Pl. 90)* displays a very rare and archaic form of decoration, though its metamorphosis of one domain into another is not uncommon in Romanesque art. Here, in the midst of luxuriant foliage, stands a (phallic) shoot which combines the attributes of a Tree of Life and a male figure—a symbolic statement which still smacks strongly of the pre-Christian fertility cult.

91–93 *Gloucester Cathedral,* as it now stands, represents a perfect and miraculous transformation of a Romanesque abbey church into a Gothic palace of light. It did not become a cathedral until 1540, but its history begins with the nuns' abbey which was founded there during the 7th century and taken over by the Benedictines in 1022, in the course of the Cluniac reforms. Nothing has survived of St Peter's, the church built by the latter. The monastic community and its church were both in a state of decay at the time of the Conquest. In 1089, one year after the beginning of the third building phase at Cluny, Serlo, the first Norman abbot of Gloucester, embarked on a completely new church there. He started with the massive *crypt (Pl. 91),* which had an apse with radiating chapels and a broad ambulatory, all constructed of ashlar-work, supported by piers, spanned by transverse arches wherever structural considerations demanded it, and surmounted by groined vaults. It is functional as opposed to aesthetic, yet impressive for the very reason that it embodies the vigour and determination of its Norman founder. In company with that of Winchester (begun 1079) and Worcester (begun 1084, *Pl. 100),* Gloucester's spacious crypt is one of the most important

11th-century structures in existence. It extends beneath the entire east end of the church, a feature pioneered by Rouen but still uncommon on the Continent at that time. The choir above it shares the same ground-plan: a three-aisled chancel with squat but massive drum-piers and an ambulatory with three radiating chapels.

The Romanesque building was probably completed *c.* 1160, together with the chapter-house and other monastery premises, the huge conflagration of 1120 having delayed work without inducing any architectural change of tack. The profane buildings are still represented by large sections of the *chapter-house (Pl. 92)*. With its human dimensions, subdued general treatment and individual touches of freedom, the blind arcading testifies, even in such an unmonumental domain, to the grandeur and dignity of High Romanesque art.

Romanesque architecture in its imposing Anglo-Normen guise is embodied in the *nave (Pl. 93)*, which is an aisled structure ten bays long, the two westernmost bays being Gothic additions. The spaciousness of the interior has been somewhat impaired by the ribbed vaults which were substituted for the original flat timber ceiling in 1242. These are not only too deep but overlap the clerestory windows (also subjected to Gothic improvement) in an unsightly way. The general appearance of the nave is principally determined by a rhythmical series of plain masonry drum-piers, 30 ft high and over 6 ft in diameter, which rise to meet cushion capitals of equal simplicity. Soaring above this austere zone are arches of the most varied design. The arcade is bounded at the head by a frieze of zigzag which runs the entire length of the nave and creates an even more bridge-like impression than that of the related cathedral at Tewkesbury *(Pl. 94)*. Romsey *(Pl. 61)* and St Frideswide's Oxford have triforia built into their tall piered arcades, but Gloucester and Tewkesbury can afford to dispense with these. Indeed, uncluttered space is precisely what endows the churches of the western group with their special majesty. No triforium surmounts the lofty arcade, simply a wall-passage with pairs of small round arches supported by cylindrical shafts, each pair framed by an arcaded arch decorated with zigzag.

94-96 *Tewkesbury Abbey* (Gloucestershire) joins Pershore Abbey and Gloucester Cathedral in forming the only Anglo-Norman group with a distinctly regional character. All three churches possess related features, but the source of their autonomous development has not hitherto been ascertained. The tall cylindrical pier, an architectural feature peculiar to the western group, exerted an influence on Oxford Cathedral and the abbey churches of Glastonbury, Romsey and Jedburgh, in all of which the drum-piers rise beyond gallery-level.

Very little is known of Tewkesbury's early history, which began in the 7th century. Its construction was decisively affected by the second wave of Anglo-Norman cathedrals. Ely was begun between 1087 and 1093, Durham in 1093, Norwich in 1096, and Tewkesbury itself in the closing years of the century. It grew slowly, built of stone from Caen and local quarries, and the consecration took place in 1123. It is probable that only the east end had been completed by then—a two-bayed presbytery, closed on three sides, an ambulatory, a transept with east chapels, of which the one in the south has survived with few changes, and the lower part of the crossing tower. The eight-bayed *nave (Pl. 94)*, probably completed towards 1140, still represents one of England's most majestic Romanesque interiors. It has unfortunately been somewhat spoilt, like that of Gloucester Cathedral *(Pl. 93)*, by the addition of 14th-century Gothic ribbed vaults. These descend as far as the pier capitals, taking the place of the flat Romanesque ceiling which used to be mounted above the clerestory windows and must have created a remarkable impression of height.

Tewkesbury's interior is sterner and more ascetic than that of its sister-church at Gloucester. The clerestory windows, though also modified subsequently, are simpler. The double arches of the wall-passage, two separate pairs to each bay of the nave, are unadorned save for the scalloped capitals on the inset shafts. The arcade arches of the nave repose on flat capitals. The soffits are equally unadorned and the treatment of the arches just as featureless, only the outer edges being slightly roll-moulded. This exemplifies the general principle that Romanesque modelling of arcade arches made less progress in the west of England than in the east or south. Arches which were rectangular in cross-section continued in use until well into the 12th century. As at Gloucester, the nave's general appearance is determined by a rhythmical series of drum-piers, though these are somewhat taller and thinner (30ft 6 ins high, 6ft 3ins thick). There are fourteen of them, equally divided into two rows which run from the crossing to the west end.

The *west front (Pl. 95)* is unique in its boldness of conception. The 14th-century turrets, the disappearance of the gabled roof, which subsided in 1614, the Gothic windows of the aisles, even the Gothicized central window so ineptly inserted in 1686—none of these things can seriously detract from the monumental effect of the recessed façade with its slender, unadorned demi-shafts and simply moulded arches. Over 60ft high, it is an eloquent symbol of the pride and majesty peculiar to Anglo-Norman architecture. Like the lofty drum-piers inside, it is an expression in vertical terms of the Anglo-Norman predilection for elongated churches.

The *tower (Pl. 96)*, erected in 1145, makes a no less monumental impression despite the paltry little corner-turrets, added in 1660 as a poor substitute for the timber spire which had collapsed a century earlier. Tewkesbury's tower is, in fact, the mightiest Romanesque tower of all (46 ft square and roughly 150 ft high). The massive lower storey, constructed during the first building phase, still carries the stone outline of the original roof on all four sides. The three upper stages, with their richly varied articulation—windows which differ in height, position and ornamentation, open arches, and enlaced blind arcading—exhibit an almost frivolous diversity. Towers of this type paved the way for those of English Gothic, which were elaborate in articulation, often square in cross-section, rhythmical in ascent, and unmistakably individual in appearance.

97-98 *Stonemason's work in St Mary's, Deerhurst* (Gloucestershire). These two examples illustrate the heights attained by architectural sculpture during the Anglo-Saxon period. They are situated in St Mary's, an Anglo-Saxon church of the first rank but one whose structural history is extremely complex and has no place in a discussion of these sculptures. The church may be attributed to the decades *c.* 900. The animal's head, which serves as the *console (Pl. 98)* of an interior arch beside the door of the west tower, is distinguished by its harmonious blend of naturalism and abstraction. It may be the head of a wild boar, since tusks can be seen in its open snout. The curved lines which delineate the nostrils, eyes and snout were once painted (traces of pigment are still visible) and display an extremely assured touch. Regular but not schematic, asymmetrical yet balanced in their composition, they at once model and enrich the head with a subtlety of nuance which denotes freedom of artistic approach. The head, too, dates from the 9th century.

The *two-light window (Pl. 97)* which opens on to the nave from the chamber in the second stage of the tower dates from the church's second structural phase and is probably subsequent to the expulsion of the Danes *c.* 930. The tower chamber may once have been a chapel. The window's two triangular heads are constructed of accurately fitted stone slabs which run right through the wall. The bands of stone encasing them project as far as the multi-stepped capitals. The wall was pierced to form two lights and the central section of masonry carved, like the jambs, to resemble pilasters resting on chamfered bases. The subtle channelling of these pilasters, which have tongues let into their upper halves to achieve an effect of light and shade, invests this finest of all surviving Anglo-Saxon double windows with a positively classical allure.

99 *Figure of St Matthew on the font at Castle Frome* (Herefordshire). It must have been the liturgical status of such fonts and a pious regard for their genealogical significance which prompted successive parochial boards to keep these vessels of lead and stone, many of them elaborately figured, in constant use down the years. England possesses more Early, High, and Late Romanesque fonts than any other country, and the font at Castle Frome may be numbered among the most important of these. Its chalice-like shape recalls the fonts at Chaddesley Corbett (Worcestershire) and Eardisley *(Pl. 110)*. It exceeds 3 ft in height and diameter, and the three beasts supporting it rise to a height of 4 ft 5 ins. Animal-shaped bases are not common in England, but in this case the animals strike a note echoed by the carving on the font itself: they represent the demonic world which is overcome by means of baptism. Interlace runs riot over the stem of the font, contrasting sharply with the neat band of triple plaiting on its lip—a common emblem of the Trinity. Situated in the zone between the disorder below and the order above are the emblems and instruments of divine aid: the winged bull of St Luke, the winged lion of St Mark, St John's eagle, and the hovering angel which symbolizes St Matthew, grasping the Holy Writ in his left hand and pointing to it with his right.

The latter figure is a fine example of mature Anglo-Norman sculpture. The head is expressive, and the wings and legs convey an impression of soaring flight. Adjoining it on the right is a portrayal of the baptism of Christ. The deep and incisive carving of the font and the profound spirituality of its themes render it a major product of the school of sculpture which flourished round Hereford and Leominster during the Late Romanesque period, a school of which more will be said in connection with Kilpeck *(Pl. 103-107)* and Eardisley. The font dates from *c.* 1170. The production of such elaborate works soon waned under Cistercian influence.

100-102 *Worcester Cathedral.* The first Bishop of Worcester was installed in the year 680, as a result of ecclesiastical reforms initiated by the Synod of Whitby. In 1084, Bishop Wulfstan started work on a new cathedral with an ambulatory on the lines of Rouen and Jumièges. This Anglo-Norman building, built on the site of the church damaged by the Danes, was transformed by the Gothic improvements which began in 1218 and took two centuries to complete. Parts of it were incorporated in the main fabric, but the bulk of it was replaced. Apart from fragmentary sections, only the crypt and chapter-house survive.

The *crypt (Pl. 100)* follows the pattern of the chancel above it, with an ambulatory, radiating chapels, and two east chapels corresponding to those of the transept. It no longer looks as it did originally, but the general impression remains strong despite alterations. The central area, corresponding to the open presbytery of the chancel, is divided into four aisles, each of eight bays, by three ranges of cylindrical piers on square plinths, with cushion capitals and plain groined vaults. The *capitals (Pl. 101)* are of the simplest cushion type, some of them grooved along the edges and others surmounted by abaci with billets adorning their bevelled undersides.

The *chapter-house (Pl. 102)* was the first of its kind to be constructed round a central column, and became a model for many of England's circular or polygonal chapter-houses. The groined vaults radiate from the central column in ten segments, each reinforced by a central rib. The chamber has a diameter of 55 ft and is only slightly exceeded in size by the largest examples, Lincoln and Westminster. Unfortunately, the windows were enlarged during the 15th century, necessitating alterations to the vaults and detracting from the room's appearance. The walls are neatly constructed of alternate courses of white and green stone. The area immediately above the chairs displays niche-like blind arches, plain and very shallow, whereas the central area is occupied by intricately enlaced blind arcading.

103-107 *St Mary and St David, Kilpeck* (Herefordshire), a small church dating from about the middle of the 12th century, is a uniquely important example of English Romanesque for three reasons: first, it is excellently preserved and has undergone very few alterations since it was built; secondly, its rich scupltural content can be seen in situ, integrated in the fabric and essentially unimpaired, so that we can for once assess the iconographic programme to which the author of the church gave deliberate expression; and, thirdly, it is an outstanding product of a regional school of sculpture which exploited the most varied assortment of religious and decorative motifs.

The buildings belongs to the three-celled type and consists of a nave, chancel and apse, the total length being roughly 60 ft. The chancel is separated from the nave by a chancel arch, and the apse from the choir by a second, smaller arch. The *apse (Pl. 104)* is lit by three small round-arched windows with the roll-moulded exterior surrounds typical of the western group of churches, and the chancel and nave by six windows, the one in the west wall *(Pl. 103)* being larger and very richly ornamented in an almost mannered way. Access to the interior is provided by the south doorway *(Pl. 105)*, which is offset to the west. The walls consist of coursed rubble and vary in thickness between $27^1/_2$ and $33^1/_2$ ins, a feature normally exclusive to Anglo-Saxon buildings.

The church has Anglo-Norman undertones. It is assumed that the Romanesque builders—Benedictines who founded a priory here in 1134—used part of an earlier, probably ruined, Anglo-Saxon church in their new building. Another derivative of Anglo-Saxon architectural ideas may be observed in the hewn stone pilasters on the exterior (cf. *Pl. 32*), which are not merely buttresses but also relics of timber construction translated into stone. This is clearly shown by the west wall *(Pl. 103)*, where the central pilaster meets the cornice (the equivalent of the old tie-beam) immediately below the west window. This approximation to the Anglo-Saxon probably had a regional origin as well, since Kilpeck, which lies off the beaten track, seven or eight miles southwest of Hereford, is situated on the erstwhile border between Wales and Mercia, the Anglo-Saxon kingdom which Offa tried to secure against Celtic raiders late in the 8th century by building a massive rampart stretching from the Dee in Flintshire to the Severn at Sedbury in Gloucestershire. In view of Kilpeck's location, it is hardly surprising that its sculptural decoration, too, should embody various elements drawn from other areas and earlier periods.

Round the top of the church walls runs a corbel table adorned with zigzag and comprising seventy-four enriched corbels. Not all of them are by the same hand, but all are thematically part of the programme which finds fulfilment in the south doorway and the figures on the chancel arch. These *corbels (Pl. 104)*, most of them very expressive and many caricaturistic, portray heads, masks, animals, mythical beasts, bulls, rams, lions, pigs, dogs, hares, birds' heads resembling beak-heads, dragons biting their own tails, wrestlers, dancers accompanied by a musician bowing his rebec in a contorted manner—even a Sheila-na-gig, that unashamedly erotic, self-prostituting female figure so often found on early Irish churches. The whole world of pleasure, passion and sensuality, of demonic temptation and menace, is graphically and unaffectedly set out with the extreme realism which is a recurrent feature of Romanesque churches and cathedrals. The pilasters of the west wall *(Pl. 103)* culminate in three sets of monstrous, protruding jaws which gape to reveal long curling tongues. This is a definite echo of imported motifs, a recollection of the Viking practice of finishing off the beam-ends of timber buildings in a similar fashion. The 'evil' in the frieze is concentrated, as it were, in these three sets of jaws on the west front. Potential salvation confronts this evil twice in the shape of a Lamb and Cross, once as a corbel above the central window of the apse, through which the light of divine grace shines from the east, and a second time on the south wall of the nave, where the doorway gives access to the interior.

The church's sculptural programme, which the 12th-century Christian regarded primarily as religious instruction—a sermon preached by frieze, capital and portal—and only secondarily as decoration, reaches its climax in the *south doorway (Pl. 105)*. Carved in local red sandstone like the rest of the sculptures, this doorway is a comparatively simple structure, with shafts, capitals and abaci, archivolts, flat jambs, lintel and tympanum. What endows it with importance is its extremely rich sculptural treatment, which testifies that a great master was at work. The outermost arch, a hood-mould with a pair of monsters snapping upwards at either end (ornamentation almost obscures their animal associations), is filled with beaded bands woven into medallions linked by inverted masks. Discernible in these nine medallions are, reading from the left, four assorted birds, a dragon-like monster with a snout resembling the prow of a Viking ship, then another bird, possibly a peacock, in seventh place the sign of Pisces, then another of those monstrous man-beast hybrids which were so common during the Romanesque period, and, finally, two entwined mythical beasts. The innermost order, bordering the tympanum is merely double-moulded. The next is carved into a band of zigzag, radial as opposed to the vertical chevrons on the lintel. The dragons at the extremities of the main order, one feathered and the other interlaced, repose on abaci decorated with saltire crosses. The arch itself is roll-moulded, and its ornamentation includes seven beak-heads of extremely advanced design. On the left can be seen an animal's head with a zebra-like linear pattern, and above it a dragon looped into a figure-of-eight. Then comes a lion with a human head followed by three assorted animal masks, two of them with twin tongues which themselves culminate in animals' heads. On the right of the arch are monsters and dragons biting their own tails. This order, too, illustrates the demonic world which must be left behind by anyone crossing the threshold of the house of God. Monsters and reptiles congregate round churches to prevent the Christian from attaining salvation, but aid and deliverance are promised here just as they were by the Lamb of God on the frieze: the two voussoirs at the vertex of the arch carry symbols of salvation. The one on the right displays an angel with a harp, praising God's eternal mastery over the Devil. This figure should not be construed as David the Psalmist, a common convention, since the patron of this church is St David of Wales, an abbot-bishop of the 6th century, and his partner and counterpart, St Dubricius, is venerated at St Devereux (Herefordshire). On the seventh voussoir from the left can be seen a phoenix, the mythical bird which, according to the *Physiologus*, plunges into the flames and rises from the ashes on the third day—a symbol of Christ, of purity, resurrection, and life.

The elaborately carved jambs, which are of unusual composition in that the outer shafts rise straight to the abacus without any capitals, pursue this theme further. The outer shafts depict fearful reptilian dragons, pointing downwards on the left and upwards on the right. An unmistakable warning to the sinner, these are related to the gaping jaws of the west front, which possess a like significance. The two groups are also stylistically related, since both hail from the pagan Nordic world. (It is probable that the Ringerike style, which should be recalled here, originated in Britain and reacted on Scandinavia.) The serpents, with their aura of paganism, are linked with the capitals, which depict, on the left, dragons fighting, and, on the right, a mask seemingly devouring some foliage very similar to that on the tympanum. On the shaft beneath is an orderly arrangement of foliate scroll-work inhabited by birds. The two figures in the scroll-work on the left-hand shaft are on their way to Salvation. They are warriors dressed in ribbed garments, possibly coats of mail, and wear headdresses resembling Phrygian caps, but it is impossible to tell whom they represent. Both hold weapons in their right hands, the upper figure (possibly) a javelin and the lower one a sword. The upper figure grasps a frond with his left hand; the lower *(Pl. 106)* presents his back to the serpent and uses his left hand to indicate the door, his gaze fixed on the goal to which he aspires. Like the whole of this strange but eloquent shaft, the expressive carving of his face represents one of the finest examples of 12th-century sculpture.

The focal point of the entire programme, which should be interpreted with reference to the religious and secular ideas of the period, is the tympanum. This bears a magnificent representation of that ancient symbol of faith, the Tree of Life, executed in the same chiselled style of relief as the hood-mould. Its pictorial conception and sculptural execution, as well as its mode of composition, which eschews symmetry yet achieves a balanced interplay of branches, foliage and fruit, are of high quality. Formulations of this kind have their after-effects: a century later, the master of the timber ceiling in the stave-church of Torpo in Hallingdal (Norway), who may conceivably have been trained in England, painted a Tree of Life which could be a descendant of the one at Kilpeck.

Anyone who passes beneath the symbolic Tree of Life and enters the church finds himself in a different world. Standing before the chancel arch, altar and apse, he sees three superimposed apostles on either jamb of the chancel arch, nimbed figures which have overcome the evils of the world and become the very pillars on which the church rests. Each grasps the Holy Writ in his right hand and a palm-frond or cross in his left. A key iden-

301

tifies the central figure in the left-hand trio as *St Peter* (*Pl. 107*). The sculptural conception of these figures differs sharply from that of the external carvings. Intensity of expression, animation and movement have yielded to inward calm and tranquillity, and superficial carving to three-dimensional modelling. The figures on the chancel arch were produced by an artist who must have been familiar with other than purely Insular works. The difference between Kilpeck's south doorway and chancel arch is great, and one cannot deny that, in comparison with the Scandinavian and Iro-Celtic features of the former, the figures of the apostles contain a hint of the South. The problems of date and authorship remain open. The Benedictines arrived in 1134, but it is debatable whether the church was completed during the mid-century wars of succession, in which this district, too, was involved, or not until *c*. 1160. Kilpeck's St Peter is not so far removed from Castle Frome's St Matthew (*Pl. 99*).

108-109 *Hereford Cathedral*. Had all that was built in Hereford during the Romanesque period survived, the city could indeed lay claim to some important and remarkable buildings. War, insurrection and misfortune have, however, precluded this. The see of Hereford was founded in the 7th century. A largish church was built in the middle of the 11th century but destroyed shortly thereafter by raiders from Wales under the leadership of an English earl. Is it conceivable that the bishop installed under the Norman regime, Robert de Losinga (1079-95), a brother of the great church-builder of Norwich (*Pl. 247-254*), did not start work on a new cathedral during his sixteen years in office, even if the title 'fundator ecclesiae' went to one of his successors, Reinhelm (1107-15?). Chronicles are silent on this point. The Norman cathedral was of the triapsidal type found in Caen, with an elongated three-bayed chancel, transept, crossing tower, and aisled eight-bayed nave. Of this doubtless imposing Norman building, whose construction progressed slowly until well past the middle of the 12th century and into the Transitional period, little retains its original appearance except in the south transept.

The *east wall of the south transept* (*Pl. 109*) is still recognizable as an architectural conception of *c*. 1100 despite the restoration of 1842, which had a simultaneously decorative and debilitating effect. The chevron motif, which was emerging in Reinhelm's time and became the fashion after 1115, is nowhere to be seen on the lower reaches of the wall. The section which opens on to the south aisle of the choir is three-storeyed, whereas the southern extension of the transept wall has five levels. Below, grouped in threes and not later in style than 1105, can be seen a series of blind arches, some of which display crocket capitals alongside the cushion and scalloped varieties. Above them, one to each bay, come large and archaic-looking blind arches, the central one with inset shafts. Above them, again, is a low triforium passage with three trios of arcaded arches. Then comes a remarkable storey which testifies to the changed architectural ideas of a new generation: a row of narrow and attentuated blind arches. At the top comes the clerestory with its wall-passage triplets overlapped, here as so often elsewhere, by Late Gothic vaulting (*c*. 1430). Only at this level does there occur, on the lofty central arches in front of the clerestory windows, the chevron motif dating from the second decade of the 12th century. (The zigzag on the arched gallery opening above the south aisle of the choir is restorer's work.)

The *choir* (*Pl. 108*) preserves the customary three-storeyed system of arcade, gallery, and clerestory. The strange gabled caps on the top of the buttresses were put there when, in conjunction with the removal of the chancel apses and the addition of an ambulatory and Lady Chapel, the clerestory of the choir was modified after 1200 and the buttresses cut away to make room for the new vaulted ceiling. A change can be observed here in the choir, too. The massive semicircular side-piers of the double gallery openings in no way correspond to the compound piers of the arcade beneath. It is as though the drum-piers characteristic of the western group (Gloucester, Tewkesbury) had been tacked on to what was still, essentially, a Norman conception. The nave (almost entirely restored) was also furnished with drum-piers, though these are short and compounded with buttresses on the nave side. This work must have been completed by about the middle of the century, after which a pause ensued. The numerous Gothic alterations and additions do not concern us here, but there is one more fact which should be mentioned because it denotes the survival of Irish traditions in an area bordering the Celtic West: Hereford possesses the sole surviving preaching cross in England, erected by the Dominicans in the 14th century.

110-111 The *font in the village church of St Mary Magdalene, Eardisley* (Herefordshire), is excellently preserved and of high quality. In company with that of Castle Frome (*Pl. 99*) and the south doorway at Kilpeck (*Pl. 105*), it embodies the best features of Herefordshire's contemporary school of stone-carving. It is remarkable, in view of the troubled times through which this border area passed between 1140 and 1170, that such a homogeneous style should have evolved, and that such a compact group of closely related doorways and fonts— more compact than anywhere else in England—should have come into being as a result. We have already pointed out that the Benedictine abbey at Reading, founded by Henry I in 1121, exerted a powerful influence which reacted on the churches of this area via the Benedictine abbey at Leominster, which was taken over by Reading in 1123. The atelier at Leominster *(Pl. 114)* must have been supervised by a master who decisively influenced other stonemasons, for a number of different hands can be identified. This atelier group displays certain formal characteristics: a relief technique which concentrates, with few exceptions, on not more than two levels, and a sculptural treatment which achieves dramatic emphasis by a close apposition of light and shade. From these there follow iconographic characteristics such as ribbed clothing, bunched hair, and beasts with long talons and claws. Inspired by a common purpose but differing in nature and ability, the stonemasons of the Leominster atelier must have travelled the district to carry out their commissions, though always under the master's guidance. The rapid disappearance of this regional school *c.* 1170 may have been attributable to the latter's death.

The Eardisley font *(Pl. 110)* is goblet-shaped like the one at Castle Frome, and of comparable size. The mythical beasts which serve the latter as a base are entirely absent here, but this only enhances the dramatic nature of the scenic field. Heavy plaiting encircles the rim, as at Castle Frome, but this band is composed of three double-skeins. The division between the bowl and base is more sharply defined than at Castle Frome, where the tangled interlace on the stem encroaches on the bowl itself. The base of the Eardisley font is encircled by a pair of bands which rise and fall obliquely, intersecting at regular intervals and forming a sort of pretzel each time they resume a downward course. This produces an ornamental pattern of a kind which occurs in various forms on Irish stelae and crosses of the 8th century. The same motif survived in Ireland for hundreds of years, though it often duplicated or reduplicated itself in the course of time. Figurative representations on fonts, as on churches, fulfilled the function of pictorial sermons which demanded to be read and interpreted. In the case of the Castle Frome font, disorder is transformed into order by the pictorial scenes adorning the central zone. Eardisley differs in that the scenes are set between two neat bands of ornamentation. The sequence is as follows: a battle scene, a saint, Christ with crosier and cruciform nimbus, a man enmeshed in scroll-work, and a lion. The foliate scroll-work represents the worldly jungle in which man repeatedly becomes entangled. In fact, an examination of all these scenes discloses that only Christ, the saint and the lion are free from its toils. The Eardisley lion differs from the one at Stretton Sugwas *(Pl. 113)*. It does not represent the Evil One who 'walketh about, seeking whom he may devour' and who must be overcome. Its size, partly determined by the law of intrinsic importance, denotes that it is the 'good' manifestation of the lion familiar to medieval symbolic thought. It is the 'Lion of Judah' of Jacob's blessing (Genesis xlix, 9), and, consequently, Christ; it is the watchful lion, symbolic of the Christian who must always be on his guard against the evils of this unruly world.

Worldly strife is symbolized by the *two warriors (Pl. 110)*. This masterly piece of composition occupies a rectangular field, but rhythmically balanced diagonals play about its perpendicular central axis. The swordsman clings to the tendrils which enmesh him, and the spearsman has just transfixed his adversary's leg. Turning his back on this savage contest, a nimbed saint with the Holy Writ in his hand strides resolutely away to the right, towards Christ and the sign of the Cross. Next comes *Christ in Limbo (Pl. 111)*, a theme which has already been discussed in connection with the carving at Bristol *(Pl. 74)*. With his crosier planted firmly on the ground, Christ takes the arm of a diminutive Adam and wrests him, with a dramatic gesture, from the infernal toils which cling so stubbornly to his feet. Adam is saved despite these, as the halo round his head clearly conveys. One additional feature worth noting is the bird perched on Christ's left shoulder, which should undoubtedly be construed as the Dove of the Holy Spirit. Not mentioned in the passage from the Acts of Peter on which this scene is based, it is a piece of artistic licence which accords with the Herefordshire school's predilection for portraying birds—though no member of the school carved as many as the master of Rowlstone *(Pl. 112)*.

The great artistic and technical merit of this font encourages one to assume that it was produced by the Castle Frome master. The formal and dramatic tension of the Eardisley font suggests that it originated before the one at Castle Frome, whose modelling gives an impression of greater lucidity. Eardisley's lion naturally raises the possibility of a relationship with the lion on the tympanum at Stretton Sugwas. However, their affinity is only such as might have arisen from membership of the same school, and they are not by the same hand. The relationship to Kilpeck is a harder question to answer, since the Eardisley warriors bear an undoubted resemblance to those on the south doorway at Kilpeck. Their helmets or Phrygian caps are identical and their ribbed garments similar, even if their trousers and cummerbunds, alias girdles, differ. The arrangement of pleats differs markedly in each case, those at Eardisley being more robust and less subtle. The reverse applies where fall of drapery is concerned. This can be observed in the Eardisley Christ, whose broken hem-line explicitly conveys the swiftness of Adam's rescue in a way which the quieter and more subtle carving of the south doorway at Kilpeck could not be expected to do. The latter was the handiwork of another great master.

We can only guess at the date of the sculptures at Kilpeck, Castle Frome and Eardisley, but the Castle Frome font undoubtedly originated last—somewhere between 1160 and 1170. The Kilpeck doorway *(Pl. 105)* came into being first, at a time when twenty-odd years of armed strife were drawing to a close and anarchy was yielding to a new stability. Indeed, the face of the warrior *(Pl. 106)* betrays a sense of coming deliverance appropriate to the period *c.* 1150. The Eardisley font conforms to the mid-century trend in English sculpture towards greater three-dimensionality. Being an earlier work by the same font master, it may be attributed to the years *c.* 1145.

112 *Detail from the chancel arch in St Peter's, Rowlstone* (Herefordshire). Rowlstone is a small and secluded village situated on the Wye's ascent to the Black Mountains of Wales, which makes one wonder why its church should have been furnished with an elaborate tympanum and richly sculptured chancel arch. Everything about its sculptural decoration, which may have been a private bequest, is highly expressive and extremely individual. The sculptor went so far as to invert two of his chancel arch figures (visible on the right of our photograph). Birds were his favourite subject, and many of them appear on both doorway and chancel arch. Their treatment is founded on natural observation, which is remarkable for the period. Possibly wood-pigeons, they bill and coo, peck—even preen themselves. Two magnificent specimens adorn the capitals of the chancel arch, their wings and tails entwined in branches in a highly decorative manner. The long claw typical of the Herefordshire school is once again in evidence. On the lateral extension of the north capital, the bird is followed by a man and then by an angel. Man and angel recur on the south side (illustrated here), but head downwards. The stone was not inserted correctly, since the bird-adorned capital and its extension form a single slab. Why, then, this inversion? Should the angel be in a tutelary, external position, as on the north side? This would place him upright on the left of the saint with the Holy Writ, but is this feasible? Perhaps the inversion of angel and saint was meant to convey a severance from time and space, but this is merely conjecture. The question remains unsolved. All that is certain is that the Rowlstone master was a man with a mind of his own.

113 The *tympanum at Stretton Sugwas* (Herefordshire) was transferred to the 19th-century church of St Mary Magdalene from the doorway of the Anglo-Norman church which used to occupy the same site. It portrays Samson in combat with the lion (Judges xiv, 5–9) and dates from the third quarter of the 12th century. This tympanum, too, comes from the atelier of a stonemason of the Herefordshire school, and exhibits typical features such as the long claws of the lion and Samson's 'ribbed' coiffure. Nevertheless, it does not possess the spontaneity of Castle Frome *(Pl. 99)*, nor the linear density and spirituality of Kilpeck *(Pl. 105)*, nor the solid craftsmanship of Rowlstone *(Pl. 112)*. The Stretton Sugwas tympanum betrays an artistic imagination which had to devise a sculptural technique of its own. Hence, it possesses the simple beauty of work done by a child who boldly essays great things without the requisite training. This naive treatment of Samson's struggle with the lion recalls the apocalyptic horsewoman in Douanier Rousseau's *War*—if such a comparison be permitted. The architectural frame is reduced to the barest essentials. The lion fills the semicircular field with its paws and tail, captured in a pose more expectant than defensive. Samson's grasp on the beast's jaws is expressive, but there is no hint of the superhuman strength which alone could have guaranteed him victory.

114 The *west doorway of the priory church at Leominster* (Herefordshire) is a handsome relic of what was once a large and prosperous monastery. There are few historical pointers to its early history, which dates back certainly to the 9th century and possibly to the 7th. The monastery made a fresh start in the year 1123, when Henry I bestowed the Leominster estate on his favourite monastic foundation, Reading. The Benedictines of Reading thereupon erected an affiliated monastery at Leominster. Work on the church—an aisled building with a transept, crossing tower, ambulatory and radiating chapels on the lines of Reading Abbey—proceeded at a rapid pace. Of the Norman church, which was probably completed *c.* 1145, only parts of the nave, the tower at the west end and the west portal survive. Everything else, including the monastery buildings, has disappeared. The west doorway, executed in the red sandstone of the locality, is surprisingly simple. The archivolts rise to a slight point above the capitals of the three pairs of smooth jambshafts. This is a remarkably early example of a pointed doorway arch, but it can be accounted for by structural factors. The abaci are adorned with palmettes, beadmoulding and saltire crosses, and the capitals terminate at the foot in a cable-moulded ring. They are richly carved, of high quality, and typical of the trend towards plastic emphasis which gained ground during the middle years of the century—in contrast to the opposing trend towards shallower relief exemplified by the capitals from the chapter-house at Much Wenlock *(Pl. 116)*. Symmetry reigns between the two trios of capitals on either side of the doorway, a symmetry naturally stressed by their cushion shape. The capitals of the north jambs (illustrated here) are adorned, from left to right, with two birds which may have served as an inspiration to the Rowlstone master, two reapers bent over their sickles, and two writhing serpents entwined in foliate scroll-work, the latter reminiscent of Kilpeck (Pl. 105). It is noteworthy that the interior of this doorway bears a capital-sized representation of the Samson-and-the-Lion scene found at Stretton Sugwas. It seems certain that the smaller version does not predate the larger, but vice versa; in other words, that a member of the Leominster atelier adopted the smaller piece as a model for the entire tympanum at Stretton Sugwas.

115-116 *Much Wenlock Priory* (Shropshire) dates from the latter half of the 7th century, as—according to legend—did the priory at Leominster. Having been destroyed by the Danes *c.* 874, it was re-founded during the 11th century. The Domesday Book refers to its wealth of structural improvements. It was bestowed on the victorious Normans in return for services rendered, which is how the Priory of St Milburga at Wenlock came to be handed over to the Cluniacs *c.* 1080. The existence of the new church, on which work started somewhat later, can only be inferred from traces of its foundations, but it is debatable whether it was ever completed. All that survives of an actual church in this extremely imposing and well-tended ruined site stems from the Early Gothic work carried out during the 13th century, whereas the remains of the chapter-house and lavatorium are late 12th-century.

The latter, a free-standing octagonal structure with a pillared ambulatory, was situated in the cloister quadrangle and probably originated *c.* 1190. Its relief carvings of the Apostles and scenes from the life of Christ represent the lattermost phase of English Romanesque at its luxuriant best. The tendency towards enrichment is also manifest in the articulation of the walls of the chapter-house, built between 1160 and 1180. This chamber, which abutted on the east side of the (vanished) cloister in the normal way, is rectangular. The east wall (also destroyed) probably had three windows. Three broad arches, of which the central one was designed as a gateway, opened on to the cloister. Their archivolts display various forms of toothed and zigzag ornamentation. The chapter-house itself was rib-vaulted. The small capitals bear rosettes of original design, stars, and palmettes, all accompanied by beaded trails and all patently the products of a late stylistic phase during which stonemasons took their cue from goldsmiths. The *north wall (Pl. 115)* and *south wall (Pl. 116)* are both faced

with three tiers of enlaced blind arches, and present an even richer appearance than the somewhat earlier chapter-house at Bristol *(Pl. 76 and 77)*. All the arches are moulded and some, especially on the south wall, are adorned with beads as well. The lowest blind arcade contains recessed niches, some of them ornamented with bands of zigzag and rhombs. All this is good English Late Romanesque.

117-118 *Parish church at Melbourne* (Derbyshire). It is strange to find such a large and elaborate church in this particular spot. Although a Norman parish church, St Michael and St Mary might easily, from its appearance, have been an abbatial or diocesan centre of worship. The west front is unusual in itself. At the west end of the aisles rise twin towers, plain and massive like fortifications, flanking a portal of five orders. The west end forms a tripartite narthex with groined vaults. Inside the towers on the floor above are two chambers and a gallery opening on to the nave. This, too, is unusual, and reminds one of Central European buildings. Passing through the impressive narthex, one enters the aisled *nave (Pl. 117)*, which stretches away to the crossing in a series of six bays. The masonry drum-piers are strikingly close-set and surmounted by shallow scalloped capitals. Above the abaci rise round-headed arcade arches, stilted because of the proximity of the piers and adorned with grooving and zigzag. Immediately above the arcade— and here the church's relatively small dimensions become apparent—is a combined gallery and clerestory, the wall-passage being lit by one exterior window and three interior arches to each bay of the nave. Another three arches give on to the nave above the crossing. The articulation of the nave walls prompts one to assume that the intention was to vault it, since a pair of demi-shafts can be seen between each of the arcade arches. The proximity of the piers may also have been a symptom of this intention. The vaults were never built, however, probably because local architects lacked courage and, more particularly, experience, as the somewhat clumsy vaulting of the narthex and clerestory-cum-gallery indicates.

The crossing, which supports a tower heightened in 1602, displays arches richly carved with zigzag and capitals adorned with singular volute motifs which develop into something akin to abstract beak-heads *(Pl. 118)*. The arms of the transept project only a short distance beyond the aisle walls—yet another apparent symptom of the need to economize—and the western precincts are cramped by a 12th-century tithe barn which nestles close to the church. The east end originally consisted of an apse built on to the unaisled choir and two transeptal apses. Today, the chancel is square-ended.

Work on the church began in the first half of the 12th century and continued into the 13th, but the building underwent numerous improvements and alterations later on.

This church was undoubtedly the work of local builders and stonemasons, as the walls, vaults, and one or two isolated capitals of positively Anglo-Saxon derivation bear witness. Foreign influences are also discernible, however—principally French, though comparisons with German Romanesque, e.g. Gernrode or Hersfeld, also come to mind. Another unusual feature: a second storey, no longer extant, was built above the east end. Was it a priest's dwelling-chamber of the sort occasionally installed above church porches or in towers? Was it, again, a sanctuary to which people could withdraw in time of peril? History supplies the answer. Ethelwulf, Henry I's father confessor, was appointed first Bishop of Carlisle in 1133 and given Melbourne Manor as his country seat. By 1136 the Scots had captured Carlisle, and Ethelwulf was obliged to take up residence at Melbourne, situated in the northern marches a little way south of the Trent. This border position helped to determine the character of the church, which Ethelwulf commissioned on the lines of a cathedral. It is possible, in view of his close ties with Henry I, who had married a Saxon princess and betrothed his daughter Matilda to Emperor Henry V, that a German architect was entrusted with the supervision of the work.

119 *Sculpture in the church of St Mary and St Hardulph at Breedon-on-the-Hill* (Leicestershire). Thanks in the main to King Offa (d. 796), Mercia enjoyed its greatest prime in the 8th century. Many sculptural relics of this period—the counterpart of the Carolingian period on the Continent—are preserved in Breedon's 12th-century Norman church, though the church itself has been substantially altered. There are over 75 ft of friezes and fragmentary mouldings, as well as several reliefs, none of them in situ but all testifying to the erstwhile importance of Breedon's parish church and the high standard of Anglo-Saxon sculpture *c.* 800. The carvings include geometrical patterns of the sort found elsewhere; a remarkable section of frieze portraying birds whose animated poses betray a degree of natural observation which even surpasses that of the Rowlstone master *(Pl. 112)*; mythical creatures and man-beast hybrids of the most fantastic shapes, all executed in an astonishingly deep intaglio technique which allows light and shade to play vividly over the spurs and recesses of the work, horsemen and foliate scroll-work. All these pieces accord with the Carolingian trend towards collaboration by a number of craftsmen, notably in the field of architectural sculpture.

Finally, there are some more autonomous and restrained pieces in the shape of carved stone slabs. Typical of the fine, animated, almost frolicsome art of Mercia in the years *c.* 800 is the sculpture illustrated here, which portrays two saints in a narrow rectangular frame. The figures advance as though on tip-toe, robes fluttering about their slender limbs and hands grasping the hollowed fronds which were so much in vogue among contemporary sculptors. The two men, clearly of advanced years, are inclined towards each other as though deep in conversation. Their pose is eloquent of a refined and courtly way of life. Marked as it is by the passage of time, this relief testifies to the full flowering of a school of sculpture which needs stand in no awe of its proximity to the Carolingian renaissance.

These highly expressive rectangular sculptures of vertical format have affinities with figurative reliefs found on English high crosses dating from this period and the two succeeding centuries, erected predominantly on the west coast and in Northumbria under the influence of Irish religious and cultural ideas. In fact, 1959 saw the discovery of some fragmentary sculptures which had been embedded high up in the east wall at Breedon. These portray figures and birds in vine tendrils, and are comparable with the reliefs on the shaft of the cross at St Andrew's, Auckland *(Pl. 171)*.

120 The slender *stone cross at Gosforth* (Cumberland) is one of a series of late high crosses found in the areas bordering the north-west coast of England. These are patently influenced by relationships which existed between Scandinavia and the British Isles or between Viking settlements in Ireland and the north of England. The Gosforth cross, dating from late in the 10th century, provides the finest possible testimony to this Anglo-Scandinavian school of art.

The shape of the cross, with its shaft and annulus, hails from Ireland, but the relationship between length of shaft and diameter of ring is an independent development. In Ireland, even very tall crosses preserve a balanced relationship between height and lateral projection; in England there manifests itself, in accentuated form, the tendency towards elongation found in Scandinavian ornaments and stave-churches. The carving on this cross, which is singularly shallow and resembles a woven sheath, combines Christian motifs with motifs of pagan Scandinavian origin, of which the latter strongly predominate: dragons, convoluted, writhing serpents with closed jaws, twisted, snarling beasts, and so on. Scenes from Viking mythology are also in evidence, as compared with only one from the Gospels, namely, Christ on the Cross with Longinus and the sponge-bearer. Nevertheless, the annular cross dominates all else, symbolizing the defeat of the Scandinavian pantheon by the Christian God of Light.

121 The *high cross at Ruthwell* (Dumfriesshire), a small Scottish township on the Solway Firth, is one of the most important examples not only of Anglo-Saxon but of Early Medieval art in general. During the Early and High Middle Ages, crosses of this kind were erected in Ireland, Wales, the Isle of Man, Scotland, and England. They are most widely found in Ireland, which probably conceived and developed the idea of the high cross on behalf of the rest of this insular, North-West European area. Although fundamentally similar, carved crosses developed independently in individual districts and evolved characteristic features of their own.

The Ruthwell cross generally used to be attributed, and for plausible reasons, to the late 7th century. However, examination of the runic script on a fragment of a similar cross now points to the latter half of the 8th century as the correct date. The Ruthwell cross also bears runes. Inscribed on it are a few verses from the finest religious poem in early English literature, *The Dream of the Rood*. This describes the dream of a man to whom the Cross itself recounts the events in which it played a part: the crucifixion and death of Christ. It is now believed that the author of these verses was Cynewulf, who was born *c.* 750, either in Mercia or, more probably, Northumbria.

The stylistic approach of the Ruthwell cross displays such a firm grasp of Mediterranean motifs that the sculptor, undoubtedly an Englishman, must have been in a position to build upon a considerable and well-established tradition—a tradition which had existed in England since the time of Theodore of Tarsus, the Greek sent by Rome to become Archbishop of Canterbury in the year 669. This association, which extended to the countries of the Eastern Mediterranean and embraced Armenia, Syria, and Egypt, that hive of Christian activity, also explains the affronted pose of the Christ on the Ruthwell cross (see our photograph). Southern influences encountered the westward-flowing tide of Irish religious faith, and this confrontation became crystallized in Northumbrian illuminated manuscripts and in sculptural works of which the Ruthwell cross may be designated the most important.

The cross is carved in reddish sandstone and stands about 15 ft high. It remained intact until the middle of the 17th century, when it was smashed in the course of post-Reformation disputes. After lying embedded in the ground for almost two centuries, it was transferred to a garden. It has since been carefully restored and re-erected in the little parish church.

As in the case of almost all English high crosses, the arms of the Ruthwell cross are not enclosed by a ring. This is the first respect in which it differs from the high crosses of Ireland. An even sharper distinction is apparent in the design and execution of the foliate scroll-work which occupies the surface between the runic borders on each of the narrower sides of the cross. This consists of vine tendrils with leaves and grapes, and is inhabited by birds, an ichneumon, a lion, and other symbolic creatures, all engaged in feeding on the fruit. The tendrils flow freely across the surface of the relief, describing curves and spirals in accordance with Mediterranean conceptions. There is no hint of any geometrical stylization in the Scandinavian or Iro-Celtic manner. The broader sides of the cross, framed by borders adorned with more runes and explanatory inscriptions written in a slightly Graecized Latin script, are occupied by various figures and scenes. On what is now the west side, in descending order, we meet St John the Evangelist with eagle, John the Baptist with lamb, a large portrayal of Christ (our photograph), Anthony the Hermit and Paul of Thebes in the desert, the Flight into Egypt, and, possibly, lowest of all, a Nativity scene. On the east side: an eagle, an arche, Mary Magdalene washing Christ's feet, the healing of the man born blind, the Annunciation, and the Crucifixion. Some of the sculptures on this once monolithic cross are in poor condition, e.g. the Crucifixion, which is almost obliterated.

Although the formal message of these scenes is Mediterranean—one might almost say Romanesque—in spirit, they do not present us with a Christianity in the Roman mould but form an extension of the Irish and monastic realm of ideas. Like the cross of Moone and many other Irish crosses, the sculptured cross at Ruthwell portrays the encounter between Anthony the Hermit, the father of Egyptian monasticism, and Paul of Thebes—an ideal illustration of the ascetic approach to life extolled and exemplified by the Iro-Celtic Church and propagated by contemporary Irish missionaries in Scotland and England and on the Continent.

IRELAND

The great importance of Ireland's role in the development of Western culture stems from the fact that the island was unaffected by the death-throes of the Roman Empire, to which it never belonged, and equally unaffected, save in the closing stages, by the great migrations. It was therefore in a position to keep the spirit of Europe alive throughout those troubled centuries. England was evangelized by Irish monks during the 7th century, and at various points on the Continent monastic communities from Ireland founded and manned monasteries which soon acquired influence and reputation. Known as 'Scottish' monasteries (Scotia being the Latin name for Ireland), many of these still commemorate the missionary work of Irish monks on the European mainland.

The assumption that Irish monasticism sprang directly from Coptic, that is to say, from the tap-root of Christian monasticism as a whole, cannot be taken for granted. That they were linked via Britain and Gaul is beyond dispute, but there is little actual evidence of any direct links between Irish monks and the monasteries of the Thebaid and the Coptic Church. One pointer in that direction is the fact that accounts of the lives of the Fathers of the Church in the Egyptian desert were regularly read by Irish monastic communities, whose structure bore so many resemblances to that of the loosely-knit pre-Benedictine hermitages of Upper Egypt. It should also be remembered that, prior to the expansion of Islam in the middle of the 7th century and even thereafter, maritime trade between the Eastern Mediterranean and the mineral-rich British Isles was extremely brisk. Coptic monks may have travelled these trade routes to visit Irish 'sages', perhaps via the ports of Saintonge. Since there is at least a modicum of evidence to indicate the presence of Coptic monks in Ireland, it is possible that reports of further visits have simply failed to survive. The 'Félire' or Calendar of Oengus, a martyrology written in 799, contains the passage 'SS septem Monachos Aegyptios qui iacent in Disert Ulidh invoco'. The actual location has never been identified, but the designation 'Disert', or desert, occurs at various points in Ireland. It is doubtful whether, say, the name Dysert O'Dea implies the erstwhile existence there of a Coptic settlement, but the application of the word 'desert' to a place of hermitage does recall the Coptic, coenobitic monasticism to which the monks of Ireland aspired.

Originally independent and organized on purely monastic lines, the Irish Church took centuries to adapt itself to, and become incorporated in, the Roman system. The slow process of transformation was boosted by the conversion of the Scandinavians who had migrated to Ireland and settled there, for their bishops, Irish-born by the second half of the 11th century, were the first entirely non-monastic prelates to wield diocesan authority. One of them, an active supporter of the new order, became the first papal legate in Ireland at the beginning of the 12th century.

The momentous and long-enduring autonomy of early Irish Christianity was only partly echoed in the artistic domain and principally by the efflorescence of book illumination, which exerted a far-reaching influence on the Continent. Not so with sculpture and architecture, neither of which evolved with anything like the same degree of autonomy except in very specialized fields. Thus, the one absolutely original product of Irish sculpture is the high cross. Its architectural counterpart is the round tower, which is indisputably and authentically Irish in character. In view of their peculiarities, it would seem advisable to comment on each of them generally before proceeding to examine particular examples.

THE HIGH CROSS

The origins of the high cross are so complex that no pronouncement on the subject can be regarded as anything more than a supposition based on isolated facts. The menhir tradition was still alive in Ireland when the first Christian missionaries arrived there. Menhirs marked the spot where the divine object of worship—whatever its exact designation—had come to earth. They thus became symbolic of a holy place and the centre of the believer's world. The idea of a 'navel of the world', meaning the point of contact between god and world, is common to many religions. Many sacred stones of this kind were overthrown or smashed during the Christianization of Ireland, but many others had crosses carved into them in recognition of their ancient status, thereby accomplishing the transformation into symbols and centres of Christianity. They were also regarded as an axis of sanctity by early Irish hermits, who were buried in their vicinity.

Engraved crosses assumed three-dimensional form in the course of time. The arms developed into protuberances and the stones themselves became wider. It was at this stage in the development of early Irish Christianity, probably at the turn of the 7th and 8th centuries, that there emerged a separate trend which led to the elaborately sculptured stelae of Scotland. In Ireland, the high cross continued to be the real badge of a monastery until the 9th and 10th centuries. Irish religious life found greater visible expression in high crosses than in churches and round towers. They were sacred places from which the Gospel went forth into the world through the medium of the preacher standing at the foot of the cross and his exposition of the scenes portrayed on its shaft and base.

Irish high crosses were strictly oriented. Moreover, as the St Mullins monastery plan clearly shows, the sacred precincts were disposed round them in accordance with the four cardinal points, so that divine grace flowed outwards to mankind like the four rivers of Paradise. One is led to wonder if this represents a link, largely unexplored and unexplained hitherto, with Coptic Christianity, since the Coptic liturgy demands that prayers be directed towards each of the four main quarters of the church in turn. A church is the house of God—in other words, a holy place on which the faithful converge from every point of the compass, later to emerge, full of grace, and disperse in every direction.

Thus, Irish high crosses of the 8th–12th centuries are not tombstones but symbols of redemption and aids to the overcoming of the world. Those responsible for presenting their fellow-men with such aids sought strength from the Almighty, and many crosses bear the following inscription: 'Pray for ..., who caused this cross to be erected'.

As we have already noted, stone crosses marked the spot from which the word of God was proclaimed. Indeed, preachers sometimes spoke from the foot of a high cross rather than inside an oratory which was too small to house the congregation. Most crosses were carved with small but dramatic scenes from the Old and New Testaments. In a largely illiterate land, these Bible-crosses performed a function fulfilled elsewhere in the West by the frescos, sculptured porches, capitals and friezes of Romanesque churches. Here, as elsewhere, entire programmes were carried out. As to the method of execution, it seems that the rough work was done before a cross was erected, whereas refinements and finishing touches were added after it had been transferred to its permanent site.

Another fundamental point to note is that Irish high crosses are never strictly symmetrical. True, their composition always achieves a perfect balance, but only by means of a contrast in weight and bulk. This tendency to avoid strict symmetry is typically Celtic, and became an Iro-Celtic legacy inherited by Insular Anglo-Saxon architecture and sculpture.

THE ROUND TOWER

The first round towers to be built in Ireland date from the early 10th century, a period when Viking raids and depredations were again showing an alarming increase. Although a number of these towers were doubtless built during the relatively peaceful years that followed the first wave of Viking raids, they were designed and constructed primarily as watch-towers and defensive fortifications, and continued to be so until into the 12th century. Their height enabled Scandinavian expeditionary forces to be sighted more quickly. When occasion demanded, the inmates of a monastery would seek refuge inside, taking food, water, and all their treasured possessions with them. While this did not prevent the sacking of monastery buildings, the protection afforded by these towers, which were suitably isolated, often saved church furnishings, reliquaries, and books, not to mention the lives of the monks themselves. Built of stone, the round tower was almost invulnerable to the weapons of the day, battering-rams

included, and the Vikings seldom indulged in protracted sieges. In a few cases, the stone towers seem to have been used as permanent strong-rooms. Once a besieger managed to set fire to the interior, however, the tall high-windowed structures acted as funnels, and there was no escape from the soaring flames.

Obscurity still surrounds the origin of these towers. One is naturally reminded of the free-standing round tower of S. Apollinare in Classe, influenced by Roman architectural tradition, built in the third quarter of the 9th century, and undoubtedly designed as a watch-tower. By contrast, the round towers of the St Gall monastery plan were conceived as straightforward stairways, which the round towers of Ireland were not. It seems reasonable to enlist the numerous round towers of East Anglia in an attempt to solve the problem, even though these are of later date and were invariably annexed to the main fabric of a church. Bearing in mind the traditionally circular shape of the stone huts of ancient Ireland, however, one is tempted to ask whether an indigenous conceptual and formal impulse may not have transformed itself, with a rapidity dictated by the pressure of threatening conditions, into buildings which fulfilled their purpose in an entirely functional way. This would mean that the towers' tall and cylindrical design evolved from the archetypal hut or stele. Attribution to predominantly native impulses would also help to explain why the round towers of Ireland have an average diameter-height ratio of 1 : 6, whereas their East Anglian counterparts are nearer 1 : 3 and can even go as low as 1 : 2. There was no essential difference between the design of the earliest round towers, in so far as this can still be ascertained, and that of the latest examples. All but a handful are free-standing, and all are associated with a church. They are situated to the north- or south-west of the church's main axis with their entrance facing the church itself.

The circular ground-plan averages 16 ft in diameter. Above the stone bases, many of which have subsided, stone walls approximately 3 ft thick converge slightly until, at 90 ft or so, they culminate in conical stone caps. Proportions became modified in the course of development. The tapering grew more pronounced, some of the interior storeys were indicated on the exterior by simple stone string courses, and the neatly constructed masonry surrounding the entrance was sometimes lightly picked out with roll-moulding.

There are no apertures in the base of a tower. The entrance, which is seldom more than shoulder-wide, barely the height of a man and almost twice that distance from the ground, could not be reached except with the aid of a ladder. The separate storeys—as many as seven of them—have wooden floors and are linked only by wooden ladders. A few of the intermediate storeys have windows, but these are invariably small and face in different directions. The only fair-sized windows are to be found right at the summit, just beneath the cap. The masonry varies. Sometimes it consists of courses of hewn stone, neatly dressed to follow the curve of the tower. Sometimes, rough-hewn blocks of varying sizes are bound with mortar. Sometimes, again, there is a mixture of techniques. The bases are neatly constructed as a rule, as though built at leisure, but there is a deterioration in quality higher up which almost suggests that work had to be completed in haste.

The Irish term for the round tower is 'cloictech', or 'house of bells'. To serve as a bell-tower was one of its functions but certainly not the most important, since tower-bells proper had yet to make their appearance. The bells of the period were hand-bells. Grasping them by their handles, the monks used to ring them from each of the four upper windows in turn as a summons to other inmates of the monastery to return from the surrounding country-side and assemble for divine office or communal activities.

Barely a dozen round towers have survived intact and another fifty are in ruins, but there must once have been more than a hundred of them. We know this because they were a characteristic feature of every monastic complex, and Irish chronicles invariably mention them in that connection.

122-125 The name *Glendalough* (Co. Wicklow) is derived from the Gaelic 'Gleann da locha' (Valley of the Two Lakes) and accurately describes the topographical situation of the first monastic settlement there. St Kevin, a contemporary of Columba, made his hermitage beside the upper lake towards the end of the 6th century. He died *c.* 618, but it is probable that he was already the focus of a group of pious men during his lifetime. Reports of St Kevin's sanctity attracted pilgrims, and the monastic community grew. At the beginning of the 8th century or there abouts, a new monastic settlement was established further down the valley adjoining the lower lake, where the Glendasan flows through a second valley from the Wicklow Pass and joins the Glenealo. There, on a terrace protected by these two strong-flowing streams, the end of the lake and a mountain spur, a large group of new monastery buildings began to take shape. By the end of the 8th century it was reported that pilgrims were visiting the sacred hermitages in their thousands and that 'many-splendoured' Glendalough had become the 'Rome of the West'. The Irish Church seems to have been vigorous, self-assured, and not devoid of lustre during the 8th century, but its thriving existence was cut short by the Vikings about a hundred years later.

The sacred precincts of Glendalough were enclosed by the usual perimeter wall, stretches of which can still be identified today. It probably consisted of a double skin filled with earth and rubble, and may have served as a raised walk-way. Within this boundary are the remains of the cathedral, St Mary's Church, and a smaller church known as the Priest's House, together with a round tower *(Pl. 124)* and an unsculptured granite cross (visible in *Pl. 122*). Immediately outside, towards the Glenealo, stand St Ciaran's and another church popularly known as 'St Kevin's Kitchen' *(Pl. 123)*. Scattered elsewhere in the valley are the remains of Trinity Church and St Saviour's *(Pl. 125)*, both of which probably formed the centre of smallish residential agglomerations of which no distinct evidence can be found. Next to Clonmacnois (Pl. *139–142*), Glendalough is the largest monastic site in Ireland and one which, thanks to its site and lay-out, still retains something of its erstwhile splendour to this day.

Access to the sacred precincts is through the twin arches of a *gatehouse (Pl. 122)* with an almost square ground-plan. An upper storey—probably a guard-room, and directly accessible from the perimeter wall—was still in existence at the end of the 18th century. The two round arches consist of granite blocks, most of them slightly tapered, and repose on massive plinth-stones. The inner arch rises to a greater height than the outer in conformity with the rising ground. It is also noticeable that the thrust of the vaulting is echoed by a slight outward inclination in the contact surfaces of each of the two lowest hewn stone blocks, as though the arch were meant to suggest a horse-shoe. That this obliquity was intentional is illustrated by the almost elegant way in which the broader plinth-stones accommodate the angled blocks—clear evidence of premeditation and technical ability on the part of architects and stonemasons.

The dating of early Irish buildings is difficult and can seldom be determined with absolute certainty because of the traditionalism of Irish architecture. The name '*St Kevin's Kitchen*' *(Pl. 123)*, ascribed to one small but important group of buildings because of its chimney-like tower, is undoubtedly a later sobriquet of legendary origin. Although isolated components of the main building might seem to indicate an earlier date of construction, the condition of the mortar and a small but genuine stone vault in the interior demonstrate that we are dealing with a building of the late 10th century. Certainly, the main walls of this church display a lime mortar construction which presupposes a certain amount of experience on the builder's part. Only the rectangular and unsubdivided nave dates from the earliest structural phase. The small round tower perched on the west end of the roof is an 11th-century addition, as is the sacristy which abuts on the north-east corner of the church. A square-ended chancel formerly adjoined the sacristy. This chancel, which still existed in 1772, can be reconstructed from its foundations, traces of jointing on the sacristy wall, and the outline of its roof on the east wall of the nave (visible in our photograph).

Of modest dimensions, St Kevin's Church clearly illustrates the conservatism of Irish ecclesiastical architecture and is still reminiscent of its point of departure: the dry-stone prayer-cell of the early hermitage. In early oratories, as in the hermit's circular stone cell, the stone slabs were not laid horizontally but canted outwards slightly to prevent rain from seeping through. At the same time, the carefully dressed stones were laid so that the walls gradually converged to form a false vault shaped like a pointed arch and running the length of the interior. Invariably oriented, these chapels were provided with light and access by a narrow door aperture and a small window. Oratories of this type resembled boats lying keel-upwards on the shore.

Despite the addition of four foundation walls, St Kevin's still recalls one of these oratories. In the small interior, which measures a mere 22 ft 6 ins by 14 ft 6 ins, even the nave walls slope inwards slightly. In view of the thickness of the walls (46 ins), this must have been dictated less by the thrust of the roof than by memories of earlier building techniques. The roof is entirely built of stone and displays two perceptible kinks in the centre and upper third of the slope. The lower part accords with traditional practice by adopting the shape of a false vault. Then, roughly on a level with the roof-ridge of the later chancel, where the internal distance between the two slopes was small enough for Irish builders to bridge, slabs of stone were laid radially to form a proper vault. Structurally, this segmental vault looks like an outward-thrusting support for the sloping stone roof. Above the vaulted apex and beneath the ridge of the roof was a small chamber, triangular in cross-section, whose function remains obscure.

Like St Kevin's and several other ruined churches, the round tower and St Saviour's are buildings belonging to the later settlements at Glendalough. The *round tower (Pl. 124)* is among the finest of its kind in Ireland. There is a possibility that these defensive structures were wholly or partially destroyed in the course of numerous raids, and that they were rebuilt and heightened when times grew more peaceful. Masonry of various periods can be discerned in the Glendalough tower, but its over-all design remained entirely homogeneous.

Glendalough's largest church, known as the Cathedral, lost its diocesan status when the monastic precincts were incorporated in the see of Dublin in 1214. A 10th-century anta building which sustained damage in numerous Viking raids and was later rebuilt, it is still impressive even in its ruined state. The chancel measures 36 ft by 23 ft and the interior of the nave 50 ft by 30 ft, which makes it one of the most capacious of early Irish churches. By contrast, the chancel arch of *St Saviour's (Pl. 125)* is under 12 ft wide and the interior of the church, chancel included, measures approximately 55 ft by 20 ft. St Saviour's belonged to a priory founded by Abbot St Lorcan O Toole in 1162, when he was promoted Archbishop of Dublin. The last church to be built at Glendalough, it handsomely exemplifies the sturdy grandeur of Irish Romanesque in the 12th century. Viewed as a whole, Glendalough used to be a compact group of buildings with strong walls and few entrances—a sort of ecclesiastical fortress set in a remote and lonely valley.

126-127   The *high cross of Moone* (Co. Kildare), though accessible to the public, now stands on private property near the ruins of a Franciscan monastery dating from 1258. The original monastic settlement may have been founded by St Columba in the 6th century. The cross, which no longer occupies its original site, can be traced back to the 8th century. It exhibits a number of remarkable features.

Composed of granite and unusually slender, the cross is over 15 ft high and elaborately carved. Its basic shape conforms to the classic design of the early high crosses, but its proportions are wholly unusual. The socle, which is square in ground-plan and distinguished by its height, has slightly tapering sides. On it reposes a second, smaller socle component whose trapeziform sides converge to meet the base of the square shaft. The equilateral shaft rises in two stages, each defined, like the upper and lower socles, by marginal bands. The horizontal arm of the cross is disproportionately small in comparison with the emphatic vertical shaft, which creates a surprisingly elegant impression. This is enhanced by the narrow annular band which transfixes each of the arms and further intensified by the fact that the stone arms do not meet at right angles but are connected by compressed semicircles—a style initiated as early as the 7th century. This tendency towards roundness is common to both Iro-Celtic and Scandinavian ornamentation: bronze-work and illuminated books afford countless examples of it. The four concavities are also echoed by the sweep of the freely executed stone ring, which symbolizes the refulgence of God and the sun. Carvings on the ends of the cross-piece prove that they never projected further than they do now, but the head of the cross was probably tipped with a conical cap.

The scenes on the cross, shaft and socle constitute an entire programme. The sequence begins on the east side (not visible in our photograph), facing the source of celestical light, and proceeds via the south and west sides (our photograph) to the north, the dark abode of the demons that menaced every Christian and the quarter from which the Vikings were soon to come and lay waste the holy places of Christian Ireland. Not all the sculptured areas can be interpreted. Some are adorned with spirals or interlace and others display a variety of not always identifiable animals. The latter may be signs of the zodiac, since the whole cross was seen in cosmic terms, but they may equally hail from the realm of the *Physiologus* and be intended as aids to interpreting the divine revelation. Other reliefs, again, are associated with the Old and New Testaments.

The *east side* of the annular cross bears a portrayal of Christ in Glory, the Light of the World. Clad in a long robe, he stands with his arms outstretched so that his forward-facing palms reach out into the extremities of the cross-piece. The scenes take their sequence from the course of the sun, passing from morning to noon and from noon to night in a clockwise direction. The integrated spiritual conception of the stone cross was not fortuitous, but carried on a strong pre-Christian Irish tradition, that of sun-worship and 'light-stones'. Still on the east side, the socle illustrates why the Son of God was made flesh. The Fall is portrayed with graphic simplicity, together with two other scenes—Abraham preparing to sacrifice Isaac and Daniel in the lions' den—which show that, even in Old Testament times, the true believer could expect redemption. The artist again demonstrates an intimate familiarity with sacred numerals: seven lions prowl round the God-fearing Daniel, three on his right and four on his left, symbolizing the proliferation of evil.

The *south side* of the socle *(Pl. 126,* south-west aspect) displays scenes from the Old and New Testaments: above, the three youths in the fiery furnace, construed as a prefiguration of the mystery of the Trinity; and, below, the flight of the Holy Family into Egypt. The works of Christ are evoked by a single but extremely graphic miracle: the feeding of the five thousand (St Matthew xiv, 13–21). With great artistic economy, the sculptor confined himself to showing the five loaves and two fishes mentioned in each of the Gospels. Between them, therefore, the east and south sides combine three memorable examples of divine aid from the Old Testament with two eloquent tokens of divine tutelage from the New.

The carved reliefs on the *west side (Pl. 126)* bring us to the core of the programme: Jesus Christ's redeeming death and the founding of the Church, symbolized by the twelve Apostles whose mission it was to proclaim the Gospel in every land. The Crucifixion, situated at eye-level on the upper part of the socle, adopts the typically Irish from. Longinus and the soldier with the vinegar-filled sponge and twig of hyssop take the place of Mary and John. Christ, wearing a long robe, stands imperiously erect with his arms extended sideways in the shape of a cross. On the annular cross, high above the animal-adorned shaft, serpentine monsters of the sort found elsewhere in Ireland can be seen coiling and writhing. The whole *west face of the plinth (Pl. 127)* is filled with a portrayal of the twelve Apostles, witnesses of the work of redemption. The slight variation in the faces may be attributable to their free-hand execution and to a millenium's exposure to the elements, but was never sypmtomatic of the slightest personalization or individualization. Ranged in three rows of four, the Apostles appear in their role as 'the Twelve', and their affronted pose indicates that they personify the Church as a whole. Formal representation is subordinated to thoroughgoing schematism. Each body is represented by a square and each pair of feet reduced to two opposing right angles. The arms, which might have impaired the rhythmical density of the three-by-four arrangement and spoiled the general effect, are omitted. So are the ears, though the pear-shaped heads exhibit noses and round eyes, all executed with a maximum of linear economy. It should be borne in mind that crosses were painted to enhance the impact of such scenes on the beholder. No traces of pigment have survived, granite being extremely impervious to layers of paint, but it is conceivable that the Apostles' arms were once painted on their bodies. Certainly, figurative portrayals of comparable date and location do not show individual parts of the body, merely a generalized shape. Often carried to considerable lengths, this interplay between objective statement and abstraction was a Celtic legacy. To early Irish Christians, the twelve disciples of Our Lord were a symbol of the foundation, stability and unity of God's Church, a visible token of the fulfilment of what Christ had established on earth. Christianity, so ran the message of the cross of Moone, must now stand the test of the world.

Three reliefs on the *north side* supply an exemplary illustration of this. Two of them refer to the life of the father of Christian monasticism, St Anthony the Hermit, who is shown visiting his fellow-hermit Paul in the Thebaid and undergoing temptation—scenes which appear on other crosses. Thus, the pictorial programme does not draw on the rich history of Irish monasticism but enlists the authority of Egyptian hermits of the first half of the 4th century. This is expressive of the profound veneration which Coptic hermits inspired in the monks of Ireland.

128 *St Brendan's Cathedral at Ardfert* (Co. Kerry), a simple aisleless church, was not built until the 12th century. The only features which mitigate its positively archaic appearance are the corner-buttresses and capitals. The Irish never bestowed as much attention on the building of churches as on round towers, nor did they show any tendency to articulate or develop their structure. At a time when magnificent Romanesque cathedrals were springing up in Normandy and England, Ireland's immediate neighbours, the Irish persisted in building rectangular churches with undivided naves and stereotyped square or rectangular chancels. The Rome-inspired basilical church, with its lofty central nave, arcades and aisles, was unknown in Ireland and remained so—discounting a few alien Cistercian buildings—until the island was conquered by the Normans late in the 12th century. There were no transepts and virtually no church towers, and doorways invariably received simple treatment. Memories of the primitive and unpretentious oratory lived on, without doubt, coupled with architectural ideas which stemmed from the first simple timber-built churches.

129 The *north cross of Ahenny* (Co. Tipperary) and the similarly shaped south cross are typical of a whole group of stone crosses in the south of Ireland. An examination of metal-work and miniatures to which they bear a marked resemblance suggests that they originated in the middle of the 8th century. The crosses of the Ahenny group all have shafts covered with interlace, trumpet-shaped ornaments, spiral and wafer motifs, and cable-moulding. Figurative carving is found sometimes on the shaft but more commonly—as in this case—on the socle.

Our photograph shows the (present) east and south sides. The west side of the socle portrays Christ *en face* and, flanking him in strict symmetry, six men wearing cowled habits and carrying Irish abbatial staffs. Christ's gesture of benediction suggests that the latter are Apostles being sent forth to preach the Gospel. On the north side, two figures can be seen riding in a two-wheeled chariot drawn by horses and escorted by mounted men. This group, which moves in a leftwards direction, has been interpreted, by reference to a letter from Columba to Pope Boniface IV, in which he speaks of Peter and Paul driving the triumphal car of Christ, as a metaphorical allusion to the missionary activities in which the monks of Ireland played so vigorous a part. The present *east side of the socle* (our photograph) may have been intended to symbolize the savagery of the world. One can discern, executed in a manner which recalls Pictish antecedents, a battle between a wide variety of animals. On the extreme left is a man holding on to a palm-tree, prob-

ably a portrayal of St Anthony the Hermit in the desert (cf. the notes on *Pl. 126* and *127* relating to the three scenes on the cross of Moone). The present south side depicts a procession. Two men, one with head bowed and the other carrying an annular cross, stride ahead of a third man with a shepherd's crook and a dog. The third man leads a donkey with a decapitated body draped over its back, legs and arms dangling, and a fourth figure brings up the rear carrying the head. It was customary to behead vanquished foes at this period, but the processional cross indicates that the body belonged to a saint. Thus, the scene on this plinth probably represents a martyr's home-coming.

If these interpretations are correct, the plinth must have been reversed when the cross was re-erected at some later date, that is to say, the east and west sides were transposed. Christ's dispatching of apostles belongs in the east, the traditional source of the Light of the World. The chariot containing God's emissaries would then proceed in a westerly direction (clockwise, in modern terminology), bound for the world in whose 'desert' the Christian must persevere, menaced by demons. Finally, the martyr is borne through the nocturnal gloom of the north side towards the light, following the processional cross as it dips towards the east in salutation.

The crosses of the Ahenny group took their shape from processional crosses of this kind, which consisted of a wooden core entirely encased in ornamented sheets of metal. Although translated into stone, the north cross of Ahenny still suggests the engraved metal overlaps and the rivet-heads which would have marked the junction of cross-pieces and segmental reinforcements in its wooden prototype. Like the earlier processional cross, stone crosses were set up at the fountainheads of Christian teaching and example. The type of ornamented stone cross represented by the Ahenny group was prefaced by the 7th-century stele of Fahan Mura (Co. Donegal), and stylistically related works are also to be found in Scotland, notably the crosses of St Columba's monastery on Iona, which became the main link between Ireland and Northern England. In addition, certain passages in the Life of St Columba suggest that Iona possessed a metal-workers' atelier.

130 The enriched *west front of Ardmore 'Cathedral'* (Co. Waterford) presents what is, for Ireland, an unwonted spectacle. Even later in date than St Brendan's Cathedral at Ardfert *(Pl. 128)*, or *c.* 1200, the church had an undivided nave to which a Gothic chancel was added subsequently. The volutes and roll-moulding of the west window are reminiscent of Norman windows, but its close proximity to the blind arches beneath renders it wholly ill-conceived. It looks very much as if stone carvings from an earlier building were preserved in a prominent position out of a sense of respect. Although many of their characteristics recall stonemason's work on high crosses of the late 10th century, they were undoubtedly produced by a minor master of the century following. This is proved by a portrayal of the Fall in which the Tree resembles Norman prototypes. Further sculptures include an Adoration of the Kings, an extremely dramatic Judgement of Solomon, and a Weighing of Souls.

131-132 One glance at *Cormac's Chapel, Cashel* (Co. Tipperary) is enough to show that it occupies a special place in Irish architecture as a whole. Like the cross of Kilfenora *(Pl. 135)*, this church demonstrates that Ireland had at last entered the realm of Romanesque imagery.

The rock of Cashel, royal seat of the Kings of Munster, makes a monumental impression as it rises abruptly from the surrounding plain. On the summit, enclosed by walls, stand a round tower of the early 10th century, a late high cross adorned with the figure of a bishop, Cormac's Chapel, a strange Gothic cathedral, and an easily defensible bishop's residence of the early 15th century—all in ruins, but preserved. St Patrick is said to have visited Cashel *c.* 450 and baptized the ruler of Munster, the south-western part of Ireland. Powerful monarchs reigned at Cashel for centuries thereafter, often combining the offices of king and bishop. Cormac I (*c.* 900), who built the round tower, was king, bishop and poet as well. Brian Boru, King of Munster, became high king of all Ireland in the year 1002. He not only defeated the Danes but won renown as a lawgiver by convening an assembly of noblemen at Cashel and securing their acceptance of his *Book of Rights.* About a century later, at a similar assembly held in 1101, King Murtagh O'Brien bestowed the entire rock on the Church. In 1152, when Kilfenora became a see, Pope Eugene III sent his nuncio, Cardinal Paparo, to deliver four pallia to the bishoprics of Armagh, Dublin, Tuam and Cashel in token of their bishops' elevation to archiepiscopal rank and of their special ties with Rome.

After Cashel had been acquired by the Church, Bishop Cormac MacCartach (1122–38) decreed the construction of a new church, an aisleless building with a square-ended chancel slightly offset to the south in an unusual manner. This impressive building, now known as Cormac's Chapel, was consecrated in 1134. It is entirely built of yellowish sandstone, and its walls consist of large blocks of ashlar, accurately dressed and neatly fitted. The Gothic cathedral came into being at about

the middle of the 13th century. Lack of space entailed that the choir and one arm of the transept not only adjoined Cormac's Chapel but actually abutted on it in places, with the result that the sculptured north doorway which once formed the main entrance to Cormac's Chapel now opens straight on to the cathedral wall. The south transept of the cathedral can be seen on the left of our photograph. Cormac's Chapel has been restored on several occasions. The rebuilt portions of the choir preserve its original design, but the obtrusive windows in the south wall and the inapt improvements to the south tower have yet to be eliminated. The two east towers *(Pl. 131)* are architecturally unusual, for Ireland, in that they adopt a square shape and are set into the nave like the arms of a transept. Equally un-Irish are the exterior and interior blind arcades, the ribbed vaults in the chancel *(Pl. 132)*, the barrel-vaulted nave, and the numerous stone string courses. The chancel arch displays a somewhat half-hearted zigzag motif reminiscent of English architectural ornamentation. The numerous heads on the chancel arch, some of which still bear traces of pigment, are worthy of special note, though the popularity of this form of decoration in 12th-century Ireland is attested by the contrasting porches at Dysert O'Dea and Clonfert *(Pl. 137)*.

On the other hand, the massive stone roof of the nave is wholly Irish. Its smooth exterior is broken only by windows designed to admit light into the interior. The construction of the roof still preserves something of the character of early Irish oratories such as the Gallarus oratory (Co. Kerry). An evolutionary thread runs from the latter, via St Kevin's Church, to Cashel, which is, in effect, the same old converging stone structure superimposed on lofty nave walls. It is not misleading to say that, just as the crosses of Moone and Kilfenora represent opposite ends of an evolutionary process whereby Irish sculpture travelled from autochthonous to European Romanesque without forfeiting its individuality, so Irish architecture also became merged with Romanesque. Apart from Irish characteristics, Cashel, in particular, betrays the influence of Romanesque prototypes—English, Norman, Gallic, and Rhenish, though these cannot be distinguished individually. A connection has been established between Cashel and Regensburg, where the Irish monk Dionysus resided between 1098 and 1121 as abbot of the so-called 'Schottenkloster' of St Jakob, a monastery with Irish inmates. Dionysus began to rebuild his monastery in 1111. The delegation which he sent to Ireland to raise funds included a stonemason named William and a carpenter named Conrad, both of them Irishmen. They visited Cashel, and it was they who exerted a decisive influence on Dionysus' plans for his new church.

133-134 Details from the *two high crosses of Castledermot* (Co. Kildare). The Ahenny type of cross *(Pl. 129)* yields to one in which ornaments are confined to segments of the annulus or side surfaces—indeed, disappear altogether. The figurative cross of the Moone type *(Pl. 126)* becomes the norm, and the tendency towards religious demonstration is reinforced by a growing number of scenic carvings. The basic design—base, shaft, cross-piece and annulus—remains the same, but the height, which was striking enough in the case of Moone, increases considerably, reaching 23ft at Monasterboice *(Pl. 145)*. More figures are in evidence, new scenes are portrayed, and 'types'—that is to say, events or personages from the Old Testament which prefigure some aspect of the New—are depicted with greater zeal. *Commentaries on the Old Testament* by Isidore of Seville (d. 636) was only one of several such works known in Ireland as early as the 7th century, and Bede's writings fulfilled a similar function in Northumbria. The 'Ordo commendationis animae' or prayers for divine aid in time of earthly affliction—of the sort which saved Noah from the Flood, Daniel from the lions, Isaac from the knife and Jonah from the belly of the whale—won increasing esteem. The religious revival which occurred *c.* 800 brought reforms in monastic life through renewed asceticism on the part of hermits in their solitude ('Dysert') and stricter religious observance. The same religious impulse promoted the development of a new form of cross. Moreover, greater importance seems to have been attached to the practice of donating crosses and adorning them with an inscription designed to honour and solicit prayers for prominent saints, abbots, or kings during their lifetime. Apart from high crosses proper, a number of smaller ones are still in existence. There must have been many more at one time, including numerous wooden crosses of which none has survived.

Castledermot also boasts the ruins of an early town and monastery buildings, together with substantial portions of a round tower built in 919 and two high crosses in a state of partial preservation. The monastery itself was founded by St Diarmuid in 812. The attribution of the two crosses to the early 9th century derives historical probability from the date of the monastery's foundation and stylistic probability from a formal affinity with the high cross of Moone, which is not far away. The Castledermot crosses are likewise hewn in granite, a local stone and one whose hardness naturally dictated a certain simplification of treatment. As the harp-playing David on the *north cross (Pl. 134)* demonstrates, the reliefs confine themselves to only two levels—surface and ground—and individual figures seem to exhibit very little modelling.

The main scenes on this cross are, on the east side, a crucified Christ surrounded by four trios of Apostles on the arms of the cross; on the west side, the Fall sandwiched between a psalmodizing David and the sacrifice of Isaac; on the shaft, inter alia, another version of the two Anthony the Hermit scenes found at Moone; and, on the socle, a portrayal of the Feeding of the Five Thousand. The latter makes a more complex and less compact impression than the one at Moone—a deterioration in quality which is evident throughout the work and proves that it originated later.

Not far away stands the *south cross*. The whole of the east side is covered with ornaments, though these were applied with great discipline and restraint. The Crucifixion scene on the *west side (Pl. 133)* provides another example of the Irish type of Rood. Christ is not nailed to baulks of timber but adopts an erect, triumphant pose, his body and outstretched arms themselves forming the Cross. On either side, as always in early Irish art, stand the sponge-bearer and spear-bearer. Flanking this 'Christus dominans' are, on his right, David playing the harp, and, on his left, Abraham preparing to sacrifice Isaac (the ram is already visible in the background). Some doubt attaches to the scenes above Christ's head, especially the one at the top, which may or may not represent his arrest. The distribution of the scenes on the shaft is significant. Adam and Eve can be clearly discerned beneath the Tree of Knowledge, its trunk encircled by the Serpent's coils. Above this portrayal of the Fall come the two desert hermits, Anthony and Paul, representing those who put their faith in God. Beneath it, Anthony undergoes temptation by demonic spirits. At the foot, symbolic of God's unfailing help in time of need, comes the story of Daniel in the lions' den.

135 *High cross at Kilfenora* (Co. Clare). Very little is known about the history of this small town in the west of Ireland. Situated south of Galway Bay, in line with the Aran Islands, Kilfenora did not reach its prime until the 12th century, when it was promoted to diocesan status. The cathedral built to mark this promotion is now in ruins, but other survivals from the same period include four high crosses of varying importance which were erected on the boundaries of the sacred precincts in accordance with ancient tradition. Only fragments of the south cross have survived. The north cross displays various ornaments. The other two crosses, one in a field and the other (illustrated here) in the graveyard, are of particular importance. Both are carved in the pale Jurassic limestone of the area.

Though typical of the development of such monuments in the 12th century, these crosses differ greatly in appearance from those at Moone *(Pl. 126)* and Monasterboice *(Pl. 145)*. Continuity had been destroyed by the post-915 recrudescence of Viking raids and depredations, and no more crosses were erected until the latter part of the 11th century. Even though their design—socle and shaft, cross and annulus—remained essentially similar, their proportions underwent a change. The ring became smaller and was set nearer the shaft, which consequently appeared more massive. The segmental apertures also grew smaller and vanished altogether in some cases, e.g. on the figurative cross at Kilfenora, where they turned into simple recesses. The annulus can also disappear, as on the magnificent cross at Dysert O'Dea (Co. Clare), which so closely approximates to the Latin form of cross commonly found on the Continent.

The shaft and arms of the cross are no longer divided into separate fields like the 'classical' picture-Bible crosses. Divisions are to be found only where self-contained ornamental motifs do not overlap or merge with adjoining areas of ornamentation, but not even this rule is consistently observed. Far more important than the ornamentation on these late crosses is the plastic treatment of figurative elements. Ornaments have become flatter and are carved in very low relief, whereas figures gain accordingly in volume and size. On the crosses at Dysert O'Dea and Kilfenora, for instance, they not only stand out against the shaft and cross-piece, rounded and free, but are sometimes executed in 'ronde bosse'. The head of the Dysert O'Dea Christ must formerly have been detached from the cross, and the presence of a hole proves that the bishop's arm used once to jut into space, raised in benediction.

The classic picture-Bible cross displayed whole series of scenes. 12th-century crosses confine themselves to isolated incidents such as the Fall or the sacrifice of Isaac. Christ has ceased to be a participant within the context of a scene and become 'Christus triumphans', symbolic of redemption because of his victory over death. The cross in the field at Kilfenora shows us a cosmic Christ whose body bears a central square, symbol of the Creation. Four is the number of the world, of its traditional elements, of the rivers of Eden, of the quarters of heaven. In the visions of Ezekiel, the holy place was surrounded by four 'living creatures' which were the elemental symbols of ancient Babylon and later became symbols of the Evangelists. In the cosmic Christ, all becomes one. Just such a Christ may once have adorned the west side of the cross whose east side is illustrated here. Nothing can be seen today except traces of a figure and, in the spaces between figure and annulus, four birds facing the putative Christ. The function of these late crosses was still to define the extent of consecrated ground. This is confirmed by an Erection of the Cross scene on the socle at Dysert O'Dea, similar to that on the Cross of the Scriptures at Clonmacnois (see note on *Pl. 139*).

Another historical event appears on the *east side of the graveyard cross at Kilfenora*, illustrated here. This is divided into three zones. At the foot are two heads and a bird; above them, two figures holding staffs; and, protruding into the cross at the head, a priest with a crosier. The upper arm of the cross is occupied by the priest's hat and the horizontal arms by a winged being and a bird, perched obliquely on his shoulders. Interpretation is difficult, but the location of the scene and its mode of execution indicate that it must have possessed genuinely documentary significance.

Opinions vary as to the identity of the priest holding the crosier. His head-dress is less like a bishop's mitre than a tiara of the sort worn by Popes of the 11th and 12th centuries. The two winged creatures on the man's shoulders provide a key to the correct interpretation. The angel on his right shoulder is the symbol of St Matthew, the eagle on his left that of St John, and Matthew and John were the only Evangelists to record Christ's crucial pronouncements on Peter's special apostolic status. Matthew (xvi, 18–19) reports that Jesus said: '. . . thou art Peter, and upon this rock I will build my church; and the gates of hell shall not prevail against it. And I will give unto thee the keys of the kingdom of heaven. . .' John alone supplies the second explicit reference to Peter's primacy in the passage (xxi, 15–17) in which Christ asks him three times '. . . lovest thou me?' —and, having received three affirmative answers, entrusts him with the care of his flock. Judging by the evangelistic symbols on its shoulders, the figure on the cross at Kilfenora is that of St Peter, and the shepherd's crook and tiara mark him out as the first of the Popes. This interpretation is corroborated by a second factor. Only the figure's index-finger and middle finger are extended, the thumb being laid against the other two fingers—a gesture of benediction peculiar to Christ and his representative on earth, the Pope. The downward direction of the benedictory gesture is dictated by formal considerations alone: the arm was intended to be raised.

Once we interpret this figure as that of St Peter, the Church's supreme pastor, the meaning of the entire composition on this side of the cross becomes plain. Just as 'desert' and 'worldly wilderness' were depicted on the socles at Moone and Ahenny *(Pl. 129)*, so the lowest zone here portrays the earthly afflictions of mankind. On one of the heads stands a bird, clawing at the skull of the second figure. The latter, with left arm raised, is trying to break the bird's grip. What it holds in its right hand cannot be ascertained. It was a Romanesque convention to symbolize the devilish trials of mankind in a depraved world by showing a bird ripping at the skull and eyes of a human being. The central zone portrays two men who have overcome the world's evils. They stand erect with arms linked, united in thought, desire, and action. Habit, hood and staff identify them as monks—men who serve the Word of God and combat the Devil. It is no mere coincidence that their staffs thrust downwards at the demonic bird beneath, but it is curious that these staffs should differ as they do. The monk on the left is holding a typical Irish abbatial or episcopal staff with a simple curve ending in a right angle. The other has a staff with a horizontal cross-piece. A development of 'ankh', the ancient Egyptian symbol of life, this is a so-called tau-staff of the type habitually carried by St Anthony the Hermit, founder of Coptic monasticism and Christian monasticism as a whole. Proof exists that the tradition of the tau-staff still survived during the 12th century, on the Continent as well as in England and Ireland, and the elaborate treatment of such staffs seems to justify the supposition that they were venerated as emblems of the monastic tradition. This would account for the presence of a tau-staff on the shaft of the cross at Kilfenora. The two closely conjoined monks with their abbatial staffs, representing past and present, may thus be construed as symbols of the Irish Church.

However, the Irish Church was subordinate to the supreme pastor in Rome, who, portrayed as St Peter and furnished with the tiara and spiral bishop's crosier typical of the Roman Church, dominates all else at the intersection of the cross. The purpose of the sculptures was to proclaim the nature of this hierarchy, unmistakably and on consecrated ground. The cross was not simply an expression of the fact that Kilfenora had been promoted to diocesan status after the Synod of Kells in 1152, but an acknowledgement of the Irish Church's unqualified submission to the Lex Petri. This was how a more or less contemporary cross, also portraying a Roman bishop, came to be erected at Dysert O'Dea, which never was a bishop's see. Ireland had become fully integrated in the history of the Western Church and the world of Romanesque imagery.

136-138 Like Clonmacnois, the former *monastery of Clonfert* (Co. Galway) was situated near the Shannon, whose navigability proved a disadvantage during the time of the Viking raids. As a result, nothing of the monastery itself has survived. The first monastic settlement was founded *c.* 460 by St Brendan the Voyager. Of the early anta type, that is to say, with its long walls extended slightly by pilaster-like buttresses, the small unaisled church originated in the 10th century but underwent numerous alterations. The sandstone *porch (Pl. 137)* probably owes its existence to the restoration of the church after a monastery fire in the year 1164. It is one of the finest examples of late Irish Romanesque. Although Irish ecclesiastical architects bestowed as little attention on porches as they did on the actual fabric of churches, sculptured doorways make sporadic appearances at about

the middle of the 12th century, probably under the influence of pilgrims to Rome and Santiago. The porch at Clonfert is a highly individual work whose special fascination derives from a blend of Irish and Continental features.

The general design is Irish. The slightly squat round-arched doorway with its triangular gable resembles a cross-section of one of those archaistic unaisled churches with precipitous stone roofs which the Irish were still building in the 11th and 12th centuries (e.g. St Kevin's Church at Glendalough and Cormac's Chapel at Cashel). The jambs are askew, but Late Gothic stonemasons of the 15th century tried to offset this by inserting an arch of pale carved limestone. Far from being dictated by structural considerations, the slanting jambs are an echo of the inward-sloping walls clearly discernible in ancient portrayals of early Irish buildings constructed of wattle, timber, or stone. This retention of Irish formal characteristics becomes all the more understandable when we reflect that practically every other feature of the porch was based on ideas which its authors had imported from elsewhere.

The embroidery-like ornamentation of the *jamb-shafts (Pl. 136)* recurs on the west portal of Lincoln Cathedral *(Pl. 193)*, which had just been completed at this time. The capitals and archivolts with their rosettes, bosses, crockets, fleurons, masks, and, biting into the detached roll-moulding of the second order, dogs' heads, bear witness to a technical proficiency which could translate the fruits of a richly stimulated imagination into visual terms—yet the squat round arch still contains an element of the primitive.

Since archaisms of this kind are always possible in Ireland and an Ibero-Celtic headstone still stands in a field not far from Kilfenora, it would be very tempting to associate the head-motif on the *gable (Pl. 138)* with Celtic archetypes. There is also a suggestion of the Gallic about it. At Clonfert, however, the subtly elongated triangles with their marguerite motif and the shape of the heads themselves are so expressive of something classically Mediterranean that a connection with Italian or Spanish works seen by pilgrims seems wholly plausible. Doorways with reduplicated surrounds and a similar wealth of sculpture were particularly common in the Norman South of Italy. The porch at Clonfert was undoubtedly painted at one time, so coloured bodies must once have been visible beneath the heads in the arcaded arches. No interpretation of the fifteen heads has yet been found.

139-142 The *monastic precincts of Clonmacnois* (Co. Offaly), an impressive agglomeration of churches, towers and crosses, occupy a commanding position above the banks of the Shannon. The *view from the east (Pl. 142)* across a later graveyard gives some idea of the juxtaposition of works of varying date and type. The large ruined round tower in the right background, O Rourke's Tower, recurs in the photograph which shows it and the *Cross of the Scriptures (Pl. 140)* against the broad expanse of the river-valley. The round-arched aperture some distance from the ground was the entrance to the tower. The tower itself was carefully constructed of hewn stone slabs dressed to conform with the curve of the wall. The regular series of windows at the top indicates that the cylindrical structure has survived almost in its entirety, and that only the conical cap is missing. A cap of this type surmounts the fully-preserved *round tower of Teampall Finghin (Pl. 141*, view from the south-west), which differs from other round towers in its relationship to the church. Instead of being a free-standing structure, it actually abuts on the chancel. Together with the ruins of the latter, it retains its architectural impact to this day. Artistically, however, the most important monument at Clonmacnois is the so-called Cross of the Scriptures.

The Cross of the Scriptures (Pl. 139, east side) and the crosses of Monasterboice *(Pl. 145)* combine to form a small but well-preserved and peculiarly important group. Their material, a local sandstone, was easy to work with —so much so that the Cross of the Scriptures is monolithic. The crosses of this group display an advanced form of general design in that the intersections of the cross and annulus are accentuated by tapering arms and inset rolls. In the case of the Cross of the Scriptures, the annulus is proud of the arms on both sides and the horizontals curve upwards slightly. There has also been a development in sculptural technique. The stonemason no longer carved his scenes in low relief on two levels but—aided, of course, by the softer stone—executed them in well-rounded high relief. The figures are anatomically more lifelike. Indeed, a certain individuality of pose and physiognomy is discernible, and the figures' clothing gives some indication of the limbs beneath.

The above-mentioned crosses possess considerable artistic merit. Comparative study of the crosses at Clonmacnois *(Pl. 139)* and Monasterboice *(Pl. 145)* inclines one to regard them rather as works by two congenial contemporaries than as products of a single atelier manned by one master and his pupils. The crosses represent a mature stage in the development of the classical Irish high cross. They were produced at the beginning of the 10th century. In 875, after half a century of Viking raids on monasteries, a period of relative calm set in and a renewal of civil and ecclesiastical life became possible under the stabilizing influence of the high king Flann Sinna (*c.* 877–*c.* 915). Many new churches and monasteries were built and many crosses commissioned at this time, as witness the partly deciphered inscription at the foot of

the shaft of the 'Cros na Screaptra' (east side). This reads: '. . . (C)olman Dorro . . . ssa Ar . . . Flaind' (Colman caused this cross to be erected for King Flann').

The crosses of this period were richly carved. Their pictorial canon had been enlarged by a modification of traditional themes, by the introduction of unwonted themes from the Old and New Testaments—indeed, by the representation of historical events. On the west side of the Cross of the Scriptures, apart from some shaft reliefs which do not permit of conclusive identification, we find a Crucifixion scene. A naked Christ with fettered feet occupies the centre of the cross. As at Moone, Longinus thrusts his spear into Christ's right side while Stephaton raises his vinegar-steeped sponge on the left. This reversal of positions accords with an Eastern iconographic tradition which was as widespread in Ireland as the conventional Latin one. Stephaton is here construed as a personification of the Synagogue, and Longinus, towards whom blood and water flow, of the Church.

The east side *(Pl. 139)* carries an Irish version of the Last Judgement. Christ stands *en face* at the intersection of the cross, the Serpent beneath his feet, the Dove of the Holy Spirit above his head, an angel with a trumpet on his right, and an averted devil on his left. Inside the horizontal arms of the cross, facing towards and away from him respectively, are the hosts of good and evil. Christ is clad in a long robe. His left hand holds the martyr's cross, which rests obliquely across his shoulder, his right hand the leafy branch of Resurrection. This variant of Christ, often found in Ireland but comparatively rare in England, possesses special significance because it is underlaid by ancient Egyptian conceptions of the resurrected god Osiris, with his sceptre and frond. The Osiris-Christ is the Irish manifestation of Christ in Judgement. Romanesque portrayals of the same theme often embodied symbols of the Evangelists. These are no more in evidence here than the aura or mandorla, though the latter's place is taken by the annular aureole which surrounds the whole scene. The annulus and the four discs are ornamented with interlace and spirals. Two Evangelists do appear on the edges of the cross. In the three fields on the south side—Christ's right—are St John and the eagle, David with his harp, and, at the bottom, some ornamentation. The upper field on the north side shows the angel with Matthew, who holds a tau-cross, the lower field Michael vanquishing a demon, and the central field a female flautist with her feet resting on lions (the Sibyl of Erythraea) and beside her a cat licking itself with its legs doubled up—a symbol of carnal pleasure. The scenes carved on the socle are arranged in two tiers and illustrate the propagation of the Gospel by apostles, either mounted or riding in chariots.

This cross, too, embodies a modification of an entire programme. The three scenes on the east side of the shaft take us from the Messianic promise to its fulfilment and, thus, into the realm of Christian history. The relief immediately beneath Christ depicts a 'Traditio Legis' of the type present on the west side of the Muiredach cross at Monasterboice *(Pl. 145)*. Christ, seated in the centre, hands Peter the key and Paul the new Law. The significance of the central relief is uncertain, but the swords carried by the two bearded men suggest a relationship with the scene at the foot. They may be representatives of God's world order—possibly a high king and an abbot, many abbots being more warlike and powerful than their kings. This would make the lowest scene wholly historical and particularly significant in the present context, since it appears immediately above Colman's dedication to Flann. It doubtless lent added authority to the erection of this didactic cross because it portrayed the founding of the monastery of Clonmacnois itself, a solemn ceremony performed in unison by the wielders of spiritual and secular authority. Abbot and king are shown thrusting the shaft of the cross into the ground. Thus, the two figures are probably those of St Ciaràn (516–549) and King Diarmait I, who together founded what was destined to become one of the most important monastic settlements in Ireland.

143 *Mellifont Abbey* (Co. Louth), the first Cistercian settlement in Ireland, was founded in 1142 by Donchadh O Carrol, ruler of the North Irish kingdom of Uriel, at the instigation of the Bishop of Down, later St Malachy. Its founding thus coincided exactly with the reformation of the Iro-Scottish Church and its orientation towards Rome. Inspired by Bernard of Clairvaux, Malachy sent a number of Irish monks to be schooled and trained at Clairvaux itself, and it was they who founded Mellifont Abbey with the assistance of one or two fellow-monks from France. Within a few years, numerous filial establishments had sprung up throughout Ireland. This annexation to a pan-European movement produced a radical change in Irish monasticism and the whole of Irish monastic architecture.

The abbey church was consecrated in the year 1157, in the presence of Cardinal Paparo, the papal legate. It must have presented a grandiose spectacle in those days —an aisled building 200 ft long, with a transept, side apses, a large square-ended chancel, a cloister, and monastery annexes—but foundations are all that can be seen of it in the charming valley today. The only conspicuous features are a few arches and sections of wall belonging to the partly restored and somewhat later *lavatorium*, visible in our photograph. These demonstrate that, although Mellifont's layout came from Burgundy, its formal idiom was closely related to that of Cistercian buildings such as Fountains Abbey *(Pl. 174–177)* and Rievaulx Abbey *(Pl. 178–179)* in Yorkshire.

144-146 Ruined buildings and well-preserved monuments stand side by side in the *monastery precincts of Monasterboice* (Co. Louth). The group consisting of the *north church and round tower (Pl. 144)* may be regarded as typical. The tower rises in front of the west end of the main fabric, slightly south of the east-west axis. Layers of ash and fragments of bone unearthed in the course of excavations show that, here as so often elsewhere, the ruinous state of the buildings is attributable to fire. Contemporary chronicles, which record disasters of this kind, state that the monastery's treasured possessions were burned in the cloictech, or round bell-tower, of Monasterboice in 1097.

As to the superb *south cross (Pl. 145,* east side), which is remarkably well preserved, stylistic analysis suggests a date of origin early in the 10th century. An inscription at the foot of the shaft (west side) reads 'OR DO MUIREDACH LAS NDERNAD CHROSSA'. Engraved subsequently, though before the turn of the century, it establishes the authorship of the cross beyond all doubt. Monasterboice had two abbots named Muiredach. The noble work under discussion must date back to the time of the second and more important of them, who presided over the monastery from 887 until 923.

The Muiredach cross represents a very advanced type of pictorial or Bible-cross. Its treatment is characteristic of the complex, ornate, over-refined phase which occurs in any process of stylistic development, but its general appearance is peculiarly massive. The cross not only rises to a considerable height (over 17 ft) but possesses a remarkably thick shaft. The pyramidal base, which makes an equally massive impression, is adorned with interlace and animals and animal scenes which defy individual interpretation. The apex of the cross is well preserved. As in the case of the west cross at Monasterboice and the Cross of the Scriptures at Clonmacnois *(Pl. 139)*, it is shaped like a miniature one-celled church and has a shingled saddleback roof with crossed gable-beams. The Irish were still building churches of this type and continued to do so for some time. Indeed, the gabled roof of the 12th-century church at Ardfert *(Pl. 128)* may well have looked like this.

The pictorial themes on the *west side* are: in the centre of the cross, a Crucifixion; at the head, Moses assailing the heavens with unremitting prayers, supported, by Aaron and Hur; and, on the shaft, the 'Traditio Legis', the scene with Thomas, and the arrest of Christ. This side of the cross is emphatically rhythmical in composition. Disposed above and below the finely articulated Crucifixion, the four three-figure scenes display bold plastic treatment coupled with artistic discipline. Their style approximates to that of the Cross of the Scriptures at Clonmacnois, which incorporates some two-figure scenes as well.

The *east side of the Muiredach cross*, illustrated here, positively teems with figures. The light reflected by the multitude of little heads creates an ornamental half-tone effect. It is hardly surprising that the edges of the cross should be limited to pure ornament, very fine interlace, foliage inhabited by birds reminiscent of the cross at Ruthwell *(Pl. 121)*, and a field of spirally-arranged nodes. The sharp contrast between the west and east sides of the shaft suggests that they were produced by different artists, the more individual of the two being closer to the cross at Clonmacnois. If so, the master of the east side of the Muiredach cross must have been a highly developed late-comer.

The east side of the shaft is adorned with four rectangular reliefs of horizontal format. Their abundance of figures is attributable partly to a juxtaposition of different scenes and partly to the introduction of supplementary dramatis personae. In the lowest frame, for instance, we find a combination of *the Fall and the murder of Abel (Pl. 146)*, two scenes which had always been portrayed separately hitherto. This was a deliberate clarification of the picture-Bible practice of presenting the two scenes as cause and effect. Above the Adam and Cain scenes comes a portrayal of the battle between David and Goliath. The third scene from the foot shows Moses smiting the rock and the water gushing forth to revive the Israelites, whose astonishment is vividly conveyed by the position of their heads and arms. The proportions of the figures in each relief vary in a way which seems deliberate rather than fortuitous—a supposition confirmed by the rhythmical flow, which runs from left to right but proceeds from an alternation of standing and seated figures. This applies throughout, from the base of the shaft to the Adoration of the Kings immediately beneath the annulus. The little round knob above the Child's head is the Star of Bethlehem, so shaped because its rays were originally added in paint.

The cross attains a spiritual and artistic climax in the horizontal arms. Their skilfully orchestrated complexity is so expressive of a late stylistic phase that it could only have been succeeded by reaction. In the centre, splayed feet planted firmly on the ground, stands Christ in Judgement. David, whose psalms are being whispered to him by a bird, plucks a harp at Christ's right hand. On Christ's left sits the flute-playing Sibyl of Erythraea. The lion at her feet can still be discerned despite the weathering of the stone. The Dove of the Holy Spirit hovers above Christ's head, as at Clonmacnois, but this Dove is a more animated creature, with its head turned to the right and its right wing beating the air. The three figures above it may be construed as angels paying homage. The figures in the arm of the cross on Christ's right represent the souls of the righteous. Grouped in three rows on the extreme left, they converge towards the centre, their uniform gestures leading the eye to one of their number who sits at the neck of the arm, reading aloud from the book which lists the deeds of the righteous. This ritardando is succeeded by a resumption of movement, and the procession is headed by an ambulant figure blowing a wind instrument. The opposite arm of the cross shows the damned being driven from Christ's presence by a devil with a trident. Another ritardando is introduced by a figure distorted and frozen with horror, preceded by a second devil who reads aloud from the book of transgressions and simultaneously kicks one of the damned towards the punishment he so richly deserves. The rest of the damned hurry on ahead, jostling each other as they go. Sentence has been passed: the deeds of each and every one have been weighed and assessed by the Archangel Michael. This 'weighing of souls' is here portrayed beneath Christ's feet with a vigour which recalls sculptured doorways in the mature Gothic style.

SCOTLAND

147-150 *Jedburgh Abbey* (Roxburghshire). Obscurity surrounds the origins of Christianity in Scotland. They are traditionally associated with St Ninian, who was active during the 5th century, but we reach firmer ground in 563, when Columba founded his monastery on Iona. It was from this island off the west coast of Scotland that the Gospel was brought not only to Northumbria but to the Picts of Scotland itself. Ireland, Columba's place of origin, continued to be the missionary centre for Scotland throughout the Viking troubles, and the monastic structure of the Irish Church took root in Scotland as evangelization progressed.

It is understandable that, under the impulse of the monastic reforms of the 11th and 12th centuries and as a result of tighter ecclesiastical organization, new monasteries should have sprung up in the border country between the Solway Firth and the mouth of the Tweed. The Norman conquest of England and the concomitant trend towards centralization unleashed forces which were felt as far afield as Scotland. Shortly after 1066 the Anglo-Saxon princess Margaret married Malcolm Canmore, King of Scotland. Margaret, educated at the court of Hungary, wanted to wield a civilizing influence through the medium of monasteries. She brought Benedictines to Dunfermline, the Scottish royal capital, and a similar policy was pursued by her sons, notably David I (r. 1124–52), who founded a whole series of monasteries. He settled monks from Tiron at Selkirk while still a prince and summoned Cistercians from Rievaulx Abbey to Melrose in 1136. His Constable brought the Premonstratensians to Dryburgh four years later. David himself chose Augustinians from Beauvais to head the new priory at Jedburgh, which was founded in 1138 and promoted to abbatial status in 1152.

It was at this period that work began on the church which, for all its alterations and additions, and despite damage sustained during the Anglo-Scottish border wars, still presents such an impressive and homogeneous appearance today. Chancel and transept were the first to be built and used for divine office. Then came the nave, which was begun at the west end and extended until it met the crossing. The *west front (Pl. 147)* clearly dates from the late 12th century, when Romanesque veered in the direction of Gothic. The three small gables over the portal were once occupied by figures. Complete with corner-buttresses, blind arches and a central window, the wall above them culminates in a gable pierced by a rose window. The *west doorway (Pl. 148)* is recessed into the projecting surround, an example of the final Romanesque phase in which the carving of jambs and archivolts became almost exclusively geometrical. The *doorway of the south transept (Pl. 149)* is a peculiarly subtle product of this phase. Very little can be seen of the south transept itself or of the monastery buildings which once ran down to the river Jed. The north transept and crossing tower were rebuilt at the beginning of the 16th century.

Relics of the original Romanesque building include parts of the *south transept wall and the interior walls of the chancel (Pl. 150,* view from the north-west), which were bordered, chapel-fashion, by aisles of two spans. The massive piers display a remarkable tendency towards verticality. Stout demi-shafts rise to a height midway between gallery and clerestory, where they meet the springers of the round arches. This is reminiscent of Oxford (Christ Church) and Romsey *(Pl. 61),* buildings with which Jedburgh has other features in common. As to the arches, one gains the impression that they were a belated and somewhat unwelcome afterthought, added with reluctance because they frustrated the original intention to build a proud Norman nave with lofty aisles.

151-152 *Kelso Abbey* (Roxburghshire). Abbot (later Saint) Bernard, founder of the Benedictine reformist movement based on Tiron, near Chartres, died in the year 1117. In 1119 a group of monks from Tiron accepted King David's invitation to settle in Selkirk, and in 1128 they transferred their headquarters to Kelso, on the left bank of the Tweed. Unlike the Cistercians, who con-

centrated on agriculture, the Tironais esteemed the virtues of careful craftsmanship only slightly less than those of prayer. Kelso Abbey testifies to this, both in design and execution. Apart from a transept in the east, the aisled church possessed a second, western, transept with its own crossing tower and galilee, not unlike Ely in layout. Only traces of the west end survive, but even they suffice to convey the massive building of yore, which is one of the finest examples of Romanesque in Scotland.

Our photograph of the ruined *north arm of the west transept (Pl. 151,* view from the south-east) illustrates the articulation of the interior walls: the west wall, with enlaced blind arches projecting from the base, and, above them, round-arched windows and two arcaded wall-passages, the upper one in the form of a triforium; and the north wall, differentiated by the doorway at the foot and the fenestration at the top and endowed with greater emphasis by a deeper arcaded gallery. The compound pier at the foot of the ruined wall adjoins the entrance to the former north aisle. The nave piers have scalloped capitals, as the left-hand edge of our photograph shows. They are as squat as the arcade arches are ponderous, but the Romanesque compound piers of the crossing, three of which still stand, rise to a great height and lead, by way of pointed arches, to the massive tower. The tectonic qualities of the building are so manifest that sculptural adornment would have been superfluous.

The *north face of the west transept (Pl. 152)* displays sandstone ashlar-work of neat construction. An air of solidity emanates from the symmetry of the pilaster-like buttresses, plain round-arched windows, corner-shafts and projecting porch. Features such as the angled string course testify to a sense of form which is also evident in the rhythmical crescendo of the portal, with its archivolts, flat superstructure and shallow gable. The diagonal trellis-work on the latter recalls similar work on the north transept of St Etienne at Beauvais. The five loop-holes beneath the enlaced blind arches provided a view from the look-out chamber. Churches in border areas were indeed fortresses of God.

153-154 *Dunfermline Abbey* (Fife). The Benedictine monks who founded this monastery in 1074 were sent by Archbishop Lanfranc of Canterbury at the request of Queen Margaret of Scotland. The abbey was begun in 1128, on the site of their original church, but only the nave still stands, the transept and chancel having been demolished to make room for later additions. Designed as a burial-place for the Scottish kings, the building may already have been complete by the time it was consecrated in 1150—a remarkably swift piece of work. Its whole stylistic manner certainly supports this assumption.

The abbey is stern and subdued. This is apparent in the accentuation of the *north doorway (Pl. 153)*, which is exactly the same size as the window above it but slightly differentiated by its carved surround. The heavy buttresses on either side are additions of later date. In the *interior (Pl. 154,* looking north-east), severity becomes transformed into a monumentality which manifests itself in horizontal calm as opposed to vertical division. The arcade strides ponderously towards the chancel, its progress emphasized by the gallery string course. The nave is six bays long, and some of the massive drum-piers are enriched with zigzag or spiral fluting. Dunfermline's resemblances to Durham *(Pl. 163)* are as unmistakable as its points of difference. There is no alternation of piers, and everything is far simpler. The wall seems to be pierced by the gallery arches rather than built round them, and the ribbed soffits of the arcade look feeble in comparison with the robust masonry of the walls. The nave roof is exposed, whereas the aisles are rib-vaulted.

NORTHUMBRIA

155-156 *Lindisfarne Abbey* (Northumberland). The Lindisfarne Gospels, written *c.* 720, provide the most celebrated memorial to the monastic community which once flourished on this island off the north-east coast of England, long known as Holy Island. Less well-known but also of great value to historians of the Church and of art is the sarcophagus of St Cuthbert of Lindisfarne, who was ultimately laid to rest in Durham Cathedral. On Lindisfarne itself, all that can still be seen of its once far-famed and influential monastery—apart from the scattered stones, stelae and cross-shafts which have been unearthed in the ancient graveyard there—dates from after the Norman Conquest. The older relics bear witness to the early history of Northumbria and its conversion to Christianity at the beginning of the 7th century, after a period of fierce conflict.

The second book of Bede's history of the English Church reaches a climax in his account of the evangelization of Northumbria. However, Christian Northumbria did not attain its 7th- and early 8th-century prime until there had been a systematic alliance between Iro-Celtic and Roman Christianity. This was sponsored by Oswald, the legitimate ruler of Northumbria who lived in exile at Iona, Columba's island monastery, where he became familiar with Irish Christianity and the Irish tongue. Oswald (*c.* 605-42) at once summoned Irish monks from Iona and gave them the island of Lindisfarne as a base of operations. There, Bishop Aidan and his companions built a monastic settlement of the customary

type—isolated cells grouped round a building that was more an oratory than a church.

There was no doctrinal gulf between the Celtic Church of Ireland and the Roman Church, merely a difference of emphasis and a corresponding difference in organization. In principle, the Irish Church was monastic and the Roman Church episcopal. Bede held King Oswald and Bishop Aidan in the highest esteem, but their computation of the date of Easter, which obeyed Irish ecclesiastical tradition, impressed him as repugnant and almost sinful. The Synod of Whitby resolved this question in favour of Rome, and, consequently, of Bede himself, in the year 664, whereupon Colman, third Bishop of Lindisfarne, returned to his see and the Church of Northumbria became incorporated in the great Roman hierarchy. In 669 Theodore of Tarsus arrived from Rome to become Archbishop of Canterbury and assume the direction of the entire English Church. The latter proved strong enough, not only to preserve its identity despite this process of integration, but to become a genuine source of light in a Christian Europe which was lapsing into pre-Carolingian gloom. Such was the function and mission of Northumbria both before and after 700, and Lindisfarne, Wearmouth and Jarrow were its main centres.

Bede (*H.E.* III/25) records that Aidan's successor Finan (651) also erected a church on Lindisfarne, built not of stone but of split oak logs (cf. Greensted, *Pl. 24*) and thatched with reeds 'after the manner of the Irish'. Cuthbert, Bishop of Lindisfarne between 684 and 687, was a striver after sanctity who died a hermit on a small rocky island in the Farne group. He was buried in the monastery church, and his saintly reputation attracted pilgrims to Lindisfarne. The monastery became larger and more elaborate as it developed into a religious and cultural centre. However, Lindisfarne's greatest prime was merely a last effulgence before the onset of darkness. While a new cultural centre was taking shape round Charlemagne, Northumbria found itself threatened by sea-farers from the North, who made sporadic and unexpected raids in their long-ships. In 793 the island monastery was attacked, plundered and burned by Danish pirates. Although another church was built and furnished with the aid of pilgrims' donations, times remained uncertain. Menaced by wholesale Danish invasion in 875, the monks of Lindisfarne took the relics of St Cuthbert and roamed through England for seven years before settling at Chester-le-Street. A good century later the Danes ousted them yet again, and in 995 the monastic community moved to Durham. Fearful of the Normans, who were subduing the rebellious North, the monks returned to the island for a short time in the 11th century. Then, in 1083, Lindisfarne was bestowed on the Benedictines of

Durham as a filial establishment. St Cuthbert's relics remained in Durham, so the place was maintained by a mere handful of monks. It was the Benedictines who commissioned the new church of 1093, whose majestic ruins still present such an impressive spectacle today.

The abbey church stands off the mainland coast, built of red sandstone. It was an aisled building six bays long, with a transept and east apses, a crossing, and an unaisled apsidal chancel which was replaced in the middle of the 12th century by a three-bayed, square-ended chancel. The laiety used to enter the nave through a north door, and a south door provided access to the monastery buildings. The larger west door was only used on ceremonial occasions. Jutting from the centre of the row of blind arches which marked the height of the lower storey, the doorway is triple-stepped, has inset shafts, cushion capitals and sturdy archivolts adorned with zigzag, and was probably completed c. 1140. The round-arched window immediately above and cutting into the projecting porch is a later addition, as is the 14th-century heightening of the west wall with its two loopholes. By contrast, the large round-arched window immediately beneath the interior vaulting in the third stage of the wall (Pl. 155) is extremely fine. Supported by cylindrical shafts with cushion capitals, five round arches (the central one broader than the rest) open on to the nave from the wall-passage. This links the two side-tribunes and can be reached by way of spiral staircases in the two rectangular towers flanking the west front.

As a daughter-church, Lindisfarne Abbey clearly betrays the influence of Durham in its piers. Cruciform piers with engaged shafts alternate with drum-piers, the latter adorned, like those at Durham, with an engraved and over-sized chevron motif (Pl. 156). Triforium, clerestory windows and vaults have disappeared altogether, but one zigzag-adorned diagonal rib soars boldly from the massive compound pier at the north-west corner of the crossing to meet its counterpart in the south-east. The construction of this 'rainbow', as the islanders call it, enables one to date it at about the middle of the 12th century, which means that the church took almost half a century to build. However, Lindisfarne never regained the lustre which the monastery had enjoyed c. 700. By the 15th century, church and monastery buildings had become too large or were already in decay. Such serviceable premises as remained after the Dissolution were turned into store-rooms for the army on the Scottish border.

157 The dedicatory plaque which can still be seen in in the nave of *St Paul's, Jarrow* (Co. Durham) hails from the original building. The Latin inscription refers to a specific day in the year 685, but the original church has completely disappeared. The present building consists of three interconnected parts running from west to east: a reconstructed nave of 1866; a tower with two lower stages dating from c. 800 and a superstructure built by the Anglo-Saxon monk Aldwin shortly after 1074; and a chancel which used to be an independent chapel until it was linked to the main church by the crossing tower. The original church, which stood on the site of the present nave, was demolished in 1782. The above-mentioned chapel (forming the present chancel) dates from shortly after 700. It is constructed of hewn stone slabs, largely of Roman manufacture and taken from a Roman camp near South Shields, not far away. Our photograph ignores this conglomeration in favour of another, namely, a section of *wall from the monastery buildings of Aldwin's time*, with additions dating from various periods: restorer's improvements; a Late Gothic window, half-demolished; a Norman imitation of an Anglo-Saxon triangle-headed doorway; and various stones, many Roman, some Norman and possibly a few Anglo-Saxon—something of everything, in fact, and everything slightly forlorn.

The same applies to the surroundings of St Paul's as a whole. It is melancholy to see the present state of Jarrow, which used to be an even greater centre of religious activity than Lindisfarne or Wearmouth. It was at Jarrow that Bede studied and wrote—Bede, the only Englishman whom Dante (*Divine Comedy* X, 131) deemed worthy of a place in Paradise beside Boethius, Isidore of Seville, Petrus Lombardus, Albertus Magnus, and Thomas Aquinas. The years c. 700, when Bede was active, were dark years. True, the Merovingian kingdom had created a new central authority and brought greater order to Europe, but no true cultural centre had evolved since the downfall of Rome. The general way of life was more uncouth. Cities were falling into decay, feudal estates and serfs multiplying, alien races on the move. Christian Europe had dwindled to a narrow strip of territory pinned between the heathen Germanic tribes and Scandinavians of the north, who were constantly pushing southwards, and the steady advance of Islam. The Mohammedans threatened Byzantium, advanced along the shores of North Africa, overran the Visigothic kingdom of Spain, terrorized the French and harassed the Italians. Squeezed between Islam and the Lombards and abandoned by the Byzantines, the Pope sought assistance from the north. The focus of Christendom shifted towards Central and North-West Europe, whence, emanating principally from an island on the fringe of the Continent, came a strength which exerted a protective, unifying and reassuring effect. Only this can explain the unusual interest in English Christianity which

Rome evinced by sending Theodore of Tarsus to become Archbishop of Canterbury. Only an awareness of his responsibility towards the whole of Christendom could have endowed Bede with the quiet strength to become the greatest historian of his time, almost as though he wished to record everything in writing before the hour of doom struck.

Bede's parents sent him to school at Wearmouth c. 680, when he was seven. Having accompanied the abbot to Jarrow in 685, the year of its foundation, he remained there for the rest of his life. Two visits, one to Lindisfarne and another to York, were the extent of his travels, but he voyaged the world in spirit by reading all the books available to him. His world consisted of the Bible, chronicles, Lives of the Saints, letters, cosmologies, and bestiaries. On becoming a teacher he started to write books himself, first aids to general study, then works on chronology, the Calendar, and geography. Having, as it were, examined the world and its workings in treatises of this kind, Bede passed on to higher things. He wrote commentaries on the books of the Old and New Testaments, accompanying his notes on the Acts with a geographical glossary. His essays in exegesis inspired him with a wish to record the effects of Christianity in historical terms. He studied sources and sent to Rome for copies of papal edicts and correspondence. Sifting and arranging, seeking his material at first hand and always naming his authorities, he compiled the work which was to make him the father of English historical writing and one of the foremost historians of all time. He completed his *Historiae ecclesiasticae gentis Anglorum—(Ecclesiastical History of the English Nation)* in the year 731. Ever alert to world events and, though permanently resident in Jarrow, in touch with the outside world by letter and visitor, Bede had become increasingly devoted to a historical theology which saw all that happened in the world as God's handiwork and, consequently, as the ultimate purpose of all study, purification and self-improvement. He recorded his views in a treatise on the six world epochs, which he completed in 725 and which provided a foundation for most of the universal chronicles written during the Middle Ages. Bede believed that mankind stood on the verge of Christ's second coming—a view shared by other eminent men of his day.

In addition to pursuing scholarly activities, Bede consoled and stimulated his contemporaries with biographies of St Cuthbert and the abbots of Wearmouth and Jarrow. He was spurred on to further efforts by the best of his own pupils, who in their turn transmitted and developed what they had received at his hands. Through them, he became the first in a whole series of teachers who paved the way for and sustained the Carolingian renascence. One of Bede's pupils, Egbert, became Archbishop of York. It was in his comprehensive library that Alcuin acquired the training which was to enable him to become a teacher at the court school and adviser to Charlemagne. Bede died at Jarrow in 735. A poem by Hrabanus Maurus informs us that relics of Bede were already venerated in the crypt at Fulda by the early 9th century. His mortal remains were reportedly transferred to Durham in 1020, so Jarrow no longer possesses even the bones of the man whom posterity surnamed 'Venerabilis'.

158-159 The aisled chancel of *Hexham Priory* (Northumberland) is characteristic of the Transitional style of c. 1200, whereas the transept and crossing exemplify the Early Gothic style of the early 13th century. The builders were Augustinian monks. Their original conception was grandiose, but it could never be realized in full because everything came to a halt after the disastrous Scottish onslaught of 1296. Hexham had already sustained one crippling blow in 875, when the Danes rowed up the Tyne and burned down the massive church which had been started two centuries earlier by Bishop Wilfrid. It is as though the early vicissitudes of the see of Hexham exerted a continuing influence on all that happened subsequently. First came Wilfrid, a strong individualist who, as spokesman of the Roman faction at the Synod of Whitby, made his mark by fiercely attacking the Iro-Celtic Church and its ritual (Bede, *H. E.* III/25). Archbishop Theodore installed him as Bishop of Northumbria after the Synod. Wilfrid at first brought great difficulties upon himself as a result of a long absence on the Continent, and quarrelled with the Archbishop. Exiled, he did missionary work among the South Saxons of England. After further controversy, more exile, and appeals to the Pope in Rome, the courageous but dogmatic priest evinced a willingness to compromise. He became Abbot of Ripon, with responsibility for the diocese of Hexham, and remained so until his death in 709. Wilfrid commissioned churches at York, Ripon and Hexham—three in the latter town, including the diocesan church with its impressive crypt.

The walls of this crypt were constructed of stones brought from Corstopitum, the former Roman camp not far away to the east. The marks of Roman stonemasons' tools can be seen here and there, as well as fragments of carved foliage and inscriptions and some hewn Roman stones which were incorporated as they stood. After descending a flight of steps leading from the centre of the nave, pilgrims entered an obliquely situated barrel-vaulted chamber measuring 9 ft by 4 ft 3 ins. From here, undoubtedly through a grille, they gained a view of the *main chamber of the crypt (Pl. 158)*, also barrel-vaulted but oriented and measuring 13 ft 9 ins by 8 ft 4 ins. This was where the relics collected by Wilfrid were displayed. To the north of the antechamber was another small chamber with a pointed ceiling composed of angled slabs of stone. From here, running eastwards beside the main chamber, then turning north and east once more, passages and steps led upwards and probably emerged into the open. These passages were illuminated by lights let into small niches in the wall. Another similarly angled and stepped passage leading out of yet another small antechamber enabled priests to gain access to the church from the relic-chamber. Unlike the main entrance, the pilgrims' egress and priests' ascent were blocked by later additions to the church. The passages themselves are spanned by large horizontal slabs of stone.

This series of subterranean passages and chambers, though commonly termed a crypt, would be more aptly described as a 'confessio'. This would differentiate it more clearly from crypts proper, that is to say, subterranean places of worship of the Repton type (Derbyshire, c. 698), which also occur on the Continent in areas evangelized by Iro-Celtic missionaries. Wilfrid, on the other hand, deliberately built a form of confessio which was influenced by the design of the Roman catacombs. Both types grew closer together during the Early Romanesque period until they ultimately merged.

At Hexham, the confessio is situated beneath the nave and immediately off the transept. Wilfrid's original church, of which few other traces remain, may possibly have had a square-ended chancel which only extended as far as the present crossing. Probably situated due east of this was a second small chapel terminating in an apse. Most of its foundations were identified beneath the crossing and chancel at the beginning of the present century, but their precise extent has yet to be ascertained. On the floor of the present chancel, just in front of the apex of the old apse, stands a *bishop's throne (Pl. 159)* which may date from Wilfrid's time. Hewn out of a single block of stone and unadorned save for grooves and enlaced bands which accentuate its simple lines, the ancient stone seat makes a majestic and dignified impression, and the men who occupied it must indeed have been fountainheads of authority. The traditional name for this stone throne was 'frith', or chair of peace. It was said to be associated with the law whereunder any fugitive within a radius of roughly one mile (marked by crosses) was protected from attack on pain of severe punishment until he could present his case and secure his rights.

160-166 *Durham Cathedral* (Co. Durham). The city of Durham owes its existence to the monks of Lindisfarne,

who, after long years of wandering with the relics of St Cuthbert and the head of the sainted King Oswald, finally settled on a rocky horseshoe of land enclosed by the river Wear. That was in the year 995. Durham's fame is attributable to the Normans, who started work on the new cathedral abbey in 1093, under their second bishop, William of Calais, later William de Carileph. Ten years earlier, in 1083, William had summoned Benedictines from Wearmouth and Jarrow to administer this major centre of pilgrimage and monasticism. With its aisled nave, aisled chancel, east-aisled transept, crossing tower, twin west towers and narthex, Durham was one of the most magnificent cathedrals in Western Europe. Spanning the tongue of land high above the steep and wooded banks of the river, it symbolized not only the Normans' strict consolidation and reorganization of the Church but also, in company with the castle which guarded the landward side of the horseshoe, their inflexible control over their subjects and their determination to guard the Scottish marches. Though frequently threatened, Durham never fell.

William de Carileph wanted a cathedral church which would stand comparison with any other. Work was already in progress on St Albans, Canterbury, Winchester, Rochester, Old Sarum, Gloucester, Lincoln, Ely, and other cathedrals and abbeys. As a Frenchman, William was familiar with the churches of Jumièges and Caen, and he wanted his cathedral at Durham to equal, if not surpass, all others of its kind. The ambition of these energetic Norman monk-bishops was boundless, even though it stemmed less from egotism than from a sense of mission. William's grand design not only became reality: the bulk of it still stands, majestic and awe-inspiring, to this day.

William died in 1096, three years after building began, but others continued his work. The chancel, apses, crossing and transept were almost completed by 1099, and St Cuthbert's remains could be ceremonially laid to rest in the east end when the cathedral was consecrated in 1104. Durham was not only one of the most splendid buildings produced in the West at the turn of the 11th and 12th centuries, but an extremely modern building for its period. It displayed what no other cathedral yet possessed in anything like the same majestic profusion, namely, ribbed vaults: over the chancel (choir aisles 1096, choir itself 1104) and over the north transept (1110). Durham thus became the first manifestation of a structural idea which paved the way for the Gothic cathedral.

When the chancel was consecrated, only the first bay of the nave and the arches of the second bay had been completed, so as to support the crossing. By 1133 the vaulted nave and the lower storeys of the west towers were finished. The whole of this vast edifice was constructed within a mere forty years—a period which, in France, witnessed the building of churches at Angoulême and Paray-le-Monial, St Lazare at Autun, large parts of Vézelay, and, above all, the third church at Cluny; in Spain, substantial sections of Santiago de Compostela; and, in Norman Apulia, S. Nicola at Bari. To quote a few more milestones in the structural history of Durham Cathedral, which was largely built of local stone from Kepier on the Wear: the narthex followed in 1175 and the west towers were completed in 1226. Early in the 13th century, cracks appeared in the ribbed vaults of *c.* 1100 which boldly spanned the choir and choir aisles. They were demolished, together with the Romanesque east end, the two rectangularly walled side-apses, and the main apse (whose foundations are still visible today). A bay with a pointed arch was annexed to the two round-arched bays of the choir, the pure Gothic east transept with its nine altars added, and the choir-loft and choir-vaults reconstructed. This work was completed in 1280. The monastery buildings continued to be augmented from 1093 until well into the 16th century. The monastery itself was dissolved in 1539, but the main fabric of the church preserved its remarkable homogeneity. It remained Romanesque in conception, although changes were made in fenestration and its proportions somewhat distorted by the crossing tower. Completed in 1262 but damaged by lightning in 1429, this was rebuilt between 1470 and 1490. It is well over 200 ft high—too high, almost—and a lasting memorial to the lord bishops of Durham.

When studying the *Romanesque west towers (Pl. 162,* view from the south-east with the cloister in the foreground), we should ignore the battlements of 1801 and, in our imagination, substitute pyramidal roofs of Romanesque design. The four richly ornamented upper stages, with their alternation of tall blind arches and window apertures, are an expression of Early Gothic but fully attuned to the predetermining Romanesque keynote of the whole. The plinth-stage dates from the church's consecration in 1133 and harmonizes with the fabric of the Romanesque nave, though the south wall was refaced in the 19th century and some unexciting tracery inserted in the cloister windows in 1827. Above the west range of the cloister lies the new dormitory (built *c.* 1400) where the wooden coffin of St Cuthbert and many other treasures belonging to the former monastery are now on display.

The north door and main entrance of the cathedral, though much altered by Wyatt in the late 18th century, still bears the original *bronze door-knocker (Pl. 160),* of which only the enamel eyes are missing. This massive piece is the work of a master with a superlative sense of composition. Framed by solar rays resembling a lion's mane, the skull, brows and cheeks are so elaborately stylized that the monster looks positively real. One can detect an intrinsic resemblance to the more or less contemporary beasts at Kilpeck *(Pl. 105)* in that the forces of evil are conveyed by a combination of human nose, devil's ears, lion's jaws, and serpentine ring. Scandinavian influence is not present in isolation, however. The corona or lion's mane is itself an echo of Mediterranean motifs, e.g. those on the bronze doors of Bohemund I's funerary chapel at Canosa di Puglia. The ties between England and Norman Apulia were strong in those days. In view of the Insular bronze-work tradition, however, it is probable that the piece originated in England.

The *nave (Pl. 163)* comprises six bays from the north door to the crossing, two of them within the scope of the west towers. The dimensions of the nave, which is 201 ft long, 39 ft wide and 73 ft high, stand in a simple relationship to one another. This interrelationship between individual members is apparent throughout the building and represents one reason for the remarkable effect created by the interior. For all the bulk of its constituent parts, the church as a whole does not dwarf man but lends dignity and poise to his relationship with the divine. The arcade arches are enormous, yet their proportions seem to harmonize with those of the gallery and clerestory. Framed by an alternation of piers, the nave progresses from compound pier to compound pier with the natural rhythm of quiet breathing, punctuated only by the intervening drum-piers. The ribbed vaults with their soaring, curved diagonals and slightly pointed transverse ridge-ribs pursue their measured course above the wall-shafts.

The walls are divided into three stages. The arcade arches are surmounted by twin-arched gallery openings with inset shafts and cushion capitals, each double arch being enclosed by a round arch of two orders. At the top come the five-part openings in front of the clerestory windows, each consisting of a wide central arch flanked by two pairs of shallower arches with inset shafts and cushion capitals. All the arches are roll-moulded, grooved, denticulated, or adorned with zigzag. The compound piers, which are really solid square sections of wall with demi-shafts corresponding to the various arches and diagonal or transverse ribs, are engaged with groups of semicircular shafts which rise to meet the ceiling vaults. Above the cylindrical piers in the intermediate zones the ribs rest on corbels alone. Precisely where the vaults meet the nave walls, their thrust is absorbed by arches beneath the roof of the triforium. Foreshadowing the Gothic flying buttress in function, if not appearance, they were the first of their kind to be built in England, and show the architect of Durham to have been an outstanding technician. Designed from the outset to be vaulted in stone, the cathedral was one of the most architecturally progressive buildings in Western Europe.

The *drum-piers (Pl. 164,* oblique view from the north aisle into the south aisle) are a characteristic feature of the building. Like the tall square bases on which they rest, the piers are constructed of hewn stones which were accurately dressed before erection. The height of these stone cylinders, 22 ft, is almost identical with their circumference. The capitals are massive blocks of stone—cushion capitals, fundamentally, but octagonal at the top and circular below, the transition being effected by means of escutcheon-shaped lunettes. Above the capitals—somewhat abruptly—rise the arcade arches and ribs, some moulded and others adorned with zigzag. The drum-piers may well have been painted at one time, but their main decoration is incised. Three forms of ornamentation are in evidence: comparatively fine fluting, a lozenge pattern with double lines and intersections, and a bold horizontal chevron or zigzag. This motif is found elsewhere in the building, e.g. on the arcade arches, transverse and diagonal ribs, and doorways. It is, in fact, Durham's basic ornamental motif, and the south pier of the north transept, completed shortly before 1104, displays the earliest example of it in England. From Durham, the zigzag band and its manifold variants became disseminated throughout English 12th-century Romanesque. A second architectural ornament makes its first appearance at Durham—yet another indication of the avant-garde character of the building—though it is not of English origin. This is the series of enlaced blind arches which occupies most of the wall below the aisle windows.

The *narthex (Pl. 165),* also known as the 'galilee' because of its association with the Easter procession, is a particularly elegant west vestibule of a type found at Vézelay. Built some decades after the main fabric, it was probably completed *c.* 1175. Bishop Hugh de Puiset, or Pudsey, had originally intended to add a Lady Chapel to the east end of the cathedral. Deterred by problems connected with the laying of foundations, he decided to build in the west instead, even though the precipitous terrain posed problems of its own. A west entrance was out of the question, so the doorway was sited on the north side. The narthex houses the tomb of Bede, whose remains were stolen from Jarrow and transferred to Durham in 1022. They have lain interred in the narthex since 1370, marked by an inscription which reads: 'Haec sunt in fossa Bedae Venerabilis ossa'. Their surroundings are not only worthy of them but magnificent. The narthex is a rectangular chamber divided into five aisles each of four bays. The arches are adorned with a bold chevron motif. The tapering spandrels and gracefully

curved capitals invest the junction of columns and upper walls with an airy elegance which is enhanced by the apparent weightlessness of the zigzag arches. Circular bases on rectangular plinths complete the vertical and supporting members, which now consist of four clustered columns, two of pale local stone and two of dark Purbeck marble. The pale columns had to be inserted in the 15th century, when buttresses were added to the west wall and the ceilings of the aisles heightened in order to reinforce the fragile structure. The appearance of the interior was originally determined by the pairs of dark columns alone.

The *Prior's Portal (Pl. 166),* situated immediately beside the south transept and leading from the nave into the east range of the cloister, was probably completed by 1104, though the archivolts with their multiplicity of abstract motifs were not inserted until after Bishop Pudsey's time. Isolated sections recall the articulation of the south wall of the chapter-house at Much Wenlock *(Pl. 116),* and there are understandable affinities with the large and elaborately enriched doorway which leads into Bishop Pudsey's hall in Durham Castle.

167 As a castle proper, *Durham Castle* (Co. Durham) goes back to the time of Waltheof, the Anglo-Saxon Earl of Northumberland who quarrelled with his new Norman sovereign in 1075. The native earl's prerogatives then passed to a bishop installed by the Normans. Extensive improvements, of which the main door, passages and great hall still survive, though with modifications, were made by Bishop Pudsey, whose residence the castle was.

The *chapel (Pl. 167),* which dates from the earliest phase, or late in the 11th century, has been carefully restored. We were not, however, permitted to take a new photograph. The flight of steps visible in the foreground has disappeared, though the entrance remains. Six cylindrical columns divide the smallish rectangular chamber into three aisles which are spanned by groined vaults of uniform height with sturdy transverse arches. Light entered the room via two splayed windows in the north wall. Of special note are the capitals, which exhibit the earlier form of volute (cf. *Pl. 21*). These are elaborately carved in a lapidary style which conveys its message in an exemplary manner, by means of isolated plants, flowers, fruit, monsters, heads and corner-figures, rather than scenically. The handsome Tree of Life on the extreme north-east capital faces in the direction of the altar. The chapel was probably completed in 1075, no less than a century before Bishop Pudsey's narthex.

168 The *parish church at Houghton-le-Spring* (Co. Durham) is dedicated to St Michael and All Angels. This

327

highly individual tympanum, situated above the sacristy door and beneath a simple toothed arch, portrays two entwined monsters surrounded by foliage. From each of the serpentine bodies sprout two hoofed legs, two wings, and a cock's head with comb. They are basilisks, or, as their name conveys 'little kings' of the serpent world. The composition harks back to Iro-Celtic originals, and the stonemason undoubtedly had illuminated books to work from. The basic idea was to warn Christians on the church threshold of the menacing activities of evil spirits in the outside world. Bestiaries, nourished on the 89th Psalm, the Book of Job, and Revelations, provided the raw material for this exercise of the imagination. In this tympanum, which probably dates from *c.* 1200, everything has become lighter and more frivolous. Its very freedom endows it with decorative charm, though the slight uncertainty evident in its composition indicates that a minor artist was at work. The style of carving is typically Insular.

169 The *stone cross in St Helen's, Church Kelloe* (Co. Durham), is the one surprising feature of this small and secluded church. 6 ft high, $15^1/_2$ ins wide and $5^1/_2$ ins deep, it differs entirely, not only from the crosses of Ireland but from those at Gosforth and Ruthwell *(Pl. 120* and *121).* The shaft bears scenes relating to the legendary discovery of the Cross by the patroness of the church, St Helen, whom Jacobus de Voragine included in the compilation of legends (1273) which later became renowned under the name *Legenda Aurea.* The uppermost scene depicts the dream of Emperor Constantine, who was visited by an angel before the battle of the Milvian Bridge. 'Look above you!' the angel commanded. 'And he looked up, and saw a shining cross in heaven, and on it, in golden letters, was written: In hoc signo vinces.' These four words are engraved on the horizontal arms of the cross. The central scene shows Empress Helena conversing with another crowned woman carrying a cross, presumably a personification of the Church. The third scene combines two occurrences. Helena, holding a sword, compels Judas to indicate with his spade the spot where Christ's cross is buried. At the same time, we are shown the triumphal cross itself, set with mirabilia and flanked by the sun and moon, its authenticity vouched for by the miraculous revival of the youth on the bier. The richly draped robes are a striking feature, and their upswept hems accord with court fashions in the East Mediterranean area *c.* 1190. Other symptoms of Byzantine influence and echoes of the Crusades can also be perceived. We are left with the problem of how a work without parallel elsewhere in England should have appeared in County Durham. Given that the area is noted for its figured crosses, however, it is not beyond

the bounds of possibility that this theme, coloured by Near Eastern influences, should once more, at the very end of the 12th century, have become crystallized in a votive cross.

170 The *parish church of St Lawrence at Pittington* (Co. Durham), which displays components of varying date, is noteworthy in two respects. In the first place, it has a very richly ornamented *north arcade* with an alternation of piers influenced by Durham (our photograph shows them from the east, facing the tower). The ornamentation, which in the case of the drum-piers at Durham *(Pl. 163)* was incised, is here raised in an elaborately serpentine manner characteristic of Late Romanesque. The same elaboration is evident in the chevron-adorned arcade arches, which are closely related to Bishop Pudsey's narthex at Durham *(Pl. 165).* (Pittington was another of Pudsey's residences.) The second noteworthy feature is that the Pudsey arches were let into an existing wall so that they cut into the splayed round-arched windows above them. (The clerestory windows are a later addition.) The exposed masonry of the lower storey of the tower, with its incongruous Early Gothic arch, as well as the style of the round-arched windows, indicates that the original building should be dated in the third quarter of the 11th century; that is to say, after the battle of Hastings but before the Normans had been able to exert any formative influence on the unruly population of Northern England. Anglo-Saxons were still at work in this remote area. It was not until about 1175 that this largely homogeneous world was boldly invaded by Norman influence and the Norman love of rich architectural ornamentation.

171 This *fragmentary sculpture in the parish church of St Andrew at Bishop Auckland* (Co. Durham) is one of several cross-shaft components preserved there. The foliage on the sides is inhabited by birds, four-legged animals, and an archer. The scenes on the face and reverse are bordered with cable-moulding and portray Christ, angels, and disciples. A Crucifixion scene shows Christ bound with ropes after the manner of Irish crosses. The Bishop Auckland cross is not far removed in date from the cross at Ruthwell *(Pl. 121),* to judge by its related foliage, and probably originated *c.* 800, but the relief style is shallower and the figures more frontal and less dramatic. Those who term them barbaric would seem to be guilty of misinterpretation. On the contrary, the figures are poised and their gestures calm, while their robes are draped in so stylized a way that they might have been drawn in gold on a dark ground. Herein, too, lies the probable reason for the stylistic contrast between the figurative reliefs and the foliage on the sides. The former were the work of an Insular stonemason who translated icons of Near Eastern origin—possibly Syrian or Byzantine—into stone. Hence the frontality and inherent symmetry of the angels and disciples, a symmetry which aimed at balance rather than uniform weight. We can deduce that icons came to England from the nature of Benedict Biscop's work at Monkwearmouth.

172-173 *St John's, Escomb* (Co. Durham) dates from the beginning of the 8th century and is the best-preserved church in the Jarrow-Monkwearmouth group. It is thus of particular importance to the history of ecclesiastical architecture, both in England and at large. Bede's statement that Benedict Biscop imported stonemasons from Gaul cannot be doubted, but the proportions of these churches—long, narrow, and tall—are typically Anglo-Saxon. Escomb's elongated rectangular nave measures 43 ft 6 ins by 14 ft 9 ins, and the inset chancel is roughly 10 ft square. The exposed roof has been restored. Alterations to the original fabric include the removal of a west end which may not have been there from the very first but certainly existed in Anglo-Saxon times. The south porch was added in the 12th century. Narrow lancet windows were let into the nave and choir during the 13th century and three very large windows inserted in the south wall, west wall and choir during the 19th. Since Bede makes no reference to the church whatsoever, it must have been either unconnected with any specific historical event or—an equally tenable theory—not built until after 737. No reference to the church's history occurs elsewhere, either, but its very seclusion may be responsible for its remarkable state of preservation. The church itself delves far back into history. Many of its stones are of Roman origin and were probably procured from the former Roman camp at Binchester (Vinovia), north of the Wear. One can still discern Roman inscriptions and the hatch-marks made by Roman stonemasons' tools. The ashlar blocks are large except in the upper courses, and it is conceivable that subsequent, though still Anglo-Saxon, restoration work was carried out, possibly after the roof caught fire. The massive quoins are laid in the long-and-short manner. In the centre of the *south wall (Pl. 172)* can be seen what is probably the earliest surviving Anglo-Saxon sun-dial, complete with figurative decoration (serpent, animal's head).

The five original windows are very small, but their interior surrounds are widely splayed. The west window is situated in the gable-end about 26 ft up, whereas the four windows in the side walls are roughly 13 ft from the ground. The two on the south side are surmounted by large slabs of stone whose lower edges are hewn into round arches, the two on the north side by rectangular lintels. The north face was originally pierced by a pair of rectangular entrances, but the one leading into the chancel—probably the later of the two—is now blocked up. These entrances are notable for their mode of construction. The jambs, consisting of stone slabs laid long-and-short, converge slightly like the porch at Clonfert *(Pl. 137)*.

Escomb is representative not only of Roman masonry but of Roman building techniques as well. Roman influence is clearly discernible in the construction of the *chancel arch (Pl. 173)*, with its radiating voussoirs, and there is something to be said for the theory that it was brought in toto from a Roman building at Vinovia. However, the jambs of this impressive arch, with their alternation of horizontal and vertical slabs, are not only decidedly Anglo-Saxon but so typical that similar examples are referred to as stonemasonry in the 'Escomb manner'. Had the proportions and lighting of the interior not been impaired by an excessively large 19th-century window, the chancel arch would make an even stronger impact. If, in addition, one visualizes the interior simply painted, as it originally was, one can still feel transported into the days of Northumbria's prime.

174-177 The founding of *Fountains Abbey* (Yorkshire) is associated with the decline of monastic discipline which set in when Cluny and its thousand monasteries had become too large, opulent and pretentious. Bernard of Clairvaux (1090-1153), who vehemently opposed this pomp and enervation, led an exemplary and strictly monastic life in company with a group of friends. From Cîteaux, he founded Clairvaux in 1115, and, as its abbot, became the central figure of the new Cistercian reform movement. The first Cistercian monastery in England was founded at Waverley (Surrey) in 1128. Others followed. In 1132, as a protest against persistent negligence in the fulfilment of monastic vows, Benedictines from St Mary's Abbey in York moved out into the lonely Skell Valley, south-west of Ripon, and built themselves huts and oratories of wattle. Such were the origins of Fountains Abbey, which became the most splendid monastic centre in England. The 'black' Benedictines solicited enrolment in the 'white' monastic order of Clairvaux, and Bernard of Clairvaux sent the monk Godefroi to instruct and assist them. When Hugo, the wealthy Dean of York, joined the group in 1135, resources became available for the construction of a church and monastery buildings.

Though abandoned since 1539 and now in ruins, Fountains Abbey presents a fascinating picture in its setting of trees and well-tended lawns. The entire complex—church, cloister, chapter-house, monastery premises, guest-house and extensive infirmary buildings—was completed within a few decades. Indigenous stonemasons worked under Godefroi's supervision, probably guided by plans brought from Clairvaux. The buildings there have disappeared, but the next-oldest Cistercian monastery in France, Fontenay (1139–47), still exists, and Fountains Abbey resembles it in many respects. The aisled church has a square-ended chancel and a transept with three square-ended chapels on each arm. French Cistercian churches eschewed towers on principle, only one bell being permitted, but Fountains Abbey adhered to Norman custom by allowing itself a low crossing tower of square design. This no longer stands, unlike the north tower which was erected in 1520, shortly before the dissolution. The simple east end, of which little is known, was replaced during the first half of the 13th century by a broad twin-'naved' east transept designed to accommodate nine altars—an Early Gothic architectural idea imitated by Durham. The first and most active structural phase, which produced the church, cloister and chapter-house, was probably complete by c. 1170.

The *church and monastery buildings (Pl. 175*, west aspect) convey single-minded concentration on the task in hand, namely, the construction of a compact city of God in a quiet and secluded valley. All the roofs are missing. Instead of round windows, the west front of the church displays the huge void of the Late Gothic window which was inserted in 1494. The west door provides the sole accent in an otherwise plain façade broken only by shallow buttresses and string courses. There is an air of majesty about this doorway, with its five-shafted jambs projecting and receding in rhythmical alternation beneath arches moulded with dignified restraint. The narthex which used to stand in front of it had stone arches, whereas the narthex at Fontenay was timber-built. The church is faced with well-dressed ashlar blocks taken from a quarry a short distance away to the north, and the same devotion to fine craftsmanship is apparent throughout the building.

The ground floor of the wing which extends to the south of the church contained vaulted store-chambers and the refectory of the lay brothers, whose sleeping quarters were on the floor above. In order to exclude the custodian's house, which would otherwise appear in our photograph, we have been obliged to show only twelve of the twenty windows in the austere face of this upper storey. The whole wing is over 300 ft long—longer than many cathedrals—and the sturdy ribbed vaults supported by the nineteen piers running down the centre of the cellarium and dormitorium present an imposing picture.

Beyond this wing and to the east lies the cloister, flanked on the south by a kitchen, a refectory and a warming-room with fireplace, and on the east by library rooms and other premises, residential quarters, and, last but not least, the chapter-house. Nothing has survived of the cloister proper, but the 'white' monks' renunciation of architectural adornment renders it probable that this consisted of a covered way built of timber only. However, the three massive *chapter-house entrances (Pl. 176)* and the fourth, or parlatorium, entrance all bear witness to the spiritual strength which animated the Cistercians. They did not strive after erudition, but sought divine peace through a manly renunciation of the world. Their aim was fulfilment of monastic vows, the celebration of divine office, and, in general, the performance of the opus Dei, which included nursing the sick and reconquering the Holy Land at risk of life and limb. The *interior of the chapter-house (Pl. 177)* was divided into three aisles each of six bays and had a rib-vaulted ceiling. The building was completed some time after 1160. South of it were the monks' sleeping quarters and sanitary facilities, the latter situated above the little river, and to the east lay the abbot's residence. Down-valley, beside the water, stood the separate group of buildings comprising the infirmary and its various offices—all remarkably neat and modern for their period. Extending due south of the church, the premises listed above provided accommodation for hundreds of monks, lay brothers, agricultural workers, and shepherds.

The *church (Pl. 174)* was reserved for monks and lay brothers only. Entering it today and seeing the eleven-bayed arcade of pointed arches stretching away beneath the unadorned walls with their string courses and clerestory windows—as in this westward-facing view from the transept—one cannot fail to be profoundly impressed by the purposeful unity of the place, by the deliberate submission to a grand design evident in the heavy cylindrical piers which still rise, solid and secure, from the floor of the nave. The pointed arches were dictated by structural considerations alone, not born of the Gothic spirit. Behind each of them, between the nave and outer walls, was a pointed-arched vault designed to give the aisles greater depth, as at Fontenay—a characteristic feature of Cistercian buildings and probably of Burgundian origin. The line of demarcation between each vault was provided by round-headed transverse arches resting on scalloped capitals. Discernible on the aisle side of each pier and rising to the height of the scalloped capitals are two demi-shafts whose function is not immediately obvious. There was no gallery, and it was left to a string course to provide horizontal accentuation. Another ledge runs round the massive round-arched windows of the clerestory, incorporating them in the general scheme. The nave was not vaulted, so the thrust of the aisle vaults met no corresponding resistance and caused the walls of the nave to slope inwards.

Fountains Abbey is an expression of pure architecture, devoid of enrichment, bare of sculpture or figurative painting, ascetic in manner, crystalline in its structural clarity, and born of a desire to attain the spirituality so uncompromisingly demanded by Bernard of Clairvaux. Like the pointed arches and ribbed vaults of Durham, which were conceived in the Romanesque spirit, the church of Fountains Abbey, though still a product of the Romanesque mentality, stands on the threshold of Gothic.

178-179 *Rievaulx Abbey* (Yorkshire) was the second great Cistercian monastery in England. It owed its foundation in 1131 directly to Clairvaux, and its first abbot, William, was one of Bernard's closest associates. Like Fountains Abbey *(Pl. 174)* a trifle after it, the church was typically Cistercian in layout and construction: an aisled nave with an arcade of pointed arches, rib-vaulted aisles with transverse arches, a transept without a crossing tower but with three square-ended chapels on each arm, and a square-ended chancel. Little survives of the original church, which was built between 1131 and 1150. Most of what remains—the *chancel, refectory (Pl. 179)* and other monastery buildings—dates from the second or Early Gothic structural phase of 1225-1240, a time when the monastery housed several hundred monks and lay brothers and when other foundations in addition to Fountains Abbey were in full flower.

Thanks to the topography of the Rye Valley, the builders of Rievaulx had to refrain from orienting their church in the normal way. They swivelled it southwards, so that the nave-side *wall of the transept (Pl. 178)*—in liturgical terms, the west wall—actually faced north. The lower sections of this original Romanesque wall were left intact during the rebuilding carried out in the 13th century. The transformation is particularly evident in the north arm of the transept (in reality, the east arm) on the left of our photograph, where the boundary between original fabric and Gothic improvement runs through the centre of the windows and is marked by the use of paler stone.

180 *Arcade capital in Holy Trinity, Stonegrave* (Yorkshire). A few fragmentary carvings survive from the early, 10th-century phase, when a small monastery of Irish foundation still existed here. Parts of the nave walls probably date from shortly before the Conquest. Norman stonemasons transformed the church c. 1140, notably by piercing the nave walls to form an arcade. Too much of the church was subjected to drastic restoration in 1863, but the north arcade with its cylindrical shafts and chamfered red-and-white sandstone arches— not uninfluenced by Durham—still displays capitals as noteworthy as the one illustrated here. The stonemason must have been conversant with oriental textile designs, because his motifs include Syrian rosettes, Trees of Life—even a mermaid adorning her person. The latter's inverted position may have been intended as punishment for her vanity.

181-183 *Capitals in the crypt of St Peter's Cathedral, York* (York Minster). As Bede recounts at length *(H.E. I/29; II/9-14, 16-17)*, the Christian tradition of York goes back to Easter Day in the year 627, when Paulinus, a missionary sent by Pope Gregory the Great, baptized King Edwin of Northumbria and his entire court.

When work began on the present Gothic minster in 1230, the site had already been occupied by four previous churches, the last one a Norman church which had been given a new choir and a crypt during the latter half of the 12th century. Apart from the core of the walls, only the crypt has survived.

Ribbed vaults span this extensive crypt. The capitals between the roll-moulded ribs and cylindrical shafts have annulets and octagonal abaci. They represent a late phase in Romanesque sculpture and originated c. 1170. Although produced by at least two stonemasons and of variable quality, they are wholly Romanesque in conception. Both figurative and floral reliefs are vividly carved, but there is something French about the floral capitals *(Pl. 181 and 183)*, whereas the capital with the row of figures *(Pl. 182)* is more Insular in approach. They have no connection with the school of sculpture associated with the Benedictine Abbey of St Mary, also in York.

184 *Sculpture of the Virgin and Child in the crypt of York Minster*. About 3 ft tall and mounted on the wall of the crypt, this piece is of much greater artistic merit than the capitals *(Pl. 181-183)* and occupies a unique position in English sculpture. It portrays an enthroned Virgin and Child, a version of the Byzantine Hodegetria. The material is an almost black stone from the quarries at Tadcaster, not far from York. Although this proves that it was indigenous work, the question of whether it was produced by a native or itinerant foreign stonemason remains unanswered, and datings vary widely.

The precise nature of the spatial relationship between mother and child cannot be ascertained because of lacunae, but we know that the Virgin once wore a crown. She sits facing the front, presenting the Child to the beholder. The Child, who probably faced the front too, in Hodegetria style, raises its right hand in benediction. Its left hand probably held a scroll rather than the Book of the Law. It is not actually seated on its mother's left knee but seems to float above it. The Virgin's left hand probably supported the Child's back, while her right arm clearly passes beneath its knees and was doubtless cupped over its body in an expressive manner. What was required of the sculptor was divine representation, not mundane realism. This colours the whole style of the piece, which is characterized by a lively interplay between abstraction and naturalism. The contours of drapery and hems, which consist mainly of double lines, were simultaneously objective and ornamental. The Child's feet and benedictory hand seem doubly close to reality by comparison.

In contrast to the tendency of Anglo-Saxon sculptors towards plastic development in serried, superimposed layers, this important piece of sculpture displays a spatial development which was rooted in Continental ideas. Its author was probably an Englishman, but one who had travelled. His approach was manifestly individual but based on Continental Romanesque exemplars—principally, it may be assumed, South French works of the first half of the 12th century, a phase in which pronounced linearity became compounded with an increasingly naturalistic treatment of the human body.

LINDSEY AND CENTRAL ENGLAND

185 *St Peter's, Barton-upon-Humber* (Lincolnshire) is the more important of the two spacious medieval churches in this small harbour town. To the west of its Gothic nave stand a tower and fore-building dating from before 1000. Inside the tower, the walls are pierced to east and west by two massive arches. On the west face of the east arch, beneath the tower, is a sculptured head of Christ Crucified which was probably continued in painting. This marks the east arch of the tower as a triumphal arch and the interior of the tower as part of the interior of the original church. The tower itself, which is one of the earliest examples of English church architecture, has a neatly constructed ashlar-work belfry-stage, probably built shortly before 1100. Its height, including the latter, is about 70 ft. If we ignore the superstructure and Gothic nave, we can visualize the building as it originally was: a typical three-celled church of the late 10th century. It has been possible to identify the foundations of the chancel which was obliterated by the Gothic nave. The west fore-building may, to judge by the greater irregularity of its rubble masonry, have originated somewhat earlier than the tower. In its west wall is a blocked door surmounted by two round windows of contemporary design. The west quoins are laid long-and-short. The rather clumsy construction of the windows on the north and south sides is clearly apparent.

The composition of the outer walls of the tower is of special interest. A round-arched doorway can be seen on the south side, illustrated here, whereas the sturdy doorway on the north side, now blocked up, has a triangular head composed of large obliquely laid slabs. There are pairs of corresponding windows on each side, triangle-headed above and round-arched below. The inner arches of the latter are monolithic and the central shafts turned like the centre-shafts employed in the south transept at St Albans (*Pl. 27*). The horizontal positioning of doorways and windows is asymmetrical but conforms with the blank arcading. The articulation of this tower is similar to that of Earls Barton (*Pl. 217*) but less elaborate.

The pilasters on the north and south sides are ranged in two tiers. The lower tier has round arches composed of radial blocks of stone, the second arch on each side being widened to accommodate the doorways. The upper tier of blind arches is even more arbitrary in that it stands on consoles which repose directly on the vertices of the orders below—a wholly unarchitectural arrangement. The double window in this stage is offset so far to the east that it cuts into two pilaster compartments. The pilaster strips project very slightly from the wall and consist, like the quoins of the tower, of an alternation of long and short slabs of stone. Plain blocks projecting somewhat further from the wall function as capitals. The triangular heads of the upper tier of blind arches, which consist of two slabs of stone abutted diagonally in the usual Anglo-Saxon manner, are contiguous with the string course above them. One is struck by the way in which the upper arcading is linked with the quoins by half-arches. These tiers of pilasters possess no structural significance and are merely a form of ornamentation.

Since the Gothic nave is higher than the original chancel of the three-celled church, one can still see the roof-line of the original building on the interior and observe how the outermost member of the roof-joint enters the quoin at an angle, that is to say, cuts it in two instead of resting against it. This is not typical of stone-masonry but an echo of earlier timber-building techniques which entailed the notching of wooden beams.

186 *Priory church of St Cuthbert and St Mary, Worksop* (Nottinghamshire). All that survives of the (second) Norman building is the nave, the two west towers, and the crossing, which is used as a choir. Everything else is either later or modern, and even the original fabric has been drastically restored in places. Despite this, and because of the individual articulation of the nave walls, the church emits an atmosphere all its own. The piers are alternately cylindrical and octagonal. The capitals are reduced to hollow-chamfered slabs adorned with crockets, and the abaci, like the outer orders of the carefully moulded arcade arches, display dogtooth moulding. Being nine bays long, the arcades emphasize the horizontal flow of the nave, which is further accentuated by the string course immediately above. Everything else adheres to the same principle. There are no vertical wall-shafts, and the three horizontal zones are all equally independent in their composition.

Immediately above the arcade comes the gallery, with its alternation of large and small arches. The larger arches project into the bare wall beyond the enriched string course at the base of the clerestory. However, while the larger gallery arches are structurally related to the arcade arches, the smaller gallery arches are unstructurally situated above the piers and below the large clerestory windows. Individual features of this peculiar-looking arrangement may be Romanesque, but the staggered position and varying weight of the arches exhibit a disjunctive tendency which infringes the laws relating to supporting members, both optically and structurally. Dating from c. 1180, this mode of articulating walls is representative of a transitional style which manipulated Romanesque features in a manneristic way and was a typical late flowering. Early Gothic seems to possess a refreshing clarity by comparison.

187–188 *Priory church at Blyth* (Nottinghamshire). Looking at the *south wall of the nave (Pl. 187)* today, one can only guess at the simple yet vigorously Norman appearance of the original building. Roger de Builli and his wife Muriel founded the priory in 1087 so that Benedictines brought there from Rouen could pray for King William and for the salvation of Matilda, his late consort. William died in the same year, before work on the church was properly under way, so the priory became a sort of memorial. It is understandable, in view of these strong associations, that the church's design was entirely based on Norman prototypes. It is, in fact, the most accurate reproduction of a Norman church in England.

In company with St Albans *(Pl. 26–29)* and the transepts of Winchester *(Pl. 50–51)* and Ely *(Pl. 225–226)*, Blyth Priory belongs to the first generation of post-Conquest churches. The original ground-plan, which was never modified, embodied an aisled nave, a crossing and crossing tower, an apsidal transept, and an apsidal chancel with square-ended aisles. This scheme is the same as that of S. Trinité at Caen, the church which Queen Matilda founded in 1062 and in which she was buried twenty-one years later.

The articulation of the walls at Blyth is tripartite and consists of arcade, gallery, and clerestory. The square-cored piers have engaged demi-shafts on all four sides, those on the inside of the arches being surmounted by

volute capitals adorned with simply carved heads—a feature which disappeared c. 1095 (cf. *Pl. 21–22*). The gallery arches are as wide as those of the arcade. The groined vaults and transverse arches of the *north aisle (Pl. 188)* betray hurried execution but enable one, yet again, to sense the original impact of a building erected during the very aftermath of the Conquest.

189 *St Mary's, Stow* (Lincolnshire), an imposing church whose ground-plan takes the form of a Greek cross with slightly shortened transept arms, was probably conceived in the latter part of the 10th century. The splendid crossing arches date from that period. The crossing itself is remarkable for its massivity. It is roughly 26 ft square and projects slightly into the right angles formed by the nave, transept and chancel. The crossing arches, though 30 ft high, are only about 15 ft wide. This distinguishes the crossing from the usual Norman type, which employed the full width. Only one other Anglo-Saxon crossing still exists apart from Stow, but a few more may have failed to survive. It has, however, been established that the crossing represents an exceptional feature in Anglo-Saxon architecture. The crossing arches at Stow are related in design and construction to those at Wittering *(Pl. 202)*.

190–193 *Lincoln Cathedral* (Lincolnshire) is one of England's most fascinating Gothic churches. Of the cathedral's diverse fabric, only the west front survives to convey the massive strength of the original Norman building. Bishop Rémy de Fécamp transferred his see to Lincoln from Dorchester-on-Thames following the council held at Winchester in 1072, which reorganized the structure of the English Church under Norman supremacy, ruled that sees should be situated in fortified towns, and redefined diocesan boundaries. Rémy built his cathedral on a hill in the centre of the town. The bulk of the Norman church was completed by 1092. It seems that the bishop, a former monk from Fécamp, summoned stonemasons from Normandy to carry out his great undertaking. This is indicated not only by resemblances between capitals—always a good pointer—but also by the way in which the cathedral was dovetailed into the country town. This distinguishes it from other English cathedrals, most of which are isolated from neighbouring buildings by spacious precincts.

The original Norman *west front (Pl. 191)* has been enclosed and partly obscured by additions of c. 1240. Ignoring this Gothic overlay, one can still discern the stout masonry of the Romanesque west front with its five recesses. The primitive volute capitals, e.g. those of the south recess, indicate a date of origin prior to 1092. The central recess was heightened and enriched

c. 1240. If one pictures it round-arched and reduced to its original height, one can see that the three portal recesses correspond, though slightly displaced, to the elevation of nave and aisles, whereas the two outer recesses were let into the thickness of the wall. The tall single recess at Tewkesbury *(Pl. 95)* was inspired by the same architectural idea.

Lincoln's massive Romanesque façade, which is genuinely representative of the first generation of Norman buildings in England, was rebuilt in the first half of the 12th century, probably after the major fire which severely damaged the cathedral in 1141. The two *west towers (Pl. 190)* were heightened and enriched at the same time. (The long-windowed Gothic superstructure followed in 1380.) Below, the towers have false gables with tiers of plain and enlaced blind arches and a network of paterae in the triangles at the head. The richly articulated sides of the towers follow the same general pattern but vary in detail. The first stage, still on a level with the roof, displays three large ornamented round-arched windows above a tier of delicate blind arches. Above these are some stilted and enlaced blind arches interspersed with two smaller windows. The topmost Romanesque stage is the shallowest: a windowless zone relieved by more blind arches which echo the lowest stage.

The west portals acquired their present appearance c. 1145, though it is probable that only one of them existed before that time. The *north jambs of the central doorway (Pl. 193)* reveal that the whole portal, much restored but corresponding in style to the original, is distinguished by a plethora of figurative decoration. It is of six orders, the jambs and arches being separated by scalloped capitals adorned with foliage and stellate flowers. The outer frame consists of Greek braid, the innermost order of Norman zigzag and multiform Anglo-Saxon beak-heads. Of the four inset shafts, the outer pair have lozenge-shaped patterns of geometrical flowers, leaves and stars which resemble oriental textile motifs, while the foliage on the two inner shafts is inhabited by birds, beasts, and human figures of North Irish and Mediterranean origin, symbolizing the struggle between worldly evil and spiritual salvation. The author of the original doorway must have been a stonemason of wide knowledge and experience. The side portals are not figured in any way.

The Romanesque west front acquired further sculptural enrichment in the shape of a carved frieze similar to the one on the façade of Modena Cathedral. It had long been an English tradition to decorate important sections of a building with sculptures, supplemented where necessary by painting. Here, however, the religious and formal theme was expanded. Across the *full width of the west front (Pl. 192)* runs a band of scenes from the Old and New Testaments, ranged to south and north respectively. A sermon in stone intended to convey the verities of Christianity to all true believers, the pictorial programme embraces, inter alia, the Expulsion from Paradise, the entire story of Noah as a prefiguration of the Passion and Salvation, Daniel in the lions' den, the story of Lazarus, Christ's descent into Limbo and the saving of Adam, and, finally, the Torments of the Damned. The sculptures display great artistic merit, even in their time-worn state. There is no precise indication of their date, but their style suggests that they are Late Romanesque and should not be dated before the fire of 1141.

194-198 *Southwell Minster* (Nottinghamshire) is a member of the second and more advanced generation of Anglo-Norman churches, which includes St Bartholomew's in London, Peterborough Cathedral, Leominster Priory, Rochester Cathedral and Romsey Abbey—all begun during the second and third decades of the 12th century. Southwell was the first church in this important group to possess the square-ended chancel which later became the standard English form, though it was subsequently replaced by one of Gothic design. In other respects, Southwell shares with Romsey *(Pl. 58–61)* the advantage of having undergone few changes in the course of the centuries. This may be due partly to its remoteness from major centres of urban development.

Archaeological finds clearly show that the district was favoured by the Romans, and this 'spiritus loci' seems to have exerted an effect on the Norman church. Southwell Minster displays something which is common to all the second-generation group, namely, a more open, more accessible and less constricted appearance than the first Norman buildings (cf. *Pl. 187)*—almost as if it were a visible token that conditions had become stabilized under Henry I. Southwell was never a monastic church, either, (it only became a diocesan church in 1884) but the church of a college of secular canons and, as such, more receptive to outside influence than the church of a monastic community would have been. The ecclesiastical history of Southwell is shrouded in the mists of the Anglo-Saxon period. The *tympanum (Pl. 196)* now mounted in the north transept predates the Norman church. The theme of this expressive relief—Samson and the Lion, St Michael and the Dragon—suggests that it used to be mounted on the outside of a doorway, possibly the main portal of a previous building. At all events, the tympanum is not in situ. It follows the Urnes style, that it to say, it adopts many features present in earlier Anglo-Saxon works based on Scandinavian animal-ornamentation. There is something more experimental than assured about the way in which the dragon's tails are twisted into ornaments, and this very lack of assurance indicates that the work did not originate until the stylistic idiom which it tried to imitate was already moribund—say in the third quarter of the 11th century.

The initiator of the Norman church at Southwell was Archbishop Thomas of York. Work probably began shortly after 1110. The first phase, which lasted until *c.* 1150, produced the square-ended chancel (no longer extant), the chancel aisles and apses, the transept and its apsidal chapels, and the crossing with its massive cylindrical and compound piers. These have capitals which display figurative scenes from the life of Christ executed in a more advanced style than the old tympanum but one which did not accord with the majestic conception of the building as a whole. The continuation of the first phase produced the aisled nave, crossing tower, and twin west towers. Our *view of the exterior (Pl. 194)*, showing the south transept, nave, and south-west tower, conveys the tranquil charm of the building. Its simplicity finds expression in the entire composition of the exterior walls, in the regularity of pilasters and string courses, and in the round-arched windows, which have inset cylindrical shafts, cable-moulded arches, and billet-moulded labels. The south-west tower, whose spire was rebuilt in 1880 (probably with too steep a pitch) is sparsely adorned with blind arches and windows. This element of dignified restraint may well be Southwell's most salient characteristic.

Unassuming dignity is equally apparent in the *central group (Pl. 195)*. There is an understandable growth of architectural ornamentation on the crossing tower, which, being the main tower of a Romanesque church and situated above the cross formed by its fabric, possessed symbolic importance. Its massive bulk is articulated and relieved by an encircling tier of enlaced blind arches immediately above the roof ridges. Higher still—another example of dignified restraint—comes the belfry-stage, which has seven arcaded arches on each face. The outer pairs are blind, whereas the middle three are open and relieved by inset shafts and small double arches. This photograph affords a good view of the circular clerestory windows beneath the undulating string course at the top of the transept and nave walls. Treated with the utmost simplicity, these windows are an outstanding feature of the church and one which enhances its classical allure.

The *interior of the nave (Pl. 197)* also preserves the essential character of the first, Romanesque building phase. The only incongruities are a few Late Gothic (Perpendicular) aisle windows, the large west window (also inserted in the 15th century), and the ceiling of

1880. The main impression created by the nave, here seen from the north-east, is one of pronounced horizontality. The short cylindrical piers of the arcade stand there in calm array, like the piers of a seven-span bridge. The gallery arches carry the horizontal line a stage further, in the manner of a Roman aqueduct, and the same tendency is further accentuated by the clerestory windows and wall-passage on the level above. Southwell's quiet but unmistakable distinction is thus evident in the nave as well. We have only to remember the multiform, intricate articulation of the nave walls at Worksop *(Pl. 186)* to gain an even clearer insight into Southwell's crystalline clarity.

The *drum-piers (Pl. 198)* are very neatly constructed of hewn stone. The capitals are no more than annular slabs, and their circularity is further emphasized by a multitude of incised scallops, fans, flutes, and palmettes. Arcade arches and vaults supports consist of simple ribbed arches adorned with roll-moulding and intervening fillets. The arcade arches and the somewhat more ornate gallery arches are edged with a billet frieze. The gallery, which has a lean-to roof and is unlit, creates a subdued spatial effect which further enhances the clarity of the ensemble. Southwell's architect went so far as to marry the circular clerestory windows with round-arched openings on the inside. By so doing, he created a triad of arcades—similar in shape but decreasing in size towards the roof—and so clarified the lucid simplicity of the building still more.

199 None of the large domestic halls dating from the Romanesque period in England has survived in better condition than *'Castle Hall' at Oakham* (Rutland). The name is somewhat misleading, since it was less a castle hall than the hall of a manor house which used, so excavation has proved, to be guarded by a wall and ditch. Tokens of the transition to Gothic are evident throughout the building.

Seen from the outside, the hall resembles an aisled church, though it is devoid of clerestory windows (the former windows are a later addition) because the lean-to roofs of the aisles almost rise to meet the eaves of the saddleback roof which spans the 'nave'. The central entrance, which used to be further to the east, is a simple round-arched doorway with jamb-shafts. Outside, the windows consist of pointed double-arches reposing on slender inset shafts, but inside, as this picture shows, the same windows take the form of round-arched recesses adorned with the dogtooth motif so popular in the Late Romanesque period (cf. *Pl. 186*).

The hall measures approximately 65 ft by 44 ft. Its spacious appearance is enhanced by the fact that the rafters were left exposed in the customary way. Two four-bayed arcades divide the interior into three parts. The cylindrical piers are composed of drums, and the wide and lofty arcade arches repose on moulded abaci of square design. The curves of the arches are stressed with a continuous band of dogtooth. Just above the abaci, where the arches meet, sit small stone musicians which already approximate to the Gothic style, whereas the horizontal beasts and twin heads on the consoles in the end walls are still wholly Romanesque in conception. The enriched crocket capitals, by contrast, are almost Gothic. From all these indications, we can deduce that the elegant hall was built *c.* 1190.

200-201 The nave and chancel of *St John the Baptist, Barnack* (Northamptonshire) date from the Early and High Gothic periods. What distinguishes it from a thousand similar churches, however, is its possession of a tower, tower arch and sculptured figure dating from still earlier periods. The tower belongs to the group of Anglo-Saxon towers which includes Barton-upon-Humber *(Pl. 185)* and Earls Barton *(Pl. 217)*, whose pilaster strips represent a decorative transmutation of earlier timber-building techniques. There is, however, a rustic air about the latter two towers which is entirely absent in the one at Barnack.

The *tower arch (Pl. 201)*, a remarkable example of Anglo-Saxon building technique, is constructed of large blocks which run the full depth of the wall. It is 13 ft wide and almost 20 ft high. The jambs and arch are closely bordered by an exterior band of stone, and their simple but effective appearance is enhanced by elaborately moulded imposts. These extend sideways to meet the responds of the nave arcades, formerly the abutment of the nave walls of the original Anglo-Saxon church. This pronounced moulding creates the effect of thin superimposed slabs. In reality, the whole capital-cum-abacus structure was hewn from massive blocks of stone. The capital section proper, which was meant to interrupt the flow of the arch, seems to recede rather than project, with the result that its optical effect is weakened. One is reminded, yet again, of the timber-builder's technique, which was to counteract lateral thrust and tension by using beams with mortise-and-tenon joints. A triumph of design and craftmanship, this remarkable tower arch may be dated *c.* 1000.

Controversy surrounds the dating of the *sculpture of Christ (Pl. 200)*, which is variously held to be Anglo-Saxon or Early Norman. Unanimity reigns only on the subject of its high artistic quality. The figure was first discovered in 1931, under one of the aisles, and is well preserved except for the feet, which appear to have been restored. The benedictory gesture and Book of the Law are typical of the nimbed 'Majestates' which appear on so

many tympana, e.g. that of the Prior's Portal at Ely *(Pl. 230)*. However, we are here dealing with an unmistakable niche figure 40¹/₂ ins high, 18 ins wide, and 7 ins deep. The seated figure is very snugly fitted into its recess. Only some drapery and the left elbow are in contact with the left-hand edge of the niche, whereas the right-hand edge is overlapped by knee, elbow, sleeve and hem. The upper part of Christ's body leans very slightly to the left, and this S-bend is accentuated by the ridges of material across the belly and lap. The style is sinuous. Every fold of drapery—whether over arms or legs—conforms to the general flow. The flat expanses of knee and shin seem peculiar at first sight but do not obtrude so much when one reflects that the figure used to be painted (traces of pigment can still be detected on the neck). Their flatness may be regarded as symptomatic of Insular work. Although the stonemason was undoubtedly an Anglo-Saxon of Edward the Confessor's time (1042–66), he may be assumed to have been familiar not only with manuscripts of the Winchester school but also with Continental works—possibly of Rhenish provenance.

202-203 The little church of *All Saints, Wittering* (Northamptonshire) is a remarkably well-preserved example of the two-celled Anglo-Saxon arrangement and consists of a rectangular nave and inset rectangular chancel. All the external corners of the original building have survived, together with their long-and-short alternation of verical and horizontal slabs of stone, some of which are unusually well fitted. This deliberate juxtaposition of weights and supports, this tectonic balance between thrust and tension, also finds formal expression in the unique *chancel arch (Pl. 202)*. It is differentiated from the more delicate arch at Barnack *(Pl. 201)*, which should be viewed in conjunction with the one at Bosham *(Pl. 52)*, by a massivity which also characterizes the chancel and crossing arches at Clayton *(Pl. 33)* and Stow *(Pl. 189)*.

Massive structural simplicity is more the key-note at Wittering than anywhere else. Strength has here been translated into form. Projecting from each side of the chancel wall are semicircular shafts which swell in a slightly conical fashion, both at the foot, where they repose on rectangular plinths, and at the head, where they resemble incipient capitals. The impost blocks are unadorned but slightly splayed towards the foot. Above them rise three roll-moulded arches which leave the intervening edges of the wall visible. In contrast to Clayton, these are slightly chamfered throughout. Following the contour of the entire arch, though at an unusual distance, is a stone strip of rectangular cross-section.

The chancel arch is a remarkable product of the late 10th century. A north aisle was added in the latter half of the 12th century. Its two arches repose on a central *drum-pier (Pl. 203)* with a square scalloped capital. The conformation of the arcade arches typifies the development of arch design during the Late Romanesque period in England. Anglo-Saxon architects developed and promoted the roll-moulded arch into a sculptural feature, as the chancel arch so splendidly demonstrates. The arches of the north arcade at Wittering are eloquent testimony to the fact that English Romanesque continued to cultivate this Insular motif until a late stage. They do, in fact, combine the two features most typical of English Romanesque: roll-moulded soffits and chevron-adorned archivolts.

204-207 *St Peter's, Northampton* (Northamptonshire) has been rather neglected by students of church architecture, possibly because so much of it has been modified or rebuilt. Nevertheless, the church does possess certain features which endow it with special distinction, even in a county which is not deficient in Romanesque churches. It also poses certain problems which still await elucidation. Peter is an ancient patrociny, so we may take it for granted that the site of the existing Late Romanesque church was occupied by a predecessor. Does the discrepancy between the clerestory windows and *arcade (Pl. 204)* indicate that these zigzag-adorned arches were cut into walls of an earlier building? We are virtually compelled to assume the existence of an Anglo-Saxon church. Ties of this nature are evidenced by a handsome but fragmentary *sculpture (Pl. 207)* found in the immediate vicinity. This is decoratively carved with foliage, knots, beasts, and a head. Both its putative identification (part of a cross-shaft) and its attribution to the 9th century must still be regarded as conjectural.

The church was badly neglected in the 16th century, and the tower collapsed. It was rebuilt at the beginning of the 17th century—surprisingly well, having regard to contemporary knowledge of the Romanesque style. The archivolts of the original west portal were incorporated in the *west front of the tower (Pl. 206)*. Astonishingly enough, the outer order bears precisely the same motif—concentric circles interwoven with a band looped into a four-pointed star—as the sculptured fragment referred to above *(Pl. 207)*. Is there a definite connection between the two? One is inclined to dissociate the west arch from the capitals of the nave arcades, which are totally different in style. If the latter originated in 1150, as it has been suggested, the west doorway of the same building cannot very well be much earlier. However, the foliage, crosses and floral motifs on the vestigial arch are considerably earlier, and point to the late 11th

century. This contradiction poses a still unsolved problem.

The extremely ornate *capitals (Pl. 204)*, here seen from the east, are Late Romanesque. Other influences of doubtful origin are present, but the tendency towards flatness is definitely Insular and betrays an affinity with metal-work. The stylistic diversity of the capitals in St Peter's make them outstanding examples of late-phase workmanship.

208-210 No signs of any earlier buildings have so far been discovered at *St Kyneburgha's, Castor* (Northamptonshire), though legend has it that a nuns' convent was founded on this hill by Kyneburgha, daughter of King Penda of Mercia and sister of the founder of Peterborough. Discounting a chapel sacred to her memory in Peterborough Cathedral, this church is the only one in England to be dedicated to her.

A very fine specimen of Anglo-Saxon art is mounted in the south wall of the choir. This *sculpture (Pl. 209)* is about 19 ins high and portrays a saint beneath an arch. It clearly formed the left-hand section of a work which consisted of at least five parts and probably had a Majestas Domini in the centre. The bearded figure with drilled eye-sockets carries a book adorned with four ornamentally arranged symbols of the Holy Trinity (bands entwined into three loops). This suggests that it represents St Matthew, the only Evangelist to have transmitted Christ's apostolic command in the name of the Triune God (St Matthew xxviii, 16–20). This, in turn, would suggest that the other figures were those of the remaining Evangelists. The surface of the relief is extremely well preserved. It shows arcaded arches with shoots and flowers sprouting from their capitals. A variant of this can be seen at Breedon-on-the-Hill, but the Castor relief creates a more advanced impression. It may be attributed to the middle of the 9th century, a dating supported by the style of drapery and 'tip-toe' stance.

Castor boasts another unusual feature, namely, the dedication stone of the Norman church. The date is not clearly decipherable because the terminal figures on this carefully carved stone are by another, later, hand. However, the year—probably 1124—may be regarded as stylistically confirmed in respect of the crossing and its *capitals (Pl. 210)*. These cushion capitals repose on cable-moulded annulets and semicircular shafts engaged with the massive crossing piers, which support robust and typically Anglo-Saxon roll-moulded arches. The forceful and rustic figurative style is softer than that of the Romsey capitals *(Pl. 57)* but very reminiscent of it, which tends to confirm the dating of works there by 'Robertus' at *c*. 1135. Various scenes are portrayed at Castor: on the north-west pier, foliage, birds, a splendid battle scene and a woman standing on one side; on the south-east pier, animals, foliage, and a man gathering grapes in a basket. The prototype of the latter scene has survived in a manuscript from Canterbury which also inspired various capitals in the crypt there. The north-east pier (our photograph) depicts a wild sow hunted by dogs, one of which is lying on the ground, torn asunder, and Samson in combat with the lion.

However, Castor's true claim to fame is its magnificent *crossing tower (Pl. 208)*. The massive plinth-stage is surmounted by a corbel table and the second stage has large central windows flanked by blind arches. Windows and arches are converted into double-arches by inset shafts, shorter in the case of the central windows, and enclosed by a common outer arch. Two more peculiarities: in the first place, the massive tower is relieved by cylindrical shafts located at the corners of the middle and belfry stages; and, in the second place, the stretch of wall between the top of the windows and the second string course is revetted with lozenges. The corresponding section of the belfry stage displays a shingled motif. The belfry-stage obeys the first rule of Romanesque tower articulation—greater elaboration in the upper stages to achieve an appearance of greater variety—by displaying three two-light windows flanked by blind double-arches. The arches are of uniform size and constitute a rhythmical arcade which runs all round the tower. This method of decorating towers presupposes the existence of a great tradition. Despite the dedicatory inscription of *c.* 1124, it is probable that the tower's Romanesque superstructure was not completed until the middle of the 12th century. The spire was added in the 14th century.

211–213 *Peterborough Cathedral* (Northamptonshire) is dedicated to SS Peter, Paul, and Andrew. It only became a cathedral in 1541 and was originally built as an abbey church. The name Peterborough itself signifies the monastery's erstwhile importance, since it proves that the city took its name from the monastery. Founded shortly after 653 by King Penda of Mercia, the monastery spawned a number of filial establishments, e.g. Brixworth, and grew in size and prosperity. In 870 the Danes massacred the monks and burned the monastery buildings to the ground. A new abbey church was erected and dedicated in 972, in the course of the great monastic revival which took place during the Ottonian period. When William the Conqueror seized power, he sparked off a serious rebellion by conferring the abbacy of Peterborough on a Norman. Monastery, church and town were devastated by fire in 1116. Work then started on the building which now ranks as one of the most important of England's cathedral churches and a prime example of the second and more elaborate phase of Norman ecclesiastical architecture.

The year 1143 saw the completion of the chancel and transept. It is probable that two bays of the nave were also begun, so as to buttress the crossing. The church follows the 'Benedictine' layout, the choir having a large apse and its aisles two smaller ones. Eight bays of the nave and the aisles with their round-arched ribbed vaults (influenced by Durham) were probably in existence by about the middle of the 12th century. The nave thus extended as far as the cloister in the south, which has entirely disappeared. It was clearly the intention to build a west end complete with towers, but this plan was abandoned in favour of two additional bays, completed *c.* 1180. Thus, although the building grew slowly, it retained its original character: typically English roll-moulded arches supported by drum-piers with engaged demi-shafts, double gallery openings adorned with zigzag, and a clerestory wall-passage with triplets opening on to the nave (one large round-arched aperture flanked by two narrower ones). Like all the rest, these arches reposed on cylindrical shafts with cushion capitals of varying ornamentation. The north-west tower was added over a bay of its own, whereas the south-west tower never progressed beyond the first storey. This takes us up to 1194. Shortly afterwards, in emulation of Lincoln *(Pl. 191)*, the building was given an Early Gothic façade which ran the full width of the nave, incorporating three gables, three huge recesses, and corner-turrets. The dedication of the whole fabric finally took place in 1238. Naturally, various alterations and additions were made during the centuries that followed, but the 12th-century building remains substantially intact—and this is what governs the impact made on one after penetrating the west front. Anyone entering the church finds himself in the realm of mature English Romanesque.

Even the wooden ceiling survives, though its paintwork has been restored, Probably executed *c.* 1220, it has a lozenge pattern which resembles that of the transept ceiling but is designed as a setting for representations of saints, bishops, kings, human figures menaced by beasts, musicians, comics—even a head of Janus. Needless to say, there is a deliberate message here relating to the forces of salvation and destruction which contend for the soul of man. Like the walls, with their sculptural articulation, continuous string courses and rhythmical succession of cylindrical piers, the painted ceiling draws the eye irresistibly towards the massive crossing. And, since the erstwhile screen between the layman's nave and monk's chancel no longer exists, one gets an unobstructed view of the east end, some 400 ft away, with the luminous Late Gothic retrochoir beyond.

The *choir wall (Pl. 213)* comprises four bays between crossing and apse (our photograph shows the first bay on the north side). Its ornamentation, which includes billet-moulded arches, soffits with zigzag running at right angles and therefore symptomatic of late development, and lunettes covered with diaper-work, stamps it as a fine example of mature Romanesque work carried out by English stonemasons who were masters both of technique and composition. Peterborough is the proud 'fortress of God' par excellence. Noteworthy features of the *view of the south aisle of the choir from the south transept (Pl. 212)* include the advanced ornamentation (enlaced blind arcading runs round the outer walls), the typical roll-moulded ribs of the massive vaults, and the way in which arcade arches and wall-shafts repose on cushion capitals which follow the circumference of each pier—all of them features which came to maturity in the second quarter of the 12th century.

The interior of the *north transept (Pl. 211)* possesses a magnitude and harmony which would be even more manifest if the light still streamed in through Romanesque instead of Late Gothic windows. The north wall (our photograph) is vertically segmented by two wall-shafts —not wall-shafts in the sense of vault supports, but instruments of rhythmical articulation. There are four vertical features: first the blind arches, then the round-arched windows with their double surrounds, then the slightly taller gallery openings, and, finally, the wall-passage openings of the clerestory. It would, however, be erroneous to speak of a four-storeyed wall arrangement, since the blind arches in the plinth are an integral part of the lower fenestration zone and help to make it taller than the one above. The three storeys are defined by the two string courses which cut across the wall-shafts. The amazing assurance with which height and width have been reconciled is eloquent of what the true believers of the Romanesque feudal era understood any large church to be, namely, a Palatium Dei. Confusion might reign in the outside world—indeed, it did—but underlying everything was the conception of a harmonious world which assumed visible form in church architecture.

214 The *tympanum of All Saints, Pitsford* (Northamptonshire) is typical of the numerous Romanesque tympana which can still be encountered, often quite unexpectedly, in even the smallest and most remote English churches. Like this one, they are frequently characterized by simple narrative vigour coupled with a power of expression which accrues to them from the very lack of constraint with which they present their message. These two characteristics are often joined by another: the latent but ever-present influence of Scandinavian-Celtic motifs and 'fillings', an element which invests the work of local stonemasons with a markedly Insular flavour. The shallow relief technique is also typical, as, at Pitsford, is the way in which the tail of the mythical beast turns into a beaded band and culminates in sprouting leaves, or the way in which the tail of the bird in the bottom left corner develops into an interlaced ornament.

What is portrayed here is not St Michael or St George fighting the Dragon but a battle between Virtue and Vice, that is to say, a scene from Prudentius' *Psychomachia*. This text was a favourite source of sermons and pictorial references in the middle of the 12th century. Lying in the bottom right corner is a pair of wings, cast off like theatrical props—possibly so that Virtue, an angelic figure, can tackle his monstrous and devilish adversary unimpeded. An allusion to the theatre is not inconceivable, since there was a growing vogue for presenting the *Psychomachia* in morality-play form during the 12th century. Although one is tempted to place it earlier in time, the tympanum should probably be attributed to the middle of the 12th century in view of its beak-head and chevron surround.

215 The *doorway of the parish church at Brixworth* (Northamptonshire) stands proxy for the whole building, which could not be photographed because of restoration work. With an original exterior length of 140 ft and interior width of 60 ft (the extant nave is itself 30 ft wide), All Saints, Brixworth, though incomplete, is the largest known Anglo-Saxon church in existence. It followed the basilican plan: an aisled nave, a square presbytery of nave width but without aisles, a slightly inset polygonal choir, and a two-storeyed west end. The nave was four bays long, and the clerestory windows are curiously situated above the spandrels of the arcade (cf., in the Late Romanesque period, Worksop, *Pl. 186*), with the result that there are only three on each side.

The history of the church is straightforward. The chronicler Petrus Candidus records that it was founded *c. 675* by monks from Peterborough, but the monastic community went out of existence when the monastery was destroyed during the Danish raids of *c. 870*. In the 10th century the aisles were demolished and the arcades walled up. The now aisleless building was fitted out as a parish church and given a new apse. The narthex was developed into a tower, annexed to which was a turret with a spiral staircase. This is roughly what the church looks like today.

The former arcade arches can still be seen in the outer wall. These were constructed of Roman tiles (source unknown) of the sort visible in the doorway illustrated here—reddish tiles which glow warmly against the yellow-grey limestone. The doorway formerly led from the ground floor of the tower into a porticus which no longer exists, so this arch, too, used to be an interior arch. It displays neater workmanship than the arcade arches. In the latter, many of the Roman tiles surmounting the masonry piers are not laid in a strictly radial manner, with the result that they form a V at the vertex of the arch and only meet with difficulty.

216 *St Andrew's, Brigstock* (Northamptonshire). The west end of this charming village church resembles that of Brixworth, but the origins of the two buildings are dissimilar. St Andrew's probably originated in the 9th century. Its core is an elongated rectangular nave, unaisled and only about 40 ft long. Parts of the side walls and windows can still be seen today. To the east of the Anglo-Saxon nave lay a square chancel, to the west a fore-building of similar shape and size. This made St Andrew's a three-celled church. The west fore-building was heightened to form a tower *c.* 1000. The more than semicircular turret added at the same time was made disproportionately large so as to accommodate a spiral staircase. The tower has neat long-and-short quoins, and the interior tower arch was modified during the Romanesque period.

217 *Earls Barton* (Northamptonshire). None of the many extant Anglo-Saxon towers is as elaborate as the one illustrated here, and none is as admirably situated. All Saints stands in an ancient graveyard on a hill overlooking the village. If we ignore the Gothic church proper and the incongruous battlements, we are left with a tower which has remained essentially unaltered since it was first built in the second half of the 10th century.

Set into the west face of the tower is a massive portal constructed of huge stones, so there can never have been a fore-building in the west. Anglo-Saxon roof-joints on the east side of the third stage indicate the existence of an east end. However, since the carefully dressed long-and-short quoins run all the way down the first stage, the east end must have been narrower than the tower, which is 24 ft wide. They were connected by an arch, subsequently modified.

The tower is about 60 ft high and formed the main component of the original church, a surprising fact and one which probably accounts for its elaborate surface decoration. All four sides follow the same basic pattern, though small variations occur. The windows fall into the various categories typical of Anglo-Saxon architecture, e.g. triangle-heads, pairs, and series, the latter being separated by turned balusters. The belfry-stage is formally enhanced by a five-light group in which each arch consists of a single concave block of stone.

The same decorative crescendo is apparent in the articulation of the walls. The four slightly stepped stages are separated by string courses and vertically divided by pilaster strips with an average width of just under 5 ins: in the first and tallest stage, plain strips which emphasize its verticality; in the second, somewhat shallower stage, strips accompanied by round arches which repose on the moulded string course at the foot; in the third stage, which is of the same height as the second, two tiers of inverted Vs reminiscent of the timber-building techniques on which the whole of this form of stone ornamentation is based; and, in the belfry-stage, two simple frameworks at the sides only, the centre of each face being occupied by an elaborate five-light window. One cannot deny the inherent harmony of such a composition. It is a 10th-century foreshadowing of the desire to achieve a rising crescendo in tower enrichment, a trend which found such splendid expression in mature Romanesque (cf. *Pl. 208*).

218 *St Thomas of Canterbury, Clapham* (Bedfordshire). Anglo-Saxon towers with pilaster strips, e.g. Barnack, Barton-upon-Humber *(Pl. 185)*, and Earls Barton *(Pl. 217)*, are in the minority. There are none at all north of the Humber—a well-known but unexplained fact. The majority of Anglo-Saxon towers display long-and-short quoins, possibly accompanied by a central pilaster strip as at Sompting *(Pl. 43)*, but others—and here lack of local hewn stone played a part—are wholly devoid of decoration. The tower at Clapham is one of the most striking examples of the latter category. It rises to a height of 75 ft, 60 of them Anglo-Saxon and the remaining 15 accounted for by a Romanesque belfry. The walls are built of rubble and consequently of unusual thickness (depth: 4 ft). Ashlar-work is present only in the west doorway and in the tower arch, which now opens into the small modern church (built 1861). The window surrounds are splayed on both sides. Inside, above the tower arch, is a triangle-headed doorway which once led from the roof of the nave into the first storey of the tower. The tower itself probably dates from the beginning of the 11th century. Like others of its austere kind, it conveys something of the defiance which the Normans encountered when they seized power.

ESSEX AND EAST ANGLIA

219–220 *Holy Sepulchre, Cambridge* (Cambridgeshire) tends to be regarded with a touch of condescension because everyone knows that it was not only restored a century ago but largely rebuilt—even though this was done on the basis of existing data. Additions (north aisle *c.* 1350, south aisle 1841) have weakened the church's focal tendency, which was alway centripetal despite the small fore-building in the east. Only a handful of round churches exist in England, and all have been encroached on by additions or restored. There are few cases where it can be proved that these circular buildings are connected, via the Knights Templar, with the Church of the Holy Sepulchre in Jerusalem, yet the affinity with Empress Helena's core is always apparent in some way or other, even here at Cambridge. Northampton's Holy Sepulchre, another round church, exemplifies this. Simon de Senlis, Count of Northampton, founded it after returning unscathed from the Crusades, probably in fulfilment of a vow. The same thing may apply in the case of Cambridge. Neither of these round churches was ever dependent on any monastic or knightly order.

The west doorway is of three orders and has inset shafts, scalloped capitals, and archivolts of which the central one is adorned with zigzag (like the continuous inner arch) and the outer ornamented with Greek braid. How much of all this is attributable to restoration need not concern us here. The *central chamber and ambulatory (Pl. 220)*, though partly restored, belong to the original fabric and are still an impressive sight. Eight thick cylindrical piers spanned by eight unadorned arches encircle the central area. Eight double-arches open on to the gloomy gallery, and light streams down from the octopartite dome through eight clerestory windows. The elemental figure four has here been doubled and translated into circular terms. It would seem correct to place this building on the threshold of the period when the second generation of large Norman churches was begun, i.e. between 1110 and 1120.

221–230 *Ely Cathedral* (Cambridgeshire), like Canterbury and Durham, is one of the eight abbey churches in England which are also diocesan churches, having been started as an abbey but completed as a cathedral. Diverse in structure, it comprises a west porch (Early Gothic, 1200–15), a west transept with corner towers and a west tower, an aisled nave twelve bays long (originally thirteen), a largish octagon in place of a crossing (constructed 1322–42, after the collapse of the original crossing tower, when the damaged bays of the choir were also rebuilt), an aisled east transept, an aisled choir nine bays long, and adjoining it in the north, a Lady Chapel of five bays (1349). Ely's dimensions are remarkable: height of west tower, 215 ft; overall height of nave 105 ft; length of nave, 248 ft; width of nave, 77 ft; total extent of east transept, 190 ft; overall length of cathedral, 537 ft. It is only exceeded in length by (in ascending order) Canterbury, St Albans, and Winchester, whose 555 ft make it the longest church in England.

As to Ely's history, Bede (*H.E.* IV/19–20) traces it back to Etheldreda, monastic founder and wife of the King of Northumbria. He describes Ely as an island surrounded by water and marshes. Etheldreda retired there in 673 and founded a mixed religious community. Two centuries later, in 870, the Danes descended on Ely by water in the course of their catastrophic invasion of East Anglia, looted the monastery, slaughtered the inmates, and burned the church and its annexes to the ground. Prompted by the Archbishop of Canterbury, Benedictine monks resumed monastic life at Ely during the period of religious revival which ensued in the latter half of the 10th century. A second and larger church was consecrated in 970. It was probably of the Carolingian type, similar to Centula but more modest, with an east and a west transept and two axial towers. This seems to have established a structural precedent which was later followed by the Norman cathedral, with its two transepts and two towers. Ely not only waxed rich and powerful during this second phase in its monastic history, but also, being protected by an expanse of water, developed a spirit of independence.

It was at Ely that the Norman conquest of England was finally decided. The last of William's Anglo-Saxon adversaries mustered there with the aim of checking his brutal subjugation of Northumbria, led by an Anglo-Saxon nobleman who had sacked Peterborough with Danish assistance. William had great difficulty in bringing his campaign to a successful conclusion. The monks of Ely, who wanted to preserve their monastery intact, came to terms with the Conqueror—not that this exempted them from submission to a Norman abbot. In 1081 William conferred the abbacy on Simeon, Prior of Winchester and brother of Walkelyn, Bishop of Winchester. Simeon wanted a Norman church of his own, so the existing fabric was entirely demolished.

In 1083 he started work on his grand design with hewn stone transported from Barnack by water. The ground-plan of the church followed the Benedictine pattern in having an east apse. The chancel, elongated in accordance with Norman taste, was allotted four bays like St Albans in the south (1077), Durham in the north (1093), and Norwich in the east (1096). The first consecration of the east end, which was probably incomplete at the time, took place in 1106. Work continued on the building, which from 1109 onwards ceased to be an abbey church and became the cathedral of an abbot-bishop to whom the prior and all the inmates of the monastery were subordinated. The proud edifice took shape slowly, but, despite interruptions, Simeon's original conception was always adhered to—a circumstance which lends the cathedral great homogeneity. The two transepts and towers were completed towards the end of the 12th century. Virtually all of this High and Late Romanesque work still stands today, creating an impression of vast size. We do not know exactly when the north arm of the west transept was demolished, but it was probably in the 14th century. The west front thus presents an asymmetrical appearance. The constituent parts of Ely Cathedral afford us an excellent survey of a continuous process of stylistic evolution ranging from very early to very late Romanesque. In the *south arm of the east transept (Pl. 226)*, which belongs to the earliest structural phase (begun 1083), the arcade arches of the west wall, illustrated here, display volute capitals of a type which disappeared towards the end of the century. (The low sacristy wall adorned with enlaced blind arches is naturally a later addition.) The piers are very plain, and alternate between cylindrical and cylindrical with engaged shafts, though full-length wall-shafts are still absent. The ribbed arches are purely functional and constructed of voussoirs with no form of decorative moulding. The arcade is in the Romanesque style of the first generation of Norman churches. The layout resembles that of Winchester *(Pl. 51)*, where Simeon came from and where his brother, the bishop, actively furthered the building of his own cathedral. It was also from Winchester that Ely adopted the aisled transept, the side aisles being spanned by groined vaults. The linking of the gallery with the south wall was, however, solved in a different way. At Ely, a continuous gallery was clearly dispensed with. The only link was a narrow passage, and this—as the tall, slender columns and series of enlaced blind arches imply—was inserted much later on. The compound piers of the gallery, which contrast with the monumental arches of the first phase, are as expressive of mature Romanesque as the triplets and wall-passage of the clerestory above them. It is debatable whether these grooved and roll-moulded gallery arches were already complete by the time Etheldreda's relics were transferred to Ely in 1106, or whether they only took shape during the accelerated phase of construction which began when Abbot Hervé of Brittany was appointed first bishop of Ely in 1109 and the abbey church became a cathedral.

Somewhat more advanced, though only in shades of detail, is the wall system of the *north arm of the east transept (Pl. 225)*, which is also of slightly later date. (The upper windows in the north wall are Late Gothic and the ceiling 15th-century.) The east wall, which is not visible here, still has volute capitals. The gallery, though renovated, seems to have retained its original form. Inexplicably, the alternating piers in the west wall follow a rhythm contrary to that of the piers in the south arm. Here, however, the wall-shafts engaged with the cylindrical piers begin on the aisle side, and this verticalization of the storey system becomes a constituent of the wall system in the nave.

The *nave (Pl. 223*, north wall seen from the west) progressed slowly but was completed in accordance with the principles on which it had originally been based. Its beginnings were pure Early Romanesque, and its characteristic restraint (absence of surface decoration, plain cushion capitals throughout) lends the nave bays— on which work continued for almost the whole of the 12th century—an air of splendid unity. The nave comprises no less than twelve bays. The impression of great length is reinforced not only by an unbroken expanse of timber ceiling (rather obtrusively painted in the middle of the last century) but also, and more particularly, by the vanishing lines and steady rhythm of the three storeys: arcade, twin-arched gallery, and clerestory with triplets and wall-passage. These vary little in height— indeed, their 6 : 5 : 4 ratio invests them with even greater unity. All that breaks the steady flow is an almost imperceptible alternation between drum-piers and compound piers, both in the arcade and the gallery.

However, the horizontal flow is offset by a factor which gives uncompromising expression to the other, or vertical, tendency at Ely, namely, the wall-shafts. Although no vaults were planned for the nave, each pier is engaged with a semicircular shaft which rises, mast-like, to the summit of the nave wall, mounted on a shallow buttress. The wall-shafts are twice overlapped by string courses, but this only enhances their vertical effect. Thus, in addition to being long, Ely's nave gives an impression of great height. Length and height combine to create an appearance of aristocratic poise—indeed, spirituality. The fact that so little of the wall has been left unarticulated also contributes to this. The walls are remarkably pierced and open for the middle of the 12th century. Confronted by Ely's nave, with its compromise between functional and formal considerations, we can truly speak of classical Romanesque at the zenith of its beauty.

The *west end* exemplifies the late phase of the evolutionary process which led from the richly articulated Romanesque of the last quarter of the 12th century, a style which already seems perfunctory in many respects, to the realm of Gothic design. Representing the interior is a view of the *south arm of the west transept (Pl. 224)*, with St Catherine's Chapel. The walls are richly adorned with blind arcading and billet-moulded friezes, the arches being enriched with roll-moulding and variously disposed zigzag motifs. This section was drastically restored in the middle of the 19th century, it is true, but strictly in accordance with the motifs which proliferate throughout the west end.

The same applies to the exterior of the *west end (Pl. 222)*. This view from the bishop's garden is particularly impressive. The measured rhythm of the three-storeyed nave derives from the regularity of its clerestory triplets, the gallery windows (products of Late Gothic restoration), and the round-arched windows of the south aisle. The complex articulation of the west end and the south arm of the west transept contrasts strongly with this quiet arrangement, the main vertical members being the two corner towers and the gigantic west crossing tower. (The latter's superstructure, four corner-turrets and battlements came into being *c.* 1400.) All in all, the west end resembles a wildly imaginative pen-drawing in which one vertical jostles the next, light is caught up in a mesh of lines, and shadows nestle in the depths of crannies and recesses. No contemporary building of a comparable nature exists anywhere else in England.

The *west front (Pl. 221*, section bounded by the Early Gothic porch or narthex on the left and the south-west tower of the west transept on the right) is expressive both of continuity and transmutation. The unity of Early Gothic has absorbed the diversity of Late Romanesque—and what a diversity it is! Although the plinth of the west transept (cropped, in the photograph) consists of plain buttressed masonry, the first stage displays a tier of extremely tall and narrow blind arches which not only runs round the entire wing, corner-tower included, in a horizontal band but also enhances the verticality of individual members by means of inset corner-shafts. The second, somewhat shallower stage is articulated with well-proportioned blind arches superimposed on double blind arches which create an impression of relief and depth—a typical example of late-phase trompe-l'œil. The next stage has large round-arched windows flanked by smaller blind arches. The window surrounds are deeply stepped, and the arches and jambs, some of which have no capitals, are adorned with a wealth of billet-moulding and zigzag. Even the wall above is covered with diaper-work, which creates an interplay of light and shade. The second and third stages could not be continued round the corner-towers because their horizontal spread would have conflicted with the shafts which provide the towers with vertical articulation. The towers are polygonal, but the shafts are engaged with the centre of each facet, not its edges, which proves that they were employed for decorative rather than structural reasons. This is a very late Romanesque characteristic, just as the increasingly 'Baroque' features of the fourth and fifth stages—trefoil arches, circular quatrefoil windows, pointed arches, shaft-rings and diaper-work—are expressive of an increasingly Gothic style. If it were not for the corbel tables and shafts, the decoration would disintegrate.

Structurally, the west end is related to its Early Romanesque counterparts in Germany. The surface conformation, with its interplay of ribs and recesses, light and shade, finds an echo in the churches of Charente-Maritime or Saintonge. This cross-Channel relationship is merely a rough guide to direction, however, and we must look for affinities even further south. The northeast tower of Palermo Cathedral (consecrated in 1185 under Archbishop Walter of the Mill), though not a blood-relation, as it were, is certainly related in spirit. There, in a building moulded by Saracen and Norman ideas, the motifs and modes of articulation which play such a dominant role in the west end at Ely can be found in endless profusion. Although influences of this sort cannot be verified, their presence at a period when Norman ships regularly traversed the Mediterranean is not only perceptible but understandable.

Further evidence of an artistic dialogue which spanned Europe can be seen in the magnificently sculptured *Prior's Portal (Pl. 228)*, which used to lead from the south aisle into the cloister (no longer extant). One senses the proximity of Burgundy and Northern Italy. Although the construction of the doorway is relatively simple (stepped jambs of three orders, lintel, tympanum, archivolts and hood-mould), its sculptural treatment stamps it as a fine example of mature Romanesque. Every member apart from the tympanum is covered with foliate scroll-work. The loops on the outer jambs, which culminate in contrasting city gates, are inhabited by human figures engaged in a variety of activities, both singly and in pairs. Some of the medallions depict Labours of the Months while others contain animals of the most diverse kinds, some resembling signs of the zodiac but others representative of the Romanesque menagerie of beasts which medieval sermons, whether spoken, painted, or carved in stone, cited as symbols of the demonic struggle for the soul of man. We encounter the same world of imagery in the jamb-shaft foliage, which spirals upwards and inwards on either side. Above the dragons lurking on the abaci, the outer jambs are echoed by an outer arch adorned with a frieze of palmettes and the foliage-adorned jamb-shafts by more foliage on the corresponding archivolt, also spiral but not inhabited. The inner jambs are covered with pure foliage of freely conceived design.

Our *detail of the Prior's Portal (Pl. 229)* demonstrates that the stonemason preserved the original surface of his material, a fact clearly deducible from the cylindrical shafts as well as the square inner and outer jambs. He did cut deeper in places, however, particularly on the tympanum, and the console-heads are entirely detached. The *tympanum (Pl. 230)* bears a Majestas Domini. The two angels, the almond-shaped glory, and the feet of the seated Christ all protrude beyond the tympanum area proper in a way which symptomizes an advanced phase of tympanum design. The dramatic but extremely arbitrary pose of the angels, with their hurrying feet and backward glances, was much favoured for Burgundian tympana of the second quarter of the 12th century, whereas the projecting lions and human figures on the capitals and jamb-shaft bases (almost obliterated) are attributable to North Italian influence. One is struck by the distorted way in which the angels grasp the mandorla with their raised arms—an example of the 'expressionism' which manifested itself in English sculpture at about the middle of the 12th century. There are good reasons for dating the Prior's Portal *c.* 1140, but a slightly later date, say *c.* 1155, would seem more likely.

The *Monk's Portal (Pl. 227)* makes a much more English impression. Situated further east, beside the south arm of the east transept (one of its later buttresses overlaps the doorway on the right), this door gave access to the monks' quarters. It probably dates from the same period as the Prior's Portal. This holds good for the jambs and archivolts, at least, though the enriched trefoil arch, which does not appear to be by the same hand as the jambs, was probably substituted for the original tympanum at some later date. There is an iconographic freshness about the way in which the two snarling dragons at the apex and the two kneeling monks on the cusps (possibly priors with crosiers) have been brought into some sort of didactic relationship.

231-233 *Colchester* (Essex). *St Botolph's Priory*, the first Augustinian settlement in England, was founded *c.* 1100. The unusually large church comprised a chancel, transept, aisled nave, and west end with three portals and two towers. The *central doorway (Pl. 232)* has five orders of which four are furnished with nook-shafts, ornamented cushion capitals, and archivolts enriched with intricate zigzag. Taking into account the tiers of enlaced blind arches which span the west front (cf. Castle Acre, *Pl. 244)*, as well as the large round window in the centre of the gable, one can hardly date the completion of the church prior to 1140. The building was severely damaged in the disorders of 1648 but is still impressive in its ruined state. Its method of construction is of special interest, since it consists almost entirely of rubble and large quantities of bricks from the Roman town which was the predecessor of modern Colchester and the successor of the important British settlement known as Camulodunum. Because of the nature of these materials, limitless supplies of which were available from the vast town walls, the *drum-piers of the nave arcade (Pl. 231)* have no capitals merely rings which may once have been transformed into mock capitals with the aid of plaster. The masonry is of neat construction, considering the materials used. The tall arches above the arcade were the product of a process whereby the triforium was extended into the clerestory, so that the three-storeyed arrangement of the interior wall became, in effect, two-storeyed.

Also built of Roman brick is the Anglo-Saxon *tower doorway of Holy Trinity, Colchester (Pl. 233)*. The bricks had to be used in whatever size was available, which is why several projecting slabs took the place of the strongly accentuated impost block typical of Anglo-Saxon architecture. The doorway is flanked by pilaster strips, another popular feature (cf. *Pl. 202, 203*), but these take the form of slightly projecting courses of brickwork instead of the usual stone slabs laid on end. The imposts, which project somewhat further still, are surmounted by three diagonal courses of brick—a purely decorative feature without any relieving function. The construction of the triangle-headed arch merits special note. Pitch was imparted to the rising slabs by brushing coarse mortar between them. The two sides incline towards each other at a uniform angle and culminate at the apex in a horizontal tile with three fragments of brick beneath it and filling material above. Set off by the yellow rubble and Roman brick of the surrounding wall, this neatly constructed red brick doorway possesses considerable decorative charm. Its advanced technique suggests a dating between 950 and the Conquest.

234 *Bury St Edmunds* (Suffolk). Hardly more than two or three Romanesque buildings, a few disjointed walls and two gate-towers, one Romanesque and the other Gothic, survive to mark the site of one of the largest Benedictine monasteries in England. Foundations also exist, of course, but the results of excavation have still to be assessed. The tower illustrated here, formerly a gateway leading into the extensive monastery precincts, was built between 1120 and 1150. It is still in good condition, having been used as a bell-tower for the neighbouring church of St James, and gives an impression of solid self-assurance. The entrance is unvaulted. One is reminded of a church façade by the stepped archway and the gable above it, not to mention the two buttresses, which are disguised as corner-turrets with arched recesses, enlaced blind arches, and pyramidal caps. The central part of the tower is flanked by corner-buttresses of plain masonry, of which only the one on the staircase side is provided with small lights. Above the gateway are two small twin-light windows surmounted by blind arches, and above these three blind double arches, similar to the windows but taller. Together with the round-arched windows above them, they form a large triad framed by containing arches with engaged shafts. The same plan recurs in the somewhat shallower belfry-stage, though this is given a positively classical appearance by three equally plain round-arched sound-holes above three roundels composed of rolls. This side of the tower, which faces the town, is the most elaborate of all. The gargoyle on the south side is also worthy of note. Its upper section takes the form of a jutting, four-legged, large-headed beast, but the supporting dragon's head with gaping jaws and curling tongue is very similar to the three on the west front at Kilpeck *(Pl. 103)*, which originated a little earlier.

235-236 *Orford Castle* (Suffolk) and *Helmsley Castle* (Yorkshire). These two unusual buildings are representative of the last phase of Norman military architecture, which began with the Tower of London *(Pl. 23)* and the huge castle at Colchester. *Orford Castle (Pl. 235)* was built for Henry II between 1165 and 1167. In it, the 'ingeniator' Alnoth for the first time abandoned the conventional rectangular ground-plan in favour of one which lent itself better to defence. The building has a (somewhat irregular) eighteen-sided core and a central platform overlooked at regular intervals by three inset rectangular towers. It is conceivable that this novel architectural idea, which increased the eighteen sides to twenty-one, may have had something to do with the Templars, on whom Henry II conferred extensive privileges after his marriage to Eleonor of Aquitaine in 1152. Orford's eighteen-sides-and-a-triangle scheme was rather spoilt by the addition of an annexe. This contained an antechamber and, above it, curiously enough, the chapel, for which no room was available in the main building. Conisborough Castle, also built in Henry's reign but shortly afterwards, had an entirely circular core ringed by six radiating towers.

Techniques of attack and defence were making enormous strides at the turn of the 12th and 13th centuries. The *keep at Helmsley (Pl. 236)*, built c. 1200, was inset into the middle of the castle's east wall. The side which projected eastwards had a semicircular exterior and three-sided interior, whereas the part shown here, which faced the inner bailey, adhered to the rectangular convention. This demonstrates that the central keep had been largely superseded. The castle retained its impressive appearance, but its role became increasingly residential. The upper works at Helmsley date from the 14th century.

237-238 *Carvings at Ipswich* (Suffolk). The stone-masons of Tournai did not confine themselves to producing elaborate fonts such as the one at Winchester *(Pl. 48, 49)*. This *font in St Peter's, Ipswich (Pl. 237)* is far more modest. Each of the four sides bears three ambulant lions separated by columns, some averted and others affronted. Their tails are curled between their hind legs and across their backs, and their grim but somehow innocuous-looking masks face outwards. The

paws are a conspicuous feature, and recall the long-clawed beasts of the Herefordshire school (cf. *Pl. 113*). Two tendrils and two Trees of Life are engraved on each of the four cusps bordering the concave basin let into the upper surface of the stone block, which measures $42^1/_2$ by $42^1/_2$ by 19 ins. This font should probably be dated just before the middle of the 12th century.

The remarkable *sculpture in St Nicholas, Ipswich (Pl. 238)*, measures approximately $19^1/_2$ by $31^1/_2$ ins and portrays St Michael in combat with the Dragon. To preclude any misunderstanding, the stonemason added the inscription: 'Her Sct Michael feht wid dane dracon'. The theme of Michael and the Dragon (Revelations xii) was a popular one. There are versions of it on the lintel at Southwell *(Pl. 196)* and the tympanum at Moreton Valence (Gloucestershire), but the yellowish stone tympanum at Hallaton (Leicestershire) provides the finest example of all. Classically beautiful in its design and execution, it represents one of the crowning achievements of mature English Romanesque. Moreton Valence dates from the early 12th century, and Southwell is Anglo-Saxon at latest. The Ipswich carving should be dated somewhere between Moreton and Southwell, that is to say, in the rather hazy period known as the 'Saxo-Norman overlap', when many Late Anglo-Saxon features found final expression after the Conquest. Thus, it probably originated *c.* 1100.

239 *St Peter-ad-Murum at Bradwell-juxta-Mare* (Essex) stands in an isolated position on the east coast, exposed to the North Sea gales. It is not only the earliest surviving church in Essex but the first ever to be built there. Far away on the west coast of Ireland, lashed by the gales of the Atlantic, Gallarus Oratory on the Dingle Peninsula has also withstood the assaults of time and weather. The link between these two different worlds was provided by Lindisfarne in the north of England. Bede (H.E. III/22) describes how the Irish monk Cedd and his companions were sent forth to preach the Gospel to the Saxons of the east coast. As bishop of the East Saxons, he commissioned churches in various places, notably the town of 'Ythancestir', formerly Othona, one of the nine Roman fortresses on the Saxon coast of England. Traces of the old west wall and west gate can still be discerned precisely at the spot where St Peter's now stands, built of Roman bricks, hewn stones, and quoins, some of which display the indentations left by Roman lifting gear. The church is 54 ft long, 26 ft wide and 24 ft high, and the walls are 30 ins thick.

The building in its present form consists of a rectangular chamber with a saddleback roof. The west doorway and west window are both original. The exterior walls are buttressed, notably in the west corners, where skilful overlapping has held the quoins in place. The latter predate the long-and-short technique and are laid vertically. Excavations have shown that, like Reculver, the church had a north and south porticus and an east apse of the same width as the nave. Nave and apsidal chancel were separated by a partition wall pierced by three arches built of Roman bricks.

St Peter's Bradwell is a pure example of the early type of church in south-east England. This had an apse instead of the square-ended chancel customary in the north (cf. *Pl. 172*). Above all, its proportions were not as vertical, and its more harmonious relationship between length, breadth and height was influenced by Roman and Mediterranean tradition. We may safely assume that this was the church erected by Bishop Cedd in the year 654. Its history during the time of the Danish raids is obscure, but it was taken over by the Benedictines after the Conquest. Deconsecrated in the 18th century, it continued to be used as a barn until 1920.

It seems strange at first sight that Cedd, being familiar with churches of a different type in Northumbria, should have commissioned such a church here. The answer is probably twofold. In the first place, he must have recruited local builders, possibly from Christian Kent, and they would naturally have built in their own style; and, secondly and more particularly, one of the enduring strengths of Irish evangelism was that the new faith was reconciled as closely as possible with local tradition.

240 The Late Romanesque *south doorway of St Mary's, Wroxham* (Norfolk) illustrates how undercurrents which were wholly unaffected by Mediterranean influence continued to make themselves felt for a long time in the south-east of England. The whole of the demonic world lives on here, primitive and untrammelled. The jambs have a strange air, almost reminiscent—if one may be permitted such a comparison—of the wood-carvings which Gauguin produced after fleeing from civilization to the remote world of Atuona in the Marquesas.

241-242 *St Margaret's, Hales* (Norfolk) is only one of a considerable number of Romanesque parish and village churches which have survived and are still in use. Norfolk abounds in very typical examples, and the little church at Hales is one of the finest. It stands in a field outside the village, still roofed with thatch *(Pl. 242)*. It is regrettable, of course, that the attractive rhythm of the round-arched openings and blind arches was disrupted by the insertion of several larger windows in the 13th century. However, the simplicity of the fabric as

a whole—circular west tower, nave, and slightly inset apse—more than makes up for this.

There are two entrances of which the south doorway, adorned with roll-moulding, zigzag and billets, is simpler than the *north doorway (Pl. 241)*, which is unusually elaborate for a village church. This has two pairs of cylindrical jamb-shafts reposing on chamfered bases of unwonted height. The capitals are distinguished by highly individual spiral and star motifs which bear witness to the stonemason's rich imagination. The areas of wall beside the capitals also bear chip-carved ornaments. The hood-mould spanning the doorway consists of wheel motifs linked by a band of stellate flowers. Apart from an advanced type of zigzag, which appears in the guise of idented roll-moulding on the innermost order, the doorway displays flattish areas of chevron and stars as well as a rarely-used form of bobbin motif—almost too much of a good thing, in fact. None of this could have originated until 1150 or thereafter.

This naturally raises the question of the round tower's age. Inside it, to north and south, are two circular windows in the Anglo-Saxon tradition, blocked up on the outside but still bearing the imprint of the wickerwork which was used to hold the wet mortar in place while drying. Comparing the tower arch with the outer doorways, one inclines to the view that the tower should be attributed to the period of Saxo-Norman transition—probably, in company with the nave, to the late 11th century—whereas the apse and doorways should be regarded as 12th-century additions. The tower, of a design popular in Norfolk, was also augmented during the 12th century.

Most of England's round towers, of which there are roughly 180, are to be found between the Thames and the Wash: about 10 in Essex, over 40 in Suffolk, and 119 in Norfolk alone. Most of them are Norman, some Saxo-Norman, and a handful Anglo-Saxon. Putative links with the round towers of Ravenna or Ireland cannot be verified (see the notes on Irish round towers). The fact that there is a closer relationship between height and diameter (usually 1 : 3 or 1 : 2) in the round towers of East Anglia than in those of Ireland is attributable to the almost invariable use of flint in their construction. East Anglia offers no real building stone, and its soft limestone or clunch only lends itself to interior use. Stone for large churches was brought from elsewhere by water—Ely and Norwich were built of Barnack stone—but smaller churches were constructed of flint, which is widely available. Edging difficulties could be overcome where relatively small structures were concerned. In the case of taller towers, modest though these were compared with their Irish counterparts, flint-and-mortar builders found that the self-supporting circular wall was the most suitable for their purpose.

243 The *south doorway of the parish church of St Mary, Haddiscoe* (Norfolk), is not the only notable feature of this commandingly situated building. Mention should also be made of the magnificent west tower, a round tower of mainly Anglo-Saxon construction. The pilaster-like outer jambs and outer arch of the Romanesque doorway are reminiscent of an Anglo-Saxon portal. Lightly decorated cushion capitals repose on cylindrical jamb-shafts, and the central roll-moulded arch is sandwiched between round arches adorned with scalloping and zigzag. The outer arch also bears zigzag and chip-carved patterns, and the outer jambs are covered with saltire crosses. This work originated *c.* 1130–40.

The round-arched niche and seated figure above the doorway are unusual. The arrangement of the ensemble, with its unevenly assembled roll-moulded arch and change of motifs in the outer arch, prompts one to wonder if the niche and figure were once mounted elsewhere and transferred here subsequently. The full-face figure, seated in a strikingly symmetrical pose, has been construed as a Christ of the Majestas type despite the absence of a cruciform nimbus. Cited as evidence of this is the stone fragment above the figure's head, which allegedly represents either the Sacred Dove or the Hand of God. This is pure conjecture, however. Against the Majestas interpretation there is the attitude of the figure and the way both hands are raised as though each grasped an object of some sort—a sceptre, perhaps. This is the pose assumed by Alexander the Great in portrayals of his legendary attempt to conquer the skies (e.g. at Basle), a theme much favoured by Continental Romanesque. Not, of course, that the Haddiscoe figure actually portrays Alexander, since it is clad in liturgical vestments; the above allusion is merely intended to shed light on the type of figure depicted. Enthroned in an attitude which demands respect, the figure suggests that of a priest-king invested with two forms of authority, earthly and spiritual. The sculpture is of considerable artistic merit, but its precise meaning remains obscure. It probably originated before 1100.

244 *Castle Acre* (Norfolk), a former priory, is one of the most fascinating large ruined buildings in England. The elaborate *west front*, which rises above an expanse of well-tended lawn, is better preserved than any other part of the church. Parts of the north transept have also survived, but anything else of Romanesque origin must be inferred from foundations alone. Built in the first half of the 12th century, the church had an aisled nave of six bays plus a seventh between the two west towers,

a crossing tower, a transept with an east apse on each arm, and an aisled chancel of three bays, each aisle culminating in a stepped apse—a ground-plan which matched that of the second church at Cluny. Founded *c.* 1190, Castle Acre was, in fact, the second Cluniac priory in England. However, the splendour of the third church at Cluny must have exerted a growing influence on the monks and architects of Castle Acre as work on the priory church progressed in a westerly direction, for the west front, completed *c.* 1150, became a prime example of enriched façade articulation—comparable with the west end at Ely *(Pl. 222)* though not quite as refined.

The façade of Castle Acre Priory could not exist anywhere but in England. It is a perfect illustration of the ever-increasing trend towards reduplication in English Romanesque, of the growing tendency to repeat motifs everywhere and ad infinitum. Typical of this is the contrast between the central doorway and the tiers of blind arches surrounding it. The central arch is conspicuous for its size and consists of four orders. The jamb-shafts are missing, but the archivolts display cable-moulding, various types of zigzag, bobbins, and diaper-work. The tiers of blind arches are both simple and enlaced, shallow and deep. Which is the dominant feature? Does the portal boldly interrupt the tiers of blind arcading, or do the tiers of blind arcading boldly frame the portal? Both attempt to assert themselves, and this produces an ambivalence which detracts from the structural lucidity of the whole. Façades of this kind easily acquire a 'stagey' character—a tendency which English architects, who always had some difficulty with the west fronts of their churches, endeavoured to combat by lending them special emphasis (e.g. at Lincoln, Peterborough, Ely, Salisbury, Wells, and elsewhere).

Such considerations should not, however, be allowed to obscure the fascination of the west front at Castle Acre. Its tension derives from the contrast between bare planes like those round the side portals and, say, the plant-like filigree-work of the continuous and enlaced blind arches which flow across the central section beneath a string course supported by sculptured corbels. Above this string course is a very low arcade of zigzag-work arches. These contrast with the plain or enlaced blind arches of the tower stages, which have pure roll-moulding or classical fluting. One wonders how the gable-end was articulated before the huge nave window was inserted in the 15th century. It seems reasonable to suppose that the tall blind arches filled with diaper-work, which once ran the full width of the nave, used to be surmounted by a circular window.

245-246 *Keep and church of St Lawrence, Castle Rising* (Norfolk). Castle Rising keep represents one of the last in a long line of rectangular fortresses which began with the Tower of London *(Pl. 23)* and Colchester Castle. Orford *(Pl. 235)* and Helmsley *(Pl. 236)* marked the beginning of a new series of polygonal and circular castles influenced by the Near East, but Castle Rising brought the earlier and more massive series to a magnificent conclusion. Comparable with Norwich Castle, it is distinguished by its dimensions (approximate length, breadth and height: 79, 69 and 40 ft respectively) and by the articulation of its walls: on the west side, blind arches of varying height; on the north and the *south side (Pl. 245)*, buttresses of varying width, some (the clasping buttresses) with engaged shafts whose very height creates an impression of elegance. Access to the keep was by way of an east fore-building adorned with carved beasts' heads. Leading into the upper storey of the main building is a surprisingly wide flight of steps and a portal of three orders. The lower storey, which was devoted to offices, had no external entrance. The upper storey is subdivided on the lines of Rochester *(Pl. 20)* and comprises a hall, living quarters, subsidiary chambers, and, last but not least, an elaborately articulated chapel. More a fortified residence than a fortress proper, the keep was built *c.* 1150 by William de Albini, second husband of Henry I's widow and Earl of Sussex.

The *interior of St Lawrence's (Pl. 246)* has been extensively restored. One feature of the Late Romanesque fabric does, however, strike the eye. Although only a village church, it resembles a large church in having a crossing tower with a gallery exposed to the nave by three sturdy arches.

247-254 *Norwich Cathedral* (Norfolk) is one of the finest and most complete Norman cathedral abbeys in England, and happily stands comparison with the Romanesque cathedrals of Continental Europe. One or two alterations were carried out during the Gothic period, it is true. The original east chapel was replaced by a Lady Chapel, the chancel clerestory was rebuilt in the 14th century, and vaults were built into the chancel and, later, the nave. However, thanks to the vigour of the original style and the sympathetic understanding and high artistry of subsequent builders, the homogeneous appearance peculiar to a living organism still survives and retains its impact to this day.

The Continental impulses which contributed to the genesis of Norwich underwent Insular transformation and matured into a typically Anglo-Norman structure. The cathedral is built of Caen and Barnack stone. Its ground-plan is based not only on Norman prototypes such as Rouen Cathedral (early 11th century) but also

on the third church at Cluny, so it has a chancel with an ambulatory and radiating chapels. The initiator of Norwich Cathedral was Herbert de Losinga, formerly prior of the Benedictine monastery at Fécamp, which also erected a church with an ambulatory in the 12th century. Losinga, a Lorrainer, was appointed Bishop of East Anglia in 1091 as a consequence of the Norman reorganization of the English Church. He was an extremely purposeful man, and one who did not spurn worldly means in the attainment of his exalted ends. It has been surmised, probably with justification, that the founding of a monastery and the building of an unusually splendid cathedral at Norwich were also symptomatic of private atonement. Letters to King William Rufus certainly imply as much.

The Christianization of East Anglia dates back to the first third of the 7th century (Bede, *H.E.* II/15). Felix, a Benedictine monk from Burgundy, established the original see of East Anglia at Dunwich on the Suffolk coast. Transferred to North Elmham (Norfolk) *c.* 800, the see was removed in 1075 to Thetford in accordance with the Norman ruling that diocesan sees should be based in sizable towns. This was why, in 1094, the see of East Anglia was finally transferred to Norwich, the largest city in the diocese, the third-largest city in England (after London and York), and a place of numerous churches. The Domesday Book records that Losinga's predecessor at Norwich had received a grant of land 'ad principalem sedem episcopatus', so the move from Thetford to Norwich probably took place as a result of Losinga's insistence that an earlier ruling in regard to centralization should be put into effect. Losinga's cathedral abbey itself became the new centre, and it remains the hub of Norwich to this day. The grand design which inspired the founder of Norwich Cathedral continued to govern its construction from 1096 until it was completed in the middle of the 12th century. Herbert de Losinga had probably witnessed the completion of the chancel and transept by the time he died in 1119, when work must already have been in progress on the first three or four bays of the nave and the base of the crossing tower.

The aisled *chancel (Pl. 247)* accords with the typical Norman tendency towards elongation in that, like St Albans, Durham and Ely, it has four bays. The wall system is the familiar one: ambulatory or aisle arcades, gallery arches, and clerestory windows. The latter were rebuilt in Gothic (Early Perpendicular) style after the original clerestory was destroyed by the collapse of the crossing tower in 1362. The apse is defined by a semicircle of five arches. Beneath the central arch at the extreme east end of the chancel, facing westwards in accordance with early tradition, stands the bishop's throne used at the first installation in Norwich in 1121. It is possible that parts of this (restored) sedia hail from North Elmham and go back to the 9th century. The apse piers adopt a form which recurs at Ely: segmental arches inside, suggesting the appearance of massive drum-piers, combined, on the chancel side, with flat areas of masonry covered by demi-shafts. The billet-moulded arches repose on scalloped and cushion capitals. (The arch on the left of the photograph was cut away to accommodate a memorial of later date.)

The gallery is a repetition of the arcade, with large undivided openings of the sort first exemplified by the gallery of St Etienne at Caen in 1065 and first reproduced in England at Blyth Priory *(Pl. 187)* not long afterwards. The piers are consistent here, having three stepped shafts facing the chancel. They also have small volute capitals (*c.* 1100) which gradually disappear as the building progresses westwards—another token of adherence to an original idea. The chancel aisles and the ambulatory visible beyond the apse arches were provided with groined vaults, whereas the Norman gallery had no vaults—merely a lean-to roof whose pitch can be deduced from the shafts, which are lower on the outside than the inside. The elaborately chamfered and roll-moulded gallery arches are stilted. This, too, symptomizes the desire for expansion, in height as well as length, a trend which also manifests itself in the vertical thrust of the wall-shafts, especially those on either side of the apse. What is more, unlike St Etienne or Blyth Priory, Norwich has gallery arches which are almost as tall as those of the ambulatory. The present clerestory windows are larger than the originals, of course, and we can assume that the wall-passage used to have triplet openings (as in the transept, *Pl. 251*, and the nave, *Pl. 249*). The present height of the chancel, from the floor to the ribbed vaults inserted *c.* 1500, is no less than 83 ft.

Bishop Losinga's unknown cathedral architect laid out his three ambulatory chapels in a highly individual manner. In Continental examples, these chapels always followed a radial pattern. The original east chapel at Norwich, begun with the main building in 1096 and replaced *c.* 1250 by a new rectangular Lady Chapel which was itself replaced in 1930, naturally conformed to the radial principle and had a ground-plan of horseshoe design. The other two chapels on the north and south sides of the ambulatory are quite different. The *south chapel (Pl. 252)*, formerly dedicated to St John the Baptist, is now known as St Luke's. (In front of it stands a memorial to Edith Cavell, born in the neighbourhood in 1865 and executed by the Germans in 1915.) The pronounced height of both chapels—and here they form an exception to the general rule—is attributable to the

fact that the gallery was continued round them as well as round the transept chapels. The continuous blind arcading is English, as is the peculiar layout. Each chapel consists of two intersecting parts, both curved. The larger, western part is markedly horseshoe-shaped and serves as the chapel proper; the smaller, which slightly exceeds a semicircle, as an altar-room. By this means, the architect achieved an orientation impossible in the case of radiating chapels of the Rouen type. It is as if there had been an attempt to reconcile the radial system with the stepped-apse system. Each chapel has two rounded excrescences, one connecting it with the ambulatory and the other connecting its two parts, and this invests both of them with a portly and rather self-satisfied air.

Visible on the left of the photograph is the east wall of the south transept, which still bears traces of the vanished east apse. The *interior of the south transept (Pl. 250,* showing the full extent of the east wall) presents an impressive picture. The layout and wall systems of the north and south transepts are essentially similar, though alterations were carried out subsequently. Each is unaisled and has, or had, an east apse. The compound piers separating them from the crossing *(Pl. 251)* are differentiated, the north and south arches having two shafts on each side and the east and west arches three. After the compound piers come the arcade and gallery arches of the aisles, followed, in the east, by an expanse of wall behind which spiral stairs ascend to the gallery. In the south transept this expanse of wall is enriched in a typically Insular manner with exaggeratedly tall and slender enlaced blind arches. Still further to the south comes the arched entrance to the former east apse, now blocked up. The apse of the north transept has survived. The *west wall of the south transept (Pl. 251)* naturally displays greater regularity of articulation because it had fewer functions to perform. Its lower reaches were restored in 1830. In front of the gallery and clerestory windows are typical wall-passages with triplet openings of varying size.

The *nave (Pl. 249,* north wall viewed from the east at gallery height) is splendidly harmonious. The wall system—arcade arches, undivided gallery openings, clerestory with triplet windows and wall-passage—extends without a break for fourteen bays. The nave of Norwich Cathedral testifies with great eloquence to a desire on the part of the best architects in England during the first half of the 12th century to lay walls open and combat their appearance of bulk by allowing the eye to penetrate them freely. A slight alternation of piers is again suggested. This extremely subtle formative differentiation (is it permissible to use the word 'artistic' in connection with a medieval cathedral?) occurs throughout, and provides relief from the unchanging system of arcade arches, gallery arches, and clerestory triplets.

Apart from constants, changes and alterations are also evident in the construction of the building, though not in its basic character. The volute capitals frequently employed in the east end almost disappear. From the fourth bay of the nave onwards, the billet motifs used in the chancel and transept are joined by zigzag, which started to gain ground in England after 1115. So much for one change. The other affects the system. An attempted break manifests itself in the spiral-fluted *drum-pier (Pl. 248)* between the fifth and sixth bays from the east. It is a version of the pier in the east transept at Durham, conceived there in 1093 and soon imitated and modified elsewhere, e.g. at Dunfermline *(Pl. 154)* and Lindisfarne *(Pl. 156)*. At Norwich, round piers of this type are already represented by the third pier to the west of the crossing (later encased), which marks the exact stage reached at the time of Bishop Losinga's death. It is probable that work was resumed under a new master mason who, being impressed by Durham, tried to switch to the Durham system. If so, he did not persevere for long. After only two bays, the original plan conceived by Losinga and his architect reasserted itself and was adhered to until all the fourteen bays had been completed *c.* 1150.

The *crossing tower (Pl. 253*, taken from the south range of the cloister, shows it rising above the nave and south transept) is uniformly decorated on all four sides with an obvious love of ornamental detail. The spire, corner-spirelets and battlements are 15th-century work, whereas the square body of the tower belongs to the first Romanesque phase. The corners of the tower are emphasized at the head by polygonal turrets with blind arcading and verticalized lower down by slender shafts which give way to flat masonry at the foot. The latter marks the interior height of the crossing, which is lit by three windows set into a tier of simple arcading. The tier above consists of intersected arches which run round the wall like a balustrade, stressing the horizontal line. By contrast, the three tall round-arched openings of the belfry-stage are vertical in emphasis. Cylindrical shafts divide the face of the wall into tall arcaded fields of slightly varying width, the narrower ones decorated with strings of alternating lozenges and circles. All this draws the upper section of the tower together in a remarkable way. Above, four thicker shafts form five elongated rectangles, each of which contains two vertically connected circles, the lower one blank and the upper one pierced to serve as a sound-hole. These classical shapes are enclosed by rings of thinner cylindrical moulding which branch off, meander-fashion, at head and foot. Rectangles and circles are linked, and each of the ten ports contains a complete circle. The architect responsible for this wall decoration—probably the second to work on the cathedral, under Losinga's successor Eborardus (1121–45)—achieved a positively classical effect. The design of the tower at Norwich is High Romanesque, and precedes the Late Romanesque articulation of the west end at Ely.

Mounted in the north wall of the north transept, above the small central doorway and beneath a simple arched hood-mould, is a *sculpture of a bishop (Pl. 254)*, fully painted but restored. Flanking him closely beneath a damaged round arch are two spiral-fluted columns which rotate upwards and inwards, one with a volute capital and the other with an averted snake. The bases consist of two grotesque masks of which the one on the left recalls the archivolt heads on the portal at Kilpeck *(Pl. 105)*. The sides converge slightly towards the foot, which has prompted the theory that this relief was the lid of a stone coffin. The probability of this assumption is enhanced by indications that the feet of the figure originally reposed on a dragon. The bishop's left hand holds a crosier diagonally across his richly draped robe, and his right hand is raised in benediction. His expression is grave. Stylistically, the figure is consistent with the second quarter of the 12th century. No portrait could have been intended at that period, but whom was the memorial meant to represent? The fact that it was located on the route to Bishop Losinga's chapel invests it with special significance. Is it, as some have suggested, part of a monument to Herbert de Losinga himself, the man whose personal vision left its mark on the entire cathedral but who died in 1119, when only the east end was complete? Alternatively, does it represent his successor, Bishop Eborardus (d. 1145), who furthered Losinga's work so actively that 'ecclesiam integraliter consummavit'?

We shall never know for certain. The man has gone for ever, but his handiwork—the Romanesque cathedral—remains.

Iona

Dumferline

Kelso
Jedburgh

Lindisfarne

Ruthwell   Hexham
                        Jarrow
                        Houghton-le-Spring
            Durham Pittington
            Escomb Church Kelloe
                Auckland
Gosforth

                        Rievaulx Abbey
Monasterboice
                    Fountains   Stonegrave
            Mellifont   Abbey   York

Clonfert Clonmacnois
                                Barton-upon-Humber

Kilfenora   Blyth   Stow
            Glendalough   Worksop   Lincoln
    Durrow   Moone   Southwell
    Cashel   Castledermot
                            Melbourne
                                        Castle Rising
Ardfert   Ahenny   Breedon-on-the-Hill Oakham Barnack Castle Acre Wroxham
                            Much Wenlock Wittering   Norwich
                                    Castor Peterborough Hales
                                                    Ely   Haddiscoe
                    Leominster   Brixworth Brigstock
Ardmore   Worcester Pitsford Earls Barton Bury St. Edmunds
                Eardisley   Northampton Orford Cambridge Ipswich
            Spretton Sugwas Castle Frome
                    Hereford Tewkesbury   Colchester
            Rowlstone Kilpeck Deerhurst
                        Gloucester Oxford St. Albans Greensted Bradwell-iuxte-Mare
                    Langford   Iffley   Waltham Abbey
                        Malmesbury Dorchester London Reculver
            Bristol   Avebury   Reading   Rochester Canterbury Patrixbourne
                    Bradford-on-Avon   Barfreston
                    Knook   Staplehurst
                            Winchester Worth   Brookland
            Glastonbury   Romsey   Old Shoreham Clayton
                            Bere Regis   New Shoreham Bishopstone
                                        Chichester Sompting
Exeter   Bosham Brighton
                        Christchurch
St. Germans

ACKNOWLEDGEMENTS

The author is indebted to numerous writers, most of them from the British Isles but some from the Continent. For obvious reasons, few bibliographical references can be given here. There is no need, for instance, to list individual publications by such established authorities as G. B. Brown, A. W. Clapham, A. Gardner, T. D. Kendrick, M. D. Knowles, D. T. Rice, F. Saxl, F. Stenton and H. Swarzenski. On the other hand, express reference must be made to the following works:

TAYLOR, H. M. and J. *Anglo-Saxon Architecture*, 2 vols, Cambridge 1965

RICKERT, M. *Painting in Britain—The Middle Ages*, London 1954, in the 'Pelican History of Art' series

STONE, L. *Sculpture in Britain—The Middle Ages*, London 1955, in the 'Pelican History of Art' series

WEBB, G. *Architecture in Britain—The Middle Ages*, London 1956, in the 'Pelican History of Art' series

ZARNECKI, G. *English Romanesque Sculpture*, 2 vols, London 1951, 1953

HENRY, F. *L'Art Irlandais*, 3 vols, La Pierre-qui-vire 1963–1964, in the 'Zodiaque' series

DOUGLAS, D. C. *William the Conqueror*, London 1964

VON DEN STEINEN, W. *Der Kosmos des Mittelalters*, Berne 1959

Special thanks are due to Nikolaus Pevsner. Various volumes on individual counties from his 'Buildings of England' series served as trustworthy guides during all research and photographic trips undertaken in England. The author and photographer also gratefully acknowledge the help given by numerous rectors, vicars, churchwardens and custodians of churches and monuments, all of whom readily supplied information and facilitated their work. Their cooperative attitude was expressive of a profound appreciation of their great heritage.

Finally, special thanks are also due to Dr G. Künstler of the Schroll Verlag, Vienna, who promoted and supervised the preparation of this volume with unflagging enthusiasm. ROBERT STOLL

In addition to the photographs taken especially for this volume by Jean Roubier of Paris, negatives were also made available by the following: Bord Fáilte Eireann, Dublin (Pl. 126, 127); Courtauld Institute of Art, London (Pl. 167); National Monuments Branch, Dublin (Pl. 133, 134, 135); and Kristian Sotriffer, Vienna (Pl. 128, 130, 143).